D1520779

WITHDRAWN

Postmodernity's Histories

Culture and Politics Series
General Editor, Henry A. Giroux, Pennsylvania State University

Postmodernity's Histories: The Past as Legacy and Project
    by Arif Dirlik

Collateral Damage: Corporatizing Public Schools—A Threat to Democracy
    by Kenneth J. Saltman

Forthcoming:

*Surpassing the Spectacle: Global Transformation and the Changing Cultural
    Politics of Art*
    by Carol Becker

Postmodernity's Histories

The Past as Legacy and Project

ARIF DIRLIK

ROWMAN & LITTLEFIELD PUBLISHERS, INC.
Lanham • Boulder • New York • Oxford

ROWMAN & LITTLEFIELD PUBLISHERS, INC.

Published in the United States of America
by Rowman & Littlefield Publishers, Inc.
4720 Boston Way, Lanham, Maryland 20706
www.rowmanlittlefield.com

12 Hid's Copse Road
Cumnor Hill, Oxford OX2 9JJ, England

British Library Cataloguing in Publication Information Available

Library of Congress Cataloging-in-Publication Data

Dirlik, Arif, 1940–
    Postmodernity's histories : the past as legacy and project / Arif Dirlik
    p. cm.
    Includes bibliographical references and index.
    ISBN 0-7425-0166-3 (alk. paper) — ISBN 0-7425-0167-1 (pbk. : alk.
paper)
    1. History—Philosophy. 2. History, Modern—1945–. 3. Postmodernism.
4. Historiography. I. Title II. Series.
    D16.8.D535 2000
    901—dc21   00-035293
                                                                         CIP

Printed in the United States of America

$\bigotimes^{\text{TM}}$ The paper used in this publication meets the minimum requirements of
American National Standard for Information Sciences—Permanence of Paper for
Printed Library Materials, ANSI/NISO Z39.48–1992.

To the memory of
Michael Sprinker

Ψ

CONTENTS

PREFACE

The essays in this volume continue a project that I took up in an earlier collection, *The Postcolonial Aura: Third World Criticism in the Age of Global Capitalism* (Boulder, Colo.: Westview Press, 1997): to reaffirm the importance of history as epistemology to restoring to contemporary discussions of postmodernism and postcolonialism a sense of their own historicity. Historicizing the postmodern or the postcolonial is not a goal in itself; it is, most important, a means to reinject into critical scholarship a reminder of the radical political visions that inspired it in the first place and must be an ever present source of inspiration if such scholarship is to avoid degenerating into intellectual gamesmanship, a fatalistic nihilism, or, at worst, the appropriation of putatively radical critical scholarship for conservative and reactionary causes. Historicization requires some recognition of reality of the past—a recognition that we do not just construct the past as we please but are constrained and shaped by the past even as we endow it with ever changing meanings. The perspective of history is crucial to a critical grasp of what we remember of the past and what we forget.

Colonizing the past, or, for that matter, the future, with a contemporary consciousness, in this case the consciousness of postmodernity or postcoloniality, is to abolish the possibility of distinguishing criticism from ideology. Radical causes long have been informed by futuristic hopes that put the present to the test of possible futures to justify criticism. The proliferation of "posts" in contemporary discourse provides ample evidence of the abandonment as destructive utopias of imagined futures as locations for critical perspectives on the present, as the future in such enunciation persists only in its residuality. That would seem to leave us only with the past as a repository of critical perspectives on the present. The trouble is, of course, that the past as a location for critical perspectives on the present has been associated for the past two centuries with conservative causes. It may seem odd, in view of that tradition, to call upon the past as an inspiration for radical imaginings.

There is a dilemma here, to be sure, but one that may be empowering in forcing a reconsideration of the ways in which the past may serve in a critical appreciation of the present. While I am critical in the essays here of the postmodern and postcolonial appropriations of the past, the latter have been invaluable in placing on the intellectual agenda the need for such reconsideration by calling into question in radical ways the teleologies of modernity, liberal or Marxist. Pasts suppressed or relegated to backwardness under the regime of modernity have resurfaced to make their claims on the present and the future. There is an enrichment here of the repertoire of past legacies in rethinking future possibilities, but whether or not this enriched repertoire will serve progressive causes is still very much at issue. Revivals of the past may also contribute to nourishing liberal identity politics, or worse, the proliferation of reactionary nativisms. The test may well be the ability of radicals to rethink the present through the past but also to confront past legacies with the challenges of the present, so that past legacies serve as resources for future projects rather than as justifications for mindless reaffirmation of native identities, with all the inherited oppressions and inequalities built into them. In either case, the past is all of a sudden very much on the contemporary intellectual and political agenda, and progressive radicals may ignore the problems and the possibilities it presents only at the risk of turning their backs on what may be the most crucial issue of the day.

The majority of the essays here explore these possibilities. Before such exploration is possible, it is necessary to clear the ground by pointing to the ways in which contemporary scholarship, adopting a disguise of radicalism by dressing itself in currently fashionable attire, seeks to erase memories of its own conditions of existence: the radical and radically critical scholarship that grew out of the legacies of the 1960s, to which ideas of national liberation and revolution were crucial. Interestingly, in historical hindsight, it was the self-criticism of such scholarship in the face of the betrayal of its visions that was to provide the material, once the conditions were right, for the repudiation of the visions as well. The crucial issue, needless to say, is the issue of revolution. Over the last two decades, revolutions have been taken out of history; or, more accurately, revolutions informed by visions of a more just future have been replaced by revolutions affirming the existing status quo or even representing a throwback to the inequalities and injustices of the past.

The first two essays in this volume address this question: the difference between critical revisits to the past that judge the aspirations of revolutions against their achievements, and self-defeating efforts to forget the history of revolutions. What is at issue in these essays is not only revolutions but also, and more important, the historical narratives that legitimized but were also inspired by revolutions. There is little question that Eurocentric narratives of progress and the nation have shaped our conceptions of history, which in turn have played a central part in the suppression of other possible ways of narrating the past, its relationship to the present and the future. Revolutions as we have known them have been implicated in Eurocentrism, since, from nationalism to glorious socialist visions of the future, the narrative of revolution has been informed by Eurocentric notions of progress. The second set of essays takes up the question of Eurocentrism, especially the question of the relationship between a Eurocentric writing of history and the urge to take Europe out of history altogether.

One of the fundamental achievements of postmodernity (lodged firmly in the contradictions of modernity) has been to make room for alternative modernities and alternative claims to modernity. On the other hand, it is important to remember that the claims to alternative modernities (and, therefore, alternative pasts) were made possible by the Euro-American universalization of history, which is the condition not just for contemporary politics but also for the ways in which we think about the past, the present, and the future. Critiques of Eurocentrism that ignore the Euro-American dynamics of modernity, especially the question of capitalism in history, simply introduce Eurocentrism by the back door even as they rage against it. Especially important here may be the dehistoricizing of the Euro-American legacies in history by confounding all distinctions between capitalist and Euro-American modernities represented by, say, the Enlightenment; while there is no doubt that some relationship exists between the two, the relationship is not one of seamless unity but one of contradiction. After two centuries, capitalist modernity is no longer just Euro-American and has shown itself capable of coexistence with the most reactionary political and cultural regimes. At the same time, it is arguable that the Enlightenment, while it might have been inconceivable without the rise of capitalism and the Euro-American conquest of the world, offered possibilities that have been distorted by the very capitalism of which it may have been a product. Those possibilities are still there and form the source of much of the discourse on human liberation even among those who fashionably reject Enlightenment narratives, etc. We might consider what it would mean to take the Enlightenment out of history, even as we speak of class, racial, and gender inequality, among other things, all of which are traceable to Enlightenment hopes for the future of humanity. The answer may be not to take the Enlightenment out of history but to bring to the realization of those ideals the help of other pasts, which were suppressed by Enlightenment notions of progress. These are the issues taken up in the next three essays. The essay on Ashis Nandy is especially important, as Nandy is a strong voice in the repudiation not just of Eurocentric history but of history as a Eurocentric mode of thinking.

The last three essays are more "practical" in their intention, as they address questions of radical politics under conditions of globality. Globalization and opposition to it inform these essays. It seems quite obvious by now that globalization has provided us with a new paradigm in a very real operative sense. Postmodernism and postcolonialism provided the residual discourse of the 1980s and 1990s, when there was clearly a need to call into question both bourgeois and Marxist discourses of modernity. But as residual oppositions, they could not claim anything like a paradigmatic status. Globalization has provided a badly needed paradigm, in the perspective of which postmodernity and postcoloniality make considerable sense as discourses of a transitional period in search of a new language to cope with a new world situation.

For reasons that I have explained at length elsewhere, the global has provoked opposition in the idea of the "local." The local, or the place-based, may be viewed as a last-ditch effort to resist the incursions of capital, as is implicit in the language of "resistance" that is frequently heard these days, or it may be viewed as the source of a more "proactive" politics that is as old as the history of capitalism and the nation-state but is made more plausible in our day by the very activities of capital, when the power of corporations is spread thin by their spatial stretch, so that capital can only exist by virtue of local consent and localities have some say over its operations, especially in the face of contradictions between local and global capital. Nowhere is this contradiction more apparent than in the case of indigenous peoples, who are torn apart by incorporation in the capitalist economy but who are enabled thereby to make their own political demands on governance, thus exposing deep contradictions in the very structure of capitalism.

The concluding essays suggest some connection between indigenism and the "new social movements." What they share is a defense of places that are the locations for everyday life and culture and, ultimately, for history. It is not my intention in these essays to privilege or romanticize either indigenism or place-based politics. Indeed, I identify indigenism not with the defense of native traditions of one kind or another, as is popular in New Age or conservative nativist understandings of indigenism, but with those radical indigenous projects that use the past as a resource to overcome the continued colonization of indigenous peoples and to seek to articulate indigenous pasts to contemporary challenges of class and gender inequality.

Place-based politics, a suppressed legacy of the 1960s, presents its own problems. Places are also locations of inherited inequalities and oppressions and need to be informed in a new politics by the need not just to overcome colonization by states and capital but also to address those legacies of the past; places, too, remain as projects—which explains my preference for "place" over "community," a term that is most appealing but is also a cover for the preservation of past ways, which are not always desirable. It is for the same reason that I am hesitant to dismiss out of hand, in spite of an anarchistic suspicion of centralized power, the importance of supraplace alliances, including the nation-state, that remain not only as reminders of the need for outside agencies in uncovering the inequalities built into places but also of the need of places, if they are not to become playthings at the hands of capital, for some kind of defense. There are two reasons that places are especially important at the present conjuncture as the locations for politics. First is that they are the locations of everyday life and culture, the welfare of which must be the ultimate test of human improvement and liberation. Second, at a time when the systematicity of existence, including the structures of capital, may be grasped only at the most abstract level, and systemic transformation (global or national) appears at its most elusive, building democratic spaces from the bottom up may be the only hope available for any kind of radical transformation that recognizes both totality and difference. I take up this question in the last essay in the collection.

Most of the essays in this volume were written during my year as a fellow of the Netherlands Institute for Advanced Studies in the Humanities and Social Sciences in 1998–1999. I would like to acknowledge my debt of gratitude to the staff of the institute, who were responsible for making my stay there a most pleasant and productive one, and fellow fellows, with whom I had a chance to discuss the issues that I take up below, in particular Wim van der Doel, Rogers Hollingsworth, Fred Inglis, Eric Johnson, Hagen Koo, Reinhardt Koselleck, and Henk Wesseling, the rector of the institute. Roxann Prazniak, companion and reader of almost everything I have written over the last decade—if with closed eyes on one occasion—deserves special thanks. Other friends and colleagues who have read and/or commented on one or more of the essays below include Vinay Bahl, Elizabeth Boyi, Duane Champagne, John Brown Childs, Leo Ching, Allen Chun, Ward Churchill, Bruce Cumings, Georgi Derluguian, Theo D'haen, Michael Dutton, Terry Eagleton, Ali-Rifaat Abou El-Haj, Arturo Escobar, Jonathan Friedman, Henry Giroux, Peter Gran, Wendy Harcourt, Michael Hardt, Harry Harootunian, Lane Hirabayashi, Yuji Ichioka, Troy Johnson, Dubravka Juraga, Vinay Lal, Russell Leong, Charles Locke, Victor Mair, Maurice Meisner, Martin Miller, John Mowitt, Harbans Mukhia, Dianne Newell, David Palumbo-Liu, Benita Parry, Michael Sprinker, Epifanio San Juan Jr., Orin Starn, Mette Thunoe, Immanuel Wallerstein, Ling-chi Wang, Rob Wilson, Robert Young, and Zhang Xudong. They are under no obligation to agree with any of the arguments I offer below.

The essays included in this volume have been presented at a number of forums: "Colonialism and Its Discontents" (Institute of Ethnology, Academia Sinica, Taipei, July 1997); "Legacies of Authoritarianism" (University of Wisconsin, March 1998); Humanities Seminar (Hong Kong University of Science and Technology, March 1998); "Globalization and the Future of the Humanities" (Beijing University of Language and Culture, July 1998); "Political Economy of World Systems Annual Conference" (Northwestern University, April 1998); "Beyond Dichotomies" (Stanford University, May 1998); "The China Forum" (University of Vienna, December 1998); "Inaugural Conference of Copenhagen Colonial and Postcolonial Studies" (Department of English, University of Copenhagen, April 1999); "Missing Chapter: The Historiographic Marginalization of East Asia" (University of Lyons, May 1999); "In the Wake of Eurocentrism" (McArthur Consortium, University of Minnesota, May 1999); "Turning Points in Historical Thinking: A Comparative Perspective" (East Asian Studies, SUNY–Buffalo, August 1999); "Globalization and the Construction of Chinese Culture" (Beijing University of Language and Culture, September 1999); "Globalization and Cultural Security: Migration and Negotiations of Identity" (House of World Cultures and the Toda Institute, Berlin, October 1999); "International Conference on Ecology and Literature" (Hainan Writers Association, Hainan, People's Republic of China, October 1999); "Asian American Studies: Past, Present and Future: A Thirtieth Anniversary Colloquium" (Department of Ethnic Studies, University of California–Berkeley, October 1999); "After Postcolonialism, Beyond Minority Discourse" (Department of English, Cornell University, November 1999); "China and the World in the Twentieth Century" (Institute of Modern History, Academia Sinica, Taipei, January 2000). I thank the participants in these seminars, workshops, and conferences for their comments and encouragement.

Last but not least, I would like to express my appreciation to two of the most sensitive editors whom I have dealt with over the years, Susan McEachern and Dean Birkenkamp of Rowman & Littlefield. My thanks to Henry Giroux for suggesting that I compile these essays for publication as a volume.

The volume is dedicated to the memory of Michael Sprinker, who passed away prematurely in 1999. His intellectual engagement, critical wisdom, and political commitment will be missed by all those who knew him as colleague and friend. Fraternally, Michael.

1

HOW THE GRINCH HIJACKED RADICALISM:

POSTREVOLUTIONARY HISTORIES

I take up in this chapter two questions that have become increasingly difficult to avoid for those who have witnessed the rapid expansion of the domain of the postcolonial in intellectual work over the last decade, in particular in the United States. First is the question of the identity of postcolonial intellectuals.[1] While postcolonial criticism has brought the question of identity to the fore-front of intellectual work with such insistence that nothing else seems worth speaking and writing about these days, it has been largely silent on the question of postcolonial identities beyond homilies of hybridity and in-between-ness. In a historical sense, the very idea of a postcolonial identity is a trivial one, as everyone these days is more or less postcolonial and enjoys (or suffers) one or another form of hybridity. Discussions of postcoloniality have little to say on the socially and politically crucial question of what postcolonial intellectuals might be in addition to being postcolonial. If identity is a product of complex relationships, as postcolonialists argue (which I for one find neither quite novel nor particularly controversial), this oversight is rather remarkable, as the relationships that constitute different postcolonialities should be of the greatest import in locating their social and political positions. In and of itself, the postcolonial as a self-referential term has little to tell us about those locations; except perhaps in one sense: that the ethnic and/or racial is the constituent moment of all identity—and, therefore, politics.

The second, related question is the identity of postcolonial criticism itself as an intellectual mode of inquiry and explanation. Postcolonial criticism as we have it now has acquired popularity during a period of rather remarkable transformations globally and the intellectual ferment that has accompanied those transformations. As the domain of the postcolonial has expanded, postcolonial criticism has infiltrated discourses that have origins that are quite independent of postcolonialism and in turn has been infiltrated by those discourses, so that it is quite impossible in our day to say what may be specific to postcolonialism. While this has facilitated the expansion of postcolonialism into a new academic orthodoxy, the victory has come at a significant cost: its loss of identity as a discourse. This has led, on the one hand, to exaggerated claims for postcolonial criticism and, on the other hand, to the trivialization of important social and historical questions as they are appropriated for, or even erased in the name of, questions of cultural identity. While the increasing diffuseness of the postcolonial may not matter to those who do not share in the enthusiasm over it, the appropriation for the postcolonial of diverse discourses that have arisen in response to contemporary changes undercuts a critical appreciation of postcolonialism as well as, more important, the possibility of confronting critically crucial questions of power in our day.

◆

Any effort to confront these questions must begin with a consideration of what we understand by "postcolonial," as well as of the historical circumstances of its emergence and reception. As Aijaz Ahmad has pointed out, the idea of the postcolonial itself has a history.[2] In its initial, more or less literal, temporal sense, it referred to newly liberated colonies and was quite radical in its social, economic, and political implications: breaking with the colonial past to create new societies economically, politically, and culturally. Integral to the postcolonial vision of this early period (peaking in the 1960s) were ideologies of national liberation that sought national autonomy in all realms from the colonial past as well as the neocolonial present. National liberation movements of this early period were informed for the most part by socialist programs of one kind or another, which also explains the affinity between ideologies of national liberation and Third World socialisms such as the Chinese.

These beginnings are largely forgotten in contemporary conceptions of postcoloniality, which not only have turned their back on these origins but indeed may be viewed as a negation of the original sense of the postcolonial of which they are products. The ambivalence produced by this dialectical positioning is still visible in the works of those such as Edward Said, Gayatri Spivak, and Stuart Hall who today are hailed as originators of postcolonial criticism as we have it now but whose works are nevertheless deeply marked by their points of departure in an earlier sense of the postcolonial, connected to its radical social programs even as they articulated a new discourse of culture that would ultimately negate those origins. It is not that culture was missing from earlier discussions of postcoloniality; but it is a long way from the "cultural revolutions" of national liberation movements in which culture appeared as part of a broader political program to the contemporary disappearance of radical social, economic, and political programs into the problematic of cultural discourse.

The postcolonial in its contemporary appearance is shaped by the retreat from revolution with the reconfiguration of global relations in the 1980s. This retreat is most readily visible in the abandonment in postcolonial criticism of two categories that were fundamental to earlier revolutionary discourses: nation and class. There are complex reasons, some of which I have discussed elsewhere, for the increasingly problematic nature of these two categories in our day. Here I will speak briefly to those aspects of the problem that are directly pertinent to the issues at hand.

Ironically, in our day, when formal political colonialism has all but disappeared, it is the nation and nationalism in their claims to homogeneous cultural identities that appear as the greatest foes of cultural and historical diversity and the free play of individual and group identities—including those that are the legacies of colonialism. Whereas an earlier generation experienced colonialism as erasure of real or imagined native identities and set out to recover those identities through the agency of the nation, postcolonial self-identification with hybridity, in-betweenness, marginality, borderlands, et cetera, represents in some fundamental ways the revolt against claims to authentic national identity of those whose very cultural formation was a product of the colonial encounter at home and abroad. While postcolonial criticism devotes much effort to the critique of the ideologies of colonial domination (chief among them, Eurocentrism), it ironically also represents an affirmation of the colonial past—at least of the colonial past in the postcolonial. The postcolonial celebration of hybridity and in-betweenness is a celebration against nationalist cultural claims of a culture that includes the culture of the colonizer as a constituent moment; that also reasserts the claims to cultural priority of those groups in society shaped by the colonial encounter.

The failure of postcolonial national liberation regimes to deliver on their political, economic, and cultural promises is no doubt an important factor in this turnabout. But so is the proliferation of diasporic populations that has accompanied economic and political globalization, whose demographic dispersal has created a situation in which it is no longer possible to identify cultures with national boundaries. One of the important by-products of this situation—encompassed in slogans of globalization—is increased porosity of the boundaries that earlier separated the colonizers from the colonized; that may account for the receptivity to postcolonialism among the intellectuals and institutions of metropolitan centers (unlike, say, in earlier, largely negative, responses to Third World–ist separatism).

There is also a reminder here, however, of the need for caution in generalizing the postcolonial experience, which was historically the most significant for those who experienced colonialism as a transformative cultural force. Even in those cases there is much that is problematic. The questioning of authenticity to nationalist claims has had as an underlying purpose the recognition of equal "authenticity" to those who were products of the colonial "borderlands," whose cultures include the cultures of colonialism. Unreflective promotion of borderlands, however, has gone beyond such demands for recognition to the erasure of all alternatives to the borderlands, and "borderlands" that were products of encounters other than the colonial. At a time when claims to ethnic authenticities proliferate, the preoccupation with borderlands makes for a blindness to other ways of perceiving cultural self-identification that have as much claim to their self-identifications as diasporic intellectuals and populations. Indeed, diasporic populations are hardly homogeneous, but deeply divided socially; against the insistence on cultural hybridity of diasporic elites, large sections of these populations appear to be more adamant about their cultural authenticities—traditions—than the populations at their places of departure. That the "border" claims of postcolonialism are taken more seriously at First World than in Third World locations also points to the power context for contemporary discussions of culture. There is little that is puzzling about the receptivity in metropolitan centers to postcolonialist arguments in favor of border cultures, as those arguments confirm that metropolitan cultures have become inevitable components of the colonized.

While the retreat from class presents its own problems within the context of globalization, it is not entirely unrelated to the question of the nation. One of the fundamental premises of earlier national liberation movements that distinguished them from other forms of Third World nationalism was conviction of the necessity of a social revolution as a prerequisite of national liberation and autonomy; this also explains their affinity to socialism. The reason was fairly straightforward from the perspective of a Leninist (if not just a Leninist) appreciation of the contradictions of imperialism: that colonial or imperialist domination required for its effectiveness and perpetuation the complicity of native classes—"feudal" classes bent on preserving their power against new nationalist forces, or "bourgeoisies" that were products of the importation of capitalism through the agency of colonialism and, in spite of their resentment of imperialist domination, also shared interests with the latter. Given the ties of these groups to imperialism, national liberation must be unsuccessful so long as they retained their power. Much the same pertained to nation-building as a cultural project: that the recovery of authentic national traditions also required the "renationalization" of those who had come under colonial cultural hegemony. The Chinese Cultural Revolution in the 1960s may be seen as one eloquent testimonial to the coincidence of economic, political, and cultural projects in a situation of obsessive concern with national autonomy, where the necessity of purging the culturally "contaminated" classes appeared as a primary task. Such extremist nativism was not restricted to China, needless to say, but entered in various ways speculation over the future of national cultures in all national liberation movements. It is not difficult to appreciate why the revolt against claims to national cultural authenticity on the part of those disenfranchised culturally by nativism should turn "class" itself into an undesirable category.[3] On the other hand, the abandonment of class issues deprives analysis of a major intellectual instrument in evaluating differences in claims to marginality, nourishing pretensions to ethnic unity and homogeneity.

Strong traces of the origins of the postcolonial in the colonial persist in the preoccupation with questions of race and ethnicity. And in its ideological effects, the generalization of the postcolonial has resulted also in the generalization of the problematics of ethnicity and race above all other questions. The meaning and politics of postcoloniality have been transformed as postcolonial criticism has suppressed important elements that earlier structured the concept of the postcolonial; ethnicity and race have been the chief beneficiaries of the retreat from nation and class—especially in the homelands of the new version of the postcolonial in metropolitan institutions. In the academic discourse of the early to mid-1980s, ethnicity and race appeared mostly in conjunction with class and gender, which pointed to a discursive conjuncture between feminism and the postcolonial in its original sense as a problem in culture and ethnicity as well as in the structures of political economy. Class was the first casualty as the postcolonial in its unfolding turned its back on structures of political economy. Issues of gender, too, were quickly infiltrated by issues of race and ethnicity. By the time postcolonialism in its contemporary guise appeared in the nineties, ethnicity and race had moved to the center of the discourse. Conceived to combat ethnocentrism and racism, postcolonial discourse ironically contributes presently to the racialization and ethnicization of the languages of both critical intellectual work and politics—with liberal intentions, no doubt, but at the risk, on the one hand, of covering up proliferating problems of social inequality and oppression whose origins lie elsewhere and, on the other hand, of contributing to the consolidation of the very ethnic, national, and racial boundaries that it is intended to render porous and traversible. Both risks are visible plainly in that slogan that has become dear to an emergent multiethnic globalist establishment: multiculturalism.

Intellectuals who hail from former British Commonwealth nations have played a significant part in the rephrasing of the postcolonial from a language of revolution infused with the vocabulary of political economy to a culturalist language of identity politics. What is of greatest relevance here is not these well-known reformulations of postcolonial criticism—of which Homi Bhabha's is possibly the most influential representative—but their reception and propagation in a completely transformed global environment, which would result not in the elaboration and refinement of earlier notions of the postcolonial, as in the case of a Said or a Spivak, but in their negation—and the appropriation of this reformulated postcoloniality by an emergent antirevolutionary consensus. It is arguable that the particular experiences with colonialism in

Commonwealth societies provide historical clues as to why intellectuals from these societies should be inclined toward the cultural and political orientations associated with postcoloniality. It is also quite evident, however, that such inclinations are not representative of the majority of the populations in those societies, have not always received the hearing that they do today, and are by no means restricted in their appeal only to British Commonwealth intellectuals. In other words, postcolonialism as we have it may have something to tell us about the present-day historical context; and if it appears as a growth industry most prominently in the United States, its ideological effects are global in their reach, if not with equal intensity and receptivity everywhere.

I have no wish here to go in any depth into a problem that I have discussed at length in a number of places, namely, the relationship between globalization and postcolonialism. Suffice it to say here that postcolonial concerns resonate with questions concerning the status of the nation-state, classes, identities, et cetera, in a world where globalization, real or imagined, has also captured the imagination of many; and it is hardly coincidental that the two have gained in intellectual popularity in tandem. If globalization for its promoters represents a break with an older world of colonialism, nationalism, and revolution that requires a rewriting of the past, postcolonialism offers valuable tools for doing so. Postcolonialism, in other words, enjoys wide appeal because it has something important to say about the contemporary world. This also is its predicament as a critical discourse. What is intended as a critique turns into a legitimation of a new ideology of globalization when it is mobilized in service of the latter. The failure of most so-called postcolonial critics to position themselves critically vis-à-vis the ideology of globalization—a product largely of a refusal to address questions of structure and totality—has facilitated such ideological use of postcolonialism. Such questions of structure include the legacies of colonial spaces that persist beneath the appearances of globality and continue to shape not only the configurations of power and political economy but also diasporic motions and cultural formations. An excessive attention to free-floating cosmopolitans conceals that most diasporic motions are regulated by conditions of political economy and, in the case of migrations out of former colonies, follow paths that end up in the "mother" country.

On the other hand, the projection of the postcolonial argument to the past has rendered the colonial past into just one more phase on the way to globalization, while erasing the revolutionary pasts that, for all their failures, envisioned alternatives to capitalist globality. The criticism of the nation that does not distinguish between different kinds of nationalism also serves to erase the revolutionary movements that took the nation as their premise. So does the obliviousness to questions of class. In light of what I have observed above with reference to the reevaluation of class formations in earlier national liberation movements, it may be understandable why postcolonial critics from formerly colonial societies should be reluctant to speak to issues of class, as they hail for the most part from classes that were (and are) suspect in the eyes of nativists. This makes it all the more imperative to speak to issues of class, however, as postcolonial elites are increasingly entangled in the transnational class formations produced by global reconfigurations. In the process, the postcolonial argument is mobilized to serve as an alibi for a cultural colonialism that is so thorough that it is nearly impossible to speak about it, as colonialism itself loses its meaning where it proceeds by consent of the colonized. However diluted in its dissolution of social differences into generalities about marginality or subalternity, the postcolonial argument even in its later phase initially retained a concern for the underdog, as witness the affinity postcolonial critics have expressed with the subaltern historians. By now, however, postcolonial criticism has become absorbed into institutions of power, its arguments appropriated by those who may feel marginal in certain ways but represent new forms of power in others. It may be indicative of this assimilation to transnational power that any call to disentangle postcolonialism as an intellectually and politically critical strategy from its service to new structures of power provokes censorial charges of "left-conservatism," racism, and, more colorfully, if in language reminiscent of politburo commissars, monsters arising from the netherlands.[4] It may also explain why First World muchacho postcolonials should be even more adamant than Third World postcolonial intellectuals in the defense of postcoloniality. It is even arguable that within the discourse of postcoloniality, the literally postcolonial are increasingly marginal as the postcolonial is abstracted as "method" and appropriated for First World concerns that have little to do with the colonial per se.

The increasing diffuseness of the content of the postcolonial may offer another clue to its expanding appeals. There have been a number of works published since the late 1980s that bear in their titles the term "postcolonial theory." To this writer, at least, it is a mystery what may be "theoretical" about much of the current discussion of postcoloniality, which in some fundamental ways resists theorization in its repudiation of all totalities and foundational categories. To be sure, a great deal of theory is invoked in justification of postcolonial concepts and arguments; but this use of theory must be distinguished from a theory of the postcolonial as such. It seems to me that "postcolonial" appears in our day most importantly as an umbrella term that covers all manner of social and cultural aspirations, more often than not couched in the languages of postmodernism and poststructuralism, many of which have little to do with the original sense of the postcolonial or with its origins in the idea of the colonial. I am referring here to theoretical and political positions that range from Gramscian Marxism to libertarianism and issues that range from gender and homosexuality to ethnicity, racism, nationalism, globalism, et cetera We may welcome the contribution postcolonial criticism has made to broadening the range of issues in cultural and political criticism beyond the singular concerns earlier with class, or gender, or race; but to qualify as theory, it needs to establish at least some hypothetical relationships between these various issues, which have not been forthcoming. Rather, the postcolonial appears in our day as the repository of a grab bag of issues that anyone can choose from in accordance with his or her political and intellectual inclinations, which cover such a broad range that it becomes meaningless even to speak of cultural and political positionings. No wonder that we can no longer speak of right or left, or even of right and wrong!

This broadening of the term's coverage frustrates even convinced postcolonialists, who complain of the increasing meaninglessness of the term.[5] It is in this generalized sense that "postcolonial" also has become integral to a new academic and intellectual establishment. It is tempting, and not entirely misleading, to suggest that the postcolonial is what postcolonial intellectuals do, and postcolonial intellectuals in our day represent a wide range of intellectual and political positions unified only by a common interest in the politics of cultural identity. Conversely, it would seem that the very deployment of the vocabulary of postcolonial criticism is sufficient qualification for postcolonial identity, further complicating the politics of postcoloniality. This may be quite in keeping with the spirit of overcoming boundaries and binarisms, but the intellectual and political confusion it creates is self-evident. The "postcolonial" has become a free-floating signifier, so to speak, that has no obvious relationship to either the "post" or the "colonial" that initially constituted its meaning—unless we take the colonial to serve as a paradigm for all inequality and oppression. Even that has become moot as the vocabulary of postcolonialism has found a comfortable lodging in the languages of political, institutional, and corporate power.

Accompanying this broadening of the term to cover a prolific range of problems is the spatial and temporal generalization of its applicability, so that the postcolonial now is something that may be perceived throughout history, regardless of time and space. There is no reason, of course, why a method of analysis emerging out of one social situation should not be applicable to another (which is the case with all social science, including Marxism), but such applicability requires at the least the testing of the method against the evidence of its new context, rather than the erasure of the latter. Postcolonial discourse may contribute to restoring to history what was suppressed in colonial and nationalist historiography. But in its conversion into a metahistorical method, it contributes itself to new kinds of erasures.

Among the pasts that are erased by the postcolonial are revolutionary pasts.

It is not that postcolonial criticism is responsible for this erasure. In consideration of the meaning of the postcolonial, it is also important to take note of a distinction between what is a product of the times and what is the consequence of an intellectual orientation, the confounding of which is another source of much confusion. It seems to me that one of the consequences of broadening the scope of the postcolonial is the appropriation for the postcolonial of concerns and questions that have diverse intellectual origins and share with postcolonial criticism little more than an effort to respond to changes in contemporary life and politics. The postcolonial has become a convenient way of naming and containing problems that have appeared with global reconfigurations—globalization, diasporas, emergent ethnicities, weakening of national boundaries, and all the cultural and identity questions associated with these developments. At the same time, it has offered a refuge to radicals who retreated from Marxism and socialism in the face of the global decline or abandonment of socialist alternatives in the 1980s, who have found relief in displacing their social and political radicalism to the realm of culture. To repeat what I observed above, in a trivial sense, we are all postcolonials. The obverse is that the gathering of diverse intellectual orientations under the umbrella of postcoloniality also makes it impossible to define and theorize what may be specific to postcolonial criticism. Postcolonialism has assumed something of the power of a self-perpetuating discourse (aided, no doubt, by its marketability in academia and the publishing industry). Even the critique of postcolonialism is rendered readily into a vehicle for its propagation.[6]

◆

As I have suggested elsewhere, bringing the perspective of history into the evaluation of postcolonial criticism may be crucial to disentangling some of the problems it presents as an intellectual current and a critical practice.[7] Historicizing postcolonial criticism is important not only to grasping its unfolding over the last three decades but also to placing it within a changing ideological context. This also makes it possible, second, to evaluate the history in postcolonial criticism, which is revealing of the ways in which its practitioners place themselves not only vis-à-vis the present but also with regard to radical critical practices of the past in which its own origins are entangled.

Rather than confront the question of history self-reflexively, however, postcolonial writing leaves the overwhelming impression that history is more of a hindrance than a help to grasping the past. I would like to comment briefly here on a recent work addressing questions in the historiography of modern China because it illustrates many of the points I have made above concerning the diffusion and diffuseness of postcolonial criticism, but especially because it focuses on questions of history with reference to the problem of the nation.

Prasenjit Duara's *Rescuing History from the Nation* explicitly claims postcolonialist inspiration and on that basis proceeds to offer a critique of earlier historiography, as well as an alternative historiography of its own.[8] As the author puts it: "I have been influenced by the general framework of a still vaguely defined 'postcolonialism' which informs much of this new scholarship in India and elsewhere. I think of postcolonialism as the critique of the ways in which modern, independent nation-states continue to operate within the old (colonial/Enlightenment) problematic of History and its hierarchy of different modes of living and time."[9] He then proceeds to argue that the writing of the history of modern China has been yoked to a project of nation-building and, in its commitment to a unilinear narrative of time derived from Enlightenment "History," has suppressed alternative ways of viewing "history." Instead of "unilinear" history, he offers what he describes as "bifurcated" history that accounts both for linear time and "dispersion" in time, therefore allowing for the recovery of "counter-memory." The latter part of the work offers illustrations of such bifurcated history by excursions into a number of themes in the historiography of modern China that offer alternatives to a history dominated by the nation and the Enlightenment.

To begin with what should be obvious to anyone familiar with the historiography of modern China, there is nothing novel about the themes that the author addresses that could be ascribed to "postcolonial" insight or the "bifurcation" of history. As the author's sources show sufficiently, questions of revolutionary attempts to build a nation (and a history to go with it), secret societies and their contradictions with modern revolutionaries, the modernizationist attack on popular beliefs, province/nation conflicts, issues of civil society, et cetera, have been the subject of extensive study by Chinese and foreign scholars of modern China. While the essays may be read as valuable review essays of existing literature with occasional sharp insights (as one would expect of Duara), the claim to novelty resulting from a new theoretical positioning is almost entirely vacuous. The author sustains his claims only by creating straw targets in the form of vague references to historians and others who allegedly have been wedded to nationalist or Enlightenment prejudices and by ignoring much evidence of history or historiography that points in different directions. As one Chinese reviewer has observed, most of these allegations have no subjects, which makes it impossible to pinpoint the author's arguments.[10] If the claim to "postcoloniality" here is little more than attaching a new label to historical work that has multiple sources, it inevitably also appropriates these multiple sources for the postcolonial.

The broader legitimation, presumably, is the questioning of national and Enlightenment narratives. But here, too, the author only ignores the complexity of the issues raised by Enlightenment and nationalist historiography, thereby managing to insert his work within a fashionable postcolonialism. There is no substantial discussion that while a unilinear conception of time may inform nationalist narratives, there is also a deep contradiction between the universalist claims of Enlightenment temporality and the particularistic cultural claims of nationalist history that is visible from the beginning in the divergent philosophies of history represented, say, by F. Hegel and J. G. von Herder. The argument also consistently confounds unilinear with evolutionary conceptions of time. These long have been challenged by the dialectical questioning of evolutionism in both the Hegelian and the Marxist traditions of history that represent history in terms of structural totalities, which may follow one another temporally but are not therefore unilinear or evolutionary.

The obliviousness to structuralist conceptions of history, and to structural contradictions, is most evident in the author's treatment of the nation and the relationship between nation and history. While Duara is critical of modern Chinese historians' efforts to project Chinese nationhood into the distant past, he himself questions the novelty of national consciousness as a modern phenomenon, arguing that it is possible in societies with long pasts such as China and India to find "political self-awareness."[11] While we may wonder how the possibility of premodern "political self-awareness" refutes the novelty of national consciousness, the more important issue is that national consciousness does not emerge ex nihilo but represents itself a restructuring of the past and its incorporation into a modern form of consciousness. Nor does this occur in a vacuum. The author's observation "that what is novel about modern nationalism is not political self-consciousness, but the world-system of nation-states,"[12] which he seems to view as a breakthrough discovery despite its banality, nevertheless does not seem to issue in any obligation to examine nationalism in China as an economic and political as well as a cultural phenomenon. Neither is Duara willing to pursue the implications of his own observation that nationalism in China took complex forms. The complexity of nationalism in China (or, for that matter, elsewhere) itself is an understatement, as the idea of nationalism has provided the discursive terrain for the articulation of diverse regional and social interests. What may be most important is that nationalism and the idea of the nation-state have served as the source of social and political contradictions in the new idea of political and cultural space that they generated—including new conceptions of the relationship between state and society and the relationship of the nation to race and ethnicity. Among the by-products of nationalism was the idea of citizenship, which was to play a crucial part in making visible in history those who had earlier been excluded from it—the vast majority of the population, including women.

Duara's approach to the nation and nationalism in the twentieth century also shapes his conceptualization of the relationship of history to the nation. Most historians of China are likely to wonder who the "we" might be when Duara writes that "because our own historical conceptions have shared so much with the linear History of the nation, we have tended to regard History more as a transparent medium of understanding than as a discourse enabling historical players (including historians) to deploy its resources to occlude, repress, appropriate and, sometimes, negotiate with other modes of depicting the past and, thus, the present and the future."[13] Chinese nationalists such as Liang Qichao were quite aware of the relationship between nation-building, politics, and history and devoted themselves explicitly to creating histories that would help reconstitute the inherited polity as a nation. Since then, of course, the relationship between the writing of history and the occlusion, repression, and appropriation of other modes of writing the past, with all their social and political implications, have generated ongoing controversy and the constant rewriting of the past. Even alternative temporalities to that assumed in modern conceptions of the past have not been erased by a century of nationalist historical writing but persist in the multiplicity of histories and stories that coexist with narratives of the nation. Here, too, Duara's analysis suffers from a one-dimensional conception of the nation and its implications for history. There is hardly any question, at least for this author, that there is much of intellectual and political significance in applying the paradigm of colonialism to nationalism and the nation-state; this enables a fuller grasp of the implications of modern states' claims to political power, as well as their efforts to homogenize culturally the populations they have claimed as their constituencies. In this sense, nationalism has played a part internally in societies that may parallel universalist Enlightenment ideologies globally. On the other hand, these same ideologies of colonization have not only generated their own contradictions but have also brought to the surface of history much that had been suppressed earlier. Interestingly, many of the themes that Duara takes up in the book, from problems of federalism and civil society to the recognition of the voices of the oppressed, are themselves products of "Enlightenment universalism" working through nationalist efforts to create new constituencies to legitimize and consolidate the nation. It is not possible at this point in history to argue that these constituencies, while they may or may not recognize themselves through the mirror of nationalist historiography, do so out of coercion or suppression rather than through the internalization of a sense of self that is the product of the same history. My point here is not simply that we should refrain from throwing the baby out with the bathwater. It is, rather, a simple recognition that our own histories enter in the most fundamental sense the ways in which we think both the past and the present.[14]

I have gone through this text in some detail because it illustrates my observations above concerning some of the pitfalls in postcolonial criticism. The point here is not to condemn a critical methodology by pointing to the slippery uses to which it may be put. But neither can we ignore that as postcolonial criticism has gained in popularity, it has come to legitimize scholarly practices for which it may not be responsible—and also in the process to appropriate for postcolonial criticism scholarly approaches that have emerged over the last three decades from diverse sources, further adding to the confusion. The Enlightenment, nationalism, and history have in the process come to serve as clichés that guarantee a hearing to any argument, however misguided, that invokes them as targets. One of the important consequences in the present context is the erasure of history, which deprives such arguments of a fundamental source of self-reflexiveness.

The treatment of the nation in a work such as the above is a case in point. While I find little that is problematic in the critique of the nation, or in a recognition of its inventedness, there is nevertheless something highly disturbing both intellectually and politically with the all-too-common assumption these days that we may therefore take the nation out of history. Having entered history, the nation has provided an ideological basis for self-identification, and invented or not, it has served as a historical force and continues to do so. While few would deny the connection between history and the nation, moreover, that relationship has neither erased alternative conceptualizations of the past nor been able to contain contradictions of its own generation that have issued in still greater complication of history—including, possibly, its negation. To appreciate these processes, it is important not to "rescue history from the nation" but to view the nation in history, and the history in the nation, in all its complexity.

The question of Chinese nationalism in relationship to postcolonial criticism is especially important because of the complex relationship between nationalism and revolution in the twentieth century. However we may assess the role of imperialism in modern Chinese history, it is quite evident that China presently is not just a postcolonial society but a postrevolutionary one, which offers a historical context from which to evaluate the claims of postcolonial criticism critically—in other words, to confront the epistemological claims of the latter in a historical context different from the one from which it issued. To apply the insights of postcolonialism to such a different historical context may help universalize its claims, but it also ends up erasing the particularities of the historical context and the ways in which such a confrontation may help evaluate the intellectual and political claims of the postcolonial. Decentering revolution (or nationalism) is quite a different matter from erasing it. The former helps us see the past in newer, more complex ways, in accordance with the insights of the present. The latter establishes a new domination over the past while depriving the present of the much-needed critical perspectives that the past may have to offer.

◆

If the abandonment of revolution has made possible the applicability of postcolonial criticism to revolutionary societies, postcolonial criticism has contributed in turn to the erasure of revolutions, or at the least to their further discrediting. For the same reason, however, recalling revolutions helps us place postcolonialism historically with greater accuracy than is possible only with reference to the term "colonial." But the goal here is not just to historicize postcolonial criticism. Even more important may be the necessity of the perspective of revolutionary history to a critical evaluation of postcolonial analysis and politics.

Ours are confusing times for anyone who might be foolish enough still to care to distinguish right from left (politically constructed), right from wrong (culturally constructed), or even reality from illusion (it is all in the representation). The right-left distinction lost its meaning to the historian of China when, beginning in the 1980s, former leftists were rendered into conservatives (and even rightists), and former rightists were reincarnated as progressive reformers. The same decade witnessed the considerable attenuation of judgments over right and wrong in debates (again involving China) over the cultural constructedness of human rights, so that it became nearly impossible to criticize the abuse of human beings without opening oneself to charges of cultural insensitivity—or worse, cultural imperialism. With everything being socially, politically, or culturally constructed, it was inevitable that sooner or later reality itself would be open to questioning, not for the first time, to be sure, but this time around with the aid of media that could turn deadly wars into Nintendo games.

It is tempting to suggest that human beings are programmed to experience disorientation on millennial occasions. Making Europe's millennium into everyone's millennium is likely to provoke among the politically correct anti-Eurocentric boos and hisses, but that might be relatively easy to ignore when so much of the disorientation on this particular millennial occasion seems to have something to do with what has come to be called "globalization." And what is globalization but the ultimate encompassment within a Euro-American modernity of a world that invents in resentful response many alternative modernities, including some of the most retrograde and reactionary kind? What is more difficult to ignore is the part putative progressive intellectuals play in the disorientation of contemporary life in their importunate embrace without discrimination of every claim to difference or grievance, ignoring the circumstances of the production and reception of such claims, which are also their historical circumstances. The politically correct are not to be blamed for efforts to confront the intellectual and ethical complexities that have come to the fore with the repudiation of past hegemonies that concealed such complexities within the appearance of coherence. Nor would it be fair to dismiss noble ideals because of their susceptibility to exploitation for causes for which they were not intended—as in the striking recent example of the genocidal dictator who seeks to overcome his quandary by seeking cover behind "truth and reconciliation commissions," which, he tells the world, are intended to forgive and forget past misdeeds.

It is necessary nevertheless to raise the question of the extent to which certain contemporary intellectual trends play a part in fostering the ethical and intellectual disorientation that permits this kind of self-serving duplicity; in other words, whether or not the celebration of ambivalence as a condition of tolerance also makes for a helplessness against bigotry and duplicity. Ambivalence, moreover, may be as much a construction as the certitudes of an earlier day that have been called into question over the last two decades for their constructedness, in which case it is important to inquire what it may be about contemporary historical circumstances that makes it into a desirable object of self-identification. Millennial thinking may seek to abolish history, but there is a historical context even for its desire to escape and overcome the past.

It is also possible that what is disorienting about contemporary critical work by putative radicals is that it points to nothing beyond itself; that is, meaningful change beyond the airing of past grievances and "voices of the weak." There is something millennial about the more extreme of the ideologies of globalization that seems to suggest that we are on the verge of liberation from history. More often than not, however, the end of this particular millennium seems to provide the occasion to render history into a cultural bazaar, offering a stall in compensation for past grievances to everyone who would enter the marketplace of history, as if that in itself would abolish the conditions that produced those grievances. Liberation from history is a moot question when history itself becomes meaningless, with "cultures" asserting their durability against time but still claiming a place in the bazaar, or, conversely, reinventing themselves as cultural products with timeless exchange values. Available evidence indicates that the crowding of the bazaar only adds new grievances to old ones, that the solution may lie in finding, not a place in the bazaar, but a way out of it. What is systematically ignored, if not suppressed, in contemporary critical work is the possibility of outsides to the bazaar—and futures that may correspond to those outsides. The end of the millennium concludes the millennium's work.

I would like to conclude here by revisiting a question that I have raised in an earlier discussion: how to position the postcolonial in relationship to the revolutionary past. I argued there that postcolonial criticism as it has emerged since the late 1980s is not only postcolonial but also postrevolutionary in two senses. The first sense is a temporal one; the "post" indicating not just "after," but also signaling the end to an era of revolutions, when revolutionary change globally seemed possible as an alternative to the present. This is no longer the case, and the surge of postcolonialism and its claims to radicalism are indicators of a break with this revolutionary past. The second sense has to do with the substance of the postcolonial, which is inherently antirevolutionary both in its social analytical strategies that eschew questions of totality and foundational categories—without which revolution understood as systemic change loses all relevance—and in its repudiation of social and political subjectivities that subvert the very notion of revolutionary activity—the move, in other words, from collective identities, which are undermined by charges of essentialism, to a stress on localized identity politics.

My argument in that chapter (as well as other writings on postcolonial criticism) has been informed to a large extent by my work on the history of the Chinese Revolution. The relationship between a particular history, in this case a revolutionary history, and postcolonial criticism is important to grasping not only the failures of revolutions in history, awareness of which has played a significant part in shaping contemporary thought and politics, but also the hubris of a present that pretends to have broken with the past. Recalling revolutions against their contemporary erasure is not to wish their return. It is rather to underline a need to remember that while political solutions and visions of the past may no longer be relevant, the circumstances that called them into existence are still very much with us. The problem with postcolonial criticism ultimately is not that it has turned its back on its radical origins but that, in doing so, it also has become oblivious to these circumstances and the possibility of imagining a world beyond the present. It represents in this fundamental sense not just a new way of remembering, as its proponents seem to believe, but also a new way of forgetting.

NOTES

This chapter originally appeared as "How the Grinch Hijacked Radicalism: Further Thoughts on the Postcolonial," *Postcolonial Studies* 2, no. 2 (1999): 149–63. The author gratefully acknowledges the permission of this publication to reprint the article here.

1. This discussion reformulates issues that I have described at length elsewhere, and I will forgo documenting my observations except in cases of direct attribution and quotation. Readers interested in such documentation may be referred to the essays in Arif Dirlik, *The Postcolonial Aura: Third World Criticism in the Age of Global Capitalism* (Boulder, Colo.: Westview Press, 1997).

2. Aijaz Ahmad, "The Politics of Literary Postcoloniality," *Race and Class* 36, no. 3 (1995): 1.

3. The historical context for these developments is the renunciation by national liberation states of their own pasts. Nevertheless, this does not eliminate the contradictions generated by past legacies. Thus, a state such as the Chinese has abandoned its earlier commitments to national autonomy in the economic realm, but it continues to pretend that cultural boundaries can and should be policed. This is less convincing than ever before in its contradictions with the economic policies of the regime. Arguments in favor of borderlands cultures are obviously of important critical significance in the critique of such policies. On the other hand, such state policies and postcolonial criticism may be contemporaries, especially with regard to a compartmentalized isolation of various realms of life from one another. As the Chinese state wishes to concentrate on the economic realm and is reluctant to speak to issues of culture (or even politics), postcolonial criticism focuses on issues of culture and relegates issues of political economy to the background. Such compartmentalization betrays the legacy of functionalism, which ignored that the economic is also social, political, and cultural, just as the cultural is at once social, political, and economic.

4. I am referring here to the distempered remarks by Stuart Hall with reference to an earlier critique of mine of postcolonialism: "We always knew that the dismantling of the colonial paradigm would release strange demons from the deep, and that these monsters might come trailing all sorts of subterranean material." S. Hall, "When Was the Post-Colonial? Thinking at the Limit," in *The Post-Colonial Question,* ed. I. Chambers and L. Curti (London: Routledge, 1996), 259. The "we always knew" part suggests that postcolonial criticism emerged as some premeditated strategy devised by an unnamed group, but Hall does not tell us what the occasion was for the "conspiracy." That a distinguished intellectual should be so oblivious to the history in postcolonial criticism is indicative of the pitfalls in postcolonialist thinking. I, for one, appreciate Hall's readiness to jump to the defense of his fellow "conspirators," but such name-calling avoids the issues involved—with which he would seem to agree, and that coincide with theoretical and political positions he has adopted elsewhere.

5. Bill Ashcroft, Gareth Griffiths, and Helen Tiffin, eds., *The Post-Colonial Studies Reader* (London: Routledge, 1995), 2.

6. I am thinking here of a volume such as Padmini Mongia, ed., *Contemporary Postcolonial Theory: A Reader* (London: Arnold, 1996). Nearly half of the essays included in this volume (including one by this author) are critical of postcolonial criticism, and yet the volume "contains" them within the domain of the postcolonial by its very title.

7. Arif Dirlik, "Postcolonial Criticism and the Perspective of History," introduction to *Postcolonial Aura,* 1–22.

8. Prasenjit Duara, *Rescuing History from the Nation: Questioning Narratives of Modern China* (Chicago: University of Chicago Press, 1995).

9. Duara, *Rescuing History,* 6.

10. Li Meng, "Zhengqiu sheide lishi?" (Saving whose history?), *Ershiyi shiji* (Twenty-first century) 49 (October 1998): 128–33, 129.

11. Duara, *Rescuing History,* 54.

12. Duara, *Rescuing History,* 69.

13. Duara, *Rescuing History,* 5.

14. Limitations of the discussion here preclude further elaboration of the complex issues

raised by the relationship between the Enlightenment, nation, and history. Readers who are interested may be referred to two forthcoming essays: Arif Dirlik, "History without a Center? Reflections on Eurocentrism," in *Historiographical Traditions and Cultural Identities in the Nineteenth and Twentieth Centuries,* ed. E. Fuchs and B. Stuchtey (Washington, D.C.: German Historical Institute, forthcoming); and Arif Dirlik, "Reading Ashis Nandy: The Return of the Past, or Modernity with a Vengeance?" in *Dissenting Knowledges, Open Futures: The Multiple Selves and Strange Destinations of Ashis Nandy* (tentative title), ed. Vinay Lal (New Delhi: Oxford University Press, forthcoming).

2

REVOLUTIONS IN HISTORY AND MEMORY:

THE POLITICS OF CULTURAL REVOLUTION

IN HISTORICAL PERSPECTIVE

I reflect in this chapter on certain questions that are presented by recent evaluations of the Cultural Revolution of the 1960s in China. The Cultural Revolution was an intriguing and significant historical event in its own right. What makes it particularly significant in the present context is that questions of the Cultural Revolution invite questions concerning the entirety of the Chinese revolution and, by extension, the problem of revolutions in general as phenomena of modernity. The question ultimately is what to do with revolutions in a postrevolutionary age that in its self-image postulates a break not just with the history of revolutions but with a modernity that was as much a producer as the product of revolutions.

While I make some effort below to disentangle problems of the Cultural Revolution from its contemporary representations, my primary concern in this discussion is with the latter. There are two aspects to my concern with these representations. First is the question of memory and history where revolutions are concerned. How to reconcile memory with history has emerged as a major concern over the last decade or two, most significantly with regard to questions of the Holocaust and World War II but also over questions of revolutionary legacies. While there has been much discussion of the status of memory in history, there has been relatively little discussion that I am aware of that addresses directly the question of *historians'* memories. The Cultural Revolution presents interesting problems in this regard for my generation of historians, who, provoked into radicalism by the Cultural Revolution (among other events of the 1960s), nevertheless have had a tendency in recent years to "forget" this intellectually formative event. The questions raised by this "forgetting" may not be encompassed, I suggest below, under technical historiographical questions of documentation, historical revisionism, et cetera, but are bound up with important transformations of the present, which have called into question not just the Cultural Revolution but also revolution as an idea. In our day, when "settling accounts with the past" seems to be quite widespread, it is important, I think, for historians to settle accounts with their own forgotten memories. Such confrontation is important for historical work itself because it calls for elucidation of the relationship of historians' memories to their historical evaluations and explanations. It is possible, after all, for historians to have too much memory of the experiences that have shaped them as historians; that might make for a nostalgic resistance to changed perspectives. It is also possible, at the other extreme, to dismiss past perspectives as irrelevant, not on some "objective" ground, but out of a desire to forget past perspectives that have become uncomfortable owing to changes in the historian's environment and consciousness. The question here is not just one of the relationship of the historian's present to the construction of the past, which is a perennial problem, but also of the relationship of the historian's present to his or her own past at a time of apparent discontinuity between the present and the past.

The question of historical memory and forgetting is not, needless to say, just an academic question but also is quite consequential for the ways in which we comprehend and act on our presents. Charles Maier has cautioned historians to ask "about the interests of the stakes involved in memory: the psychological or existential stakes and then the political stakes. For memory does not come in a social or political vacuum."[1] Neither memory nor forgetting is entirely innocent—nor is the historical consciousness that they inform. A central question for the present, I think, is how to distinguish critical memories of the past that also allow for a critique of the present from those memories that conform to the predispositions of the present and serve to legitimize contemporary configurations of power. Revolutions are particularly significant in this regard; the relegation to the past of a phenomenon long associated with uncompromising futuristic progressivism inevitably provokes questions about contemporary notions of the relationship between the present and the past. It also helps, I hope, to disturb some of the self-complacency of the present about the past that it has in its self-image left behind.

I reflect by way of conclusion on some of the contemporary changes that may help explain the recent turnabout in attitudes toward the revolutionary past, from revolutions as forces of social transformation and liberation to revolutions as producers of backwardness, oppression, and terror. My point of departure is a question that springs from my own experience as a historian of China but that I hope has broader implications: Why is it that revolutions, which seemed to make eminent sense only decades ago, no longer seem to make any sense? The question provokes other questions that pertain at once to history and the historian. Is it the conditions that have been transformed so drastically, revealing revolutions in all their senselessness, or is it we who have changed, so that we can no longer make sense of a phenomenon that seemed eminently sensible to many for two centuries? I think one could make a case either way, but I argue below that how the case is made is quite significant in its implications for the present. Revolutions may be historicized, or forgotten, in different ways. In the substance of the discussion below, I query the implications for the present of the manner in which revolutions are "forgotten" these days, which requires that we also "forget" a great deal about the present. One of my concerns here is to disturb the categories, among them "authoritarianism," that serve presently to contain complex phenomena of the past; I invoke revolution above all to reconsider contemporary "strategies of containment" that "contain" not just the past but also radical possibilities at the present.

I argue that while the historical perspective provided by the present enables new critiques of the past, a claim to a genuinely critical historiography may be sustained only if the critique of the past returns as its ultimate goal to the critique of the present. I hope by the banality of this premise to underscore its importance to a contemporary "regime of discontinuity,"[2] when it is practiced mostly in the forgetting, especially when it comes to the revolutionary past. That the historian makes history is hardly fresh news, especially with the postmodern stress on the author that, in its denial at the extreme of any reality to the past beyond its discursive construction, lodges history firmly in the present, however elusive that may be. It is all the more remarkable then that those who would deconstruct the past rarely extend the deconstruction to their own practices, not in some narcissistic sense of authorial self-deconstruction, which seems to represent the limit of critical self-reflection in our day, but in the more significant sense of the relationship of discursive practices to the structures of power of which discourses are at once products and producers. Another banality that might be recalled to some critical effect in discussions of revolution is the existence of a relationship between representation and power; specifically, the ways in which contemporary representations of revolution not only may resonate with the self-images of contemporary configurations of power but also stand as articulations of the power of those same configurations over the present and the past. While a sense of rupture with the past privileges more than ever the present over the past, it also conveniently places the present beyond the reach of any critical insights that may be gained from the critique of the past. With all their contradictions, revolutions may still be recalled, I suggest, to serve a much needed critical purpose and help rescue quite justifiable, and necessary, criticism of the past from intended or unintended complicity in legitimizing—perhaps even preparing the ground for—contemporary structures of power.

But the issue of revolution involves more than critical scholarship, or even criticism of existing forms of power. For all their flaws, shortcomings, failures, and occasional horrors, revolutions provided alibis for possibilities of fundamental social, political, and cultural transformation—and, in the case of socialist revolutions, the possibility of alternatives to a capitalist modernity. This may be a fundamental reason that revolutions are presently under condemnation not just for their acts of terror but also for the radical discourses that are held responsible for them. The terror discredits not just the revolutions in history as discrete historical events but the very idea of radical structural transformation, including the social and political phraseology of radical change from class to equality and even democracy. This itself is not particularly novel; it did not take the "linguistic turn" in social sciences to reveal that speaking about revolutions, or invoking the terminology of radical transformation, might speak revolutions into existence. The Guomindang regime in China in the 1930s blamed the success of Communism on loose talk about social phenomena. More than one U.S. politician in recent years has warned about speaking too much about classes lest such talk conjure classes into existence. The diagnosis of the linguistic turn that revolutionary discourses may have conjured revolutions into existence is not novel, but pervasive compliance with a linguistic turn that denies to revolutions any significant social and political basis may be revealing of the conservative turn in postmodernist/ poststructuralist social science.[3]

To recall revolutions, similarly, is not merely to single out one or another revolution for its virtues or vices but to keep open the possibility of alternative forms of social existence and organization. From radical perspectives, it is arguable that the fall of state socialisms has allowed for the recognition once again of certain kinds of radical social visions, grounded in everyday life, that have been as undesirable to a modernizationist socialism as to capitalism. Also, while the state socialist projects of the past may have failed to achieve the most fundamental of their promises, it is not clear that their revolutionary legacies are therefore little more than curiosities from a forgettable past. I would like to suggest that in transformed ways that account for the failures of the past, the legacies of revolution, and the search for alternatives that it inspired, are very much alive in our day in movements that seek to achieve from the bottom up what state socialisms sought to realize through the agency of bureaucratic states. These movements articulate a critique not just of past authoritarianism but also of the authoritarianism (among other things) that is built into the very structures of contemporary capitalism, to which democracy often means little more than market democracy, while markets provide at the same time unprecedentedly powerful means of supervision and control. Preoccupation with the flaws of the past may indeed blind us to the democratic impulse in revolutions that now finds expression in different forms in contemporary social movements. The presence of these movements—as contemporary incarnations of earlier visions of democracy and social justice that also repudiate, however, earlier means to achieve those ends—also makes it possible to recall the past as a resource without falling into a conservative or reactionary reaffirmation of the past. These movements serve as reminders that contrary to celebrations of historical discontinuity, both in the structures of power and in oppositions to them, the present and its past are linked quite intimately. It is not only in oppositional social and political movements that the legacy of revolutionary pasts is visible. The discourse on development at the highest levels of contemporary politics and power has slowly disintegrated as it has sought to come to terms with alternatives to capitalism that, while they may not have been direct products of revolutionary regimes, and may even have been subject to suppression by such regimes, nevertheless found their most powerful articulation in the demands for revolutionary change.[4]

Revolutions as we have known them may quite well be phenomena of the past. The social forces that made revolutions possible have largely disintegrated, and no amount of revolutionary discourse is likely to conjure into existence political identities that made revolutions possible; this may include national as well as class identities. On the other hand, the conditions that called forth revolutions in the past have hardly disappeared, either in terms of structural conditions or in the dislocations of life by the forces of capitalist modernity, which if anything are more powerful and unpredictable than earlier. These dislocations now give rise to identities of another type, which in their most visible forms shift opposition to existing forms of power onto other terrains, most powerful among which these days would be the terrains of religion and ethnicity. Alongside these oppositions, which are highly divisive and, to this author at least, productive of new forms of oppressive abstractions, however, are movements based in everyday life that seek to sustain and rejuvenate in transformed forms long-standing community ideals. If I may resort to a political language that has been abandoned too readily in the rush to forget revolutions, revolution has been hijacked in recent years by forces of the right. One fundamental reason for recalling revolutions of the past is once again to empower those movements of the left that retain commitments to visions of democracy and social justice.

The Cultural Revolution in China offers an important case for exploring some of these questions, both because it is still within living memory and because of its complexities that still render it relevant to the present. The Chinese revolution was at once a socialist and a Third World revolution, where nationalist and socialist goals reinforced and contradicted one another, class issues clashed with those of the state, and developmentalism came into conflict with the agrarian loyalties of a guerrilla revolution. In the end, the Chinese revolution presented itself as an alternative both to capitalism and to socialist modernizationism as represented by Soviet socialism. The Cultural Revolution proclaimed in the final phase of the revolution, which retrospectively has shaped understanding of the entire Chinese revolution, was a "revolution within the revolution," to recall Regis Debray's pithy phrase, that revealed the contradictions that beset all revolutionary regimes. In spite of the upheaval and ultimate terror of the Cultural Revolution, moreover, the Communist Party leadership has refused to abandon professions of faith in socialism even as it has opened the country ever more radically to capitalism; whatever we may make of this socialism that I have described elsewhere as postsocialism, it has interestingly allowed for some latitude of policy and experimentation that may account for the remarkable ability of the regime to survive and to flourish, at least for the time being. A most significant aspect of this latitude is the rather interesting flexibility of both the regime and the population toward the revolutionary past, which differs significantly from the urge to erase memories of the revolution among most China scholars, and some Chinese intellectuals, and may account for continued anxiety concerning China's future.

The issues that I take up below are best stated through a paradox that the Cultural Revolution presents in historical hindsight. The Cultural Revolution was launched to prevent a slide from socialism to capitalism, which Mao Zedong and his supporters perceived as an imminent possibility. Since the end of the Cultural Revolution, this is indeed what has happened, as Chinese society under Deng Xiaoping (one of the prime targets of the Cultural Revolution) has been incorporated into a capitalist world-system and is by now socialist only in name, and the persistent dictatorship of the Communist Party. In other words, the prognosis that justified the launching of the Cultural Revolution has been borne out by subsequent history. Why is it, then, that the image of the Cultural Revolution that prevails in most quarters in China and abroad is that of a historically meaningless and deviant undertaking that had little purpose beyond satisfying the craving for power or the perverse ideological attachments of its leaders and proponents?

There is probably more than one answer to this question, but whatever the answer or answers may be, it is necessary, I think, to account for two sets of problems. One set relates to the failings of the Cultural Revolution itself. Revolutions are tragic events even when they succeed in achieving their goals; a revolution that fails is likely to leave behind only memories of the naked oppressions and cruelties that revolutions inevitably unleash. In this particular case, that Chinese society has reverted to capitalism since the Cultural Revolution not only does not serve to legitimize it historically but also only underlines its futility. What stands out in historical memory is the wasteful and arbitrary cruelty it visited on millions of people.

To leave the matter here, where it is usually left these days, is to be entrapped in the ideology of the present, which seeks to erase in a teleology of the present memories of past alternatives that envisioned different historical outcomes from those that actually occurred. A genuinely critical appreciation of the Cultural Revolution is one that needs to understand it critically against its own claims and deeds, but without entrapment in this ideology of the present. Hence we need to account for a second set of problems that are epistemological and that pertain to our ways of knowing China, our understanding of revolutions (socialist or otherwise) over the last two centuries, and, last but not least, the conceptions of the present and the future that inform our understanding of the past. This task is all the more crucial in light of changes in the world situation over the last decade, when the fall of socialisms around the world and the seemingly undisputed global hegemony achieved by capitalism marks off our world from the world of the Cultural Revolution—to the point where it seems difficult even to imagine that there might have been a time when there were those audacious enough to envision a world different from the world of the present. This new ideological disposition reinforces the image of futility and arbitrariness left behind by the failures of the Cultural Revolution, making it almost impossible to speak about it critically as a historical event.

It is these two sets of issues that I take up below. I have two goals. First, I undertake to evaluate the Cultural Revolution historically, within the context both of the modern Chinese revolution and of the global history of which the revolution was an inextricable part. And second, I inquire into the relevance for the present, across the divide that I referred to above, of the political problems and aspirations that the Cultural Revolution expressed, which carry a significance not only beyond the whims and ideological predispositions of individual leaders but also beyond the boundaries of China itself.

THE VIRTUES OF AMBIVALENCE, OR THE PROFOUND AMBIGUITY OF THE CULTURAL REVOLUTION

Ambivalence usually implies moral and intellectual uncertainty or, even worse, a cowardly refusal to take a position on a problematic issue. It may, however, also serve another, less ignoble, purpose: to avoid entrapment in ideologically shaped moralities or intellectual positions in order to leave the door open for the possibility of other moral and intellectual positions.[5] Much of the problem with past and present interpretations of the Cultural Revolution lies in a refusal of ambivalence in favor of clear-cut positions that have ideologically suppressed one aspect or another of this complex historical event.

Over the last three decades, interpretations of the Cultural Revolution in the United States have gone through roughly four phases, each phase drastically revising or reversing the judgment of the previous phase. The interpretation that prevails presently, ironically, is closest to the initial responses to the

Cultural Revolution in 1966. When news of the Cultural Revolution reached the outside world in late summer 1966, the immediate interpretation placed on it was that it was a power struggle in the Communist leadership that in its extremeness and unprecedented nature confirmed the madness of the whole enterprise that was the Chinese revolution.[6] In the radical atmosphere of the late 1960s, this interpretation was challenged almost immediately by radicals, including a new generation of radical China scholars, who saw in the Cultural Revolution a Third World renewal of the promise of revolutionary socialism that had been betrayed in the Soviet Union. While conservative critiques of the Cultural Revolution never disappeared, this radical version was in the ascendancy by the early 1970s. Following President Nixon's visit to China, this unquestioning positive assessment of the Cultural Revolution spread beyond radicals to conservatives, who went even further than the radicals in lauding the Cultural Revolution; Richard Nixon himself credited the Cultural Revolution under "Chairman Mao" with instilling in the Chinese people the Protestant spirit of commitment and hard work that had been lost among the original Protestants in the United States.

The enthusiasm of this second phase was to vanish almost overnight after 1978. As support shifted to Deng Xiaoping's reform policies, both in scholarly and journalistic circles the image of the Cultural Revolution turned, following the assessments in China, into "ten years of disaster" that had taken a heavy toll both in terms of human lives and China's economic development. Now reporting from China, U.S. reporters wrote books showing that beneath the image of rosy-cheeked Red Guards lay a much harsher reality for the lives of the people; scholars began to uncover evidence that the developmental claims of the Cultural Revolution had been false; and the new socialist ethic that had so impressed visitors of the 1970s gave way to the image of a population rendered listless and immobile by political conflict and incoherence at the top. Earlier enthusiasm for Mao and the Cultural Revolution gave way to an even more exaggerated enthusiasm for Deng Xiaoping and his "democratic" policies.

Whether or not post-Tiananmen assessments of the Cultural Revolution deserve to be described as a fourth phase is problematic, for in many ways they represent an elaboration of, rather than departures from, the assessments of the 1980s. Following the Tiananmen tragedy, and especially the nearly unrestrained opening of China to capitalism after 1992, it is not so much the image of the Cultural Revolution that has changed as the image of the Chinese revolution as a whole, as the Cultural Revolution now became emblematic of the bankruptcy of the revolution as a whole (this theme was already on the emergence by the late 1980s). The Tiananmen tragedy burst illusions about Deng Xiaoping, who now joined Mao in the pantheon of "China's new emperors." The accumulation of memoirs by Chinese who had suffered under the Cultural Revolution confirmed the effects of the Tiananmen tragedy, making the whole history of post-1949 China (if not earlier) into one sorry story of corruption, ineptitude, and waste. It is not just the Cultural Revolution, but the revolution of which it was one manifestation and the regime that claims the legacy of that revolution, that is presently the object of American suspicion and hostility. On the other hand, in areas such as economic development, there has been a tendency in recent years to qualify the uniformly negative assessment of the 1980s concerning economic achievements of the Mao years.[7] This has not affected the assessment of the Cultural Revolution in other areas.

The history of representations of the Cultural Revolution remains to be written, but it is possible to observe that in spite of their divergent interpretations of the Cultural Revolution, these four phases share one thing: a refusal to acknowledge the ambiguities of the Cultural Revolution as a historical event and to incorporate such ambiguity in analysis. While there is no question that there has been an accumulation of evidence to call for new interpretations of the Cultural Revolution, these shifts in interpretation are not explainable on the basis of evidence alone. What we make of the Cultural Revolution depends on how we view it, and this view is not just a matter of evidence as it involves considerations of our perceptions of China and the world. There was always enough evidence of silliness and cruelty, if only in the language of the Cultural Revolution, and yet it was ignored so long as positive assessments prevailed. On the other hand, evidence of silliness and cruelty now seems to be the only kind of evidence that counts, ignoring the concerns that had justified earlier positive assessments. The present refusal of ambiguity is even more serious in its consequences than it was earlier. Even at the height of the positive assessments of the Cultural Revolution, there were always conservative voices that insisted on alternative assessments, making for some diversity of interpretation. In contrast, the memories of the Cultural Revolution that currently prevail are uniform in their condemnations of it as a historical event. My call for ambivalence, under the circumstances, is intended to counter this situation. I will make a brief case in its justification here, to illustrate how it may enable a less ideological and more critical historical evaluation of the Cultural Revolution.

What we mean by the Cultural Revolution is itself problematic, as it entails questions of where we draw the boundaries of the Cultural Revolution in its temporality. Different periodizations of the Cultural Revolution create different kinds of problems. If we take the Cultural Revolution in its most restricted, official sense, it refers to the years 1966–1969, and the image it yields is of chaos, mindless idol worship, political factionalism at the top and social conflict at the bottom, gratuitous violence, and an escape from the world at large. If we take the Cultural Revolution in the sense that the post-Mao official periodization takes it, as "ten years of disaster" from 1966 to 1976, the image

27

becomes that of political factionalism at the top and systematic oppression of dissidents at the bottom, with, however, quite different characteristics than the 1966–1969 period in terms of party-society relations, development policies, relationship to the world, and so on.

While this latter periodization accounts for the consequences of the "official Cultural Revolution," however, it ignores the concerns and the problems that went into the making of the Cultural Revolution, which take us back to the fateful year of 1956, when it was declared in the Eighth Party Congress that China had successfully achieved "the transition to socialism." It was conflicts over what was to be done next, with a concern for serious transformations in the global context, that were to culminate in the Cultural Revolution—not inevitably, but step-by-step as certain policies and conflict over those policies brought about the upheaval of the mid-1960s. If stress on the first two periodizations places in the foreground issues of personality and power, this broader periodization makes it necessary that we deal also with issues of policy. We may note also that in this periodization what we understand by the Cultural Revolution pertains to what we make of the "socialist phase" of the Chinese revolution, since, by the regime's own reckoning, the period before 1956 was still the period of "transition to socialism" (or "New Democracy," I would suggest), and the period after 1976 witnessed the step-by-step abandonment of socialism, contrary to claims of "socialism with Chinese characteristics." This broad periodization, finally, raises the question of the relationship between the Cultural Revolution (or the socialist phase of the revolution) and the revolution as a whole.[8]

The profound ambiguity of the Cultural Revolution arises from a deep contradiction between the policies it professed and promoted and the consequences of those policies at the ground level, which were indeed as problematic as its detractors claim. To briefly rehearse those policies, which were once the cause for the adulation of the Cultural Revolution in China and abroad, they sought, in the first place, to delink China from the capitalist world-system in order to guarantee progress toward socialism, based upon an understanding of an inevitable entrapment in capitalism that would follow from any serious involvement in the capitalist world-system.[9]

These policies, second, were intended to move China in a direction of socialism that broke with the example of the Soviet Union. As Mao noted in his reading of the texts on the Soviet economy, the process of socialist development required close attention not just to the forces but even more fundamentally to the relations of production.[10] Ignoring this problem had produced in the Soviet Union a new class structure based on the hierarchy of bureaucracy and expertise. Attention to relations of production was necessary to counter such class tendencies, as well as to evolve more democratic forms of management, both in agriculture and in industry, that required popular participation in decision making. The latter required also that more attention be given in development to popular mobilization over technology and technique. Under Chinese circumstances, this also meant a continuing emphasis on the peasantry in the process of development. In accordance with Mao's conviction about the necessity of spatial evenness in development, as expressed most cogently in his "On the Ten Great Relationships," this emphasis on the peasantry and the countryside was to bring industry to the villages in order to forestall an urban/industrial versus rural/agricultural bifurcation. Close attention to local circumstances, rather than bureaucratic fiat from the center, was basic to all these policy formulations.

Third, crucial to either set of policies was an emphasis on self-reliance at all levels, from the national level, to minimize material and intellectual dependence on advanced countries; to the level of the individual, to foster individual creativity in service of public goals. Self-reliance as an idea was inseparable from a commitment to placing public interests ahead of private ones. Growing out of earlier revolutionary experiences, especially in Yan'an, where the slogan of self-reliance had first emerged, the stress on self-reliance also addressed a fundamental problem of all Third World societies whose political sovereignty had been compromised by continuing financial and technological dependence on the capitalist and socialist blocs. Internally, it addressed the thorny question of creating a public consciousness of the process of development.

Finally, the idea of cultural revolution itself addressed the question of creating a new culture appropriate to a new, socialist mode of production. Such a culture could not emerge overnight but required continuing revolution so that development would take a genuinely socialist course, rather than move in the direction of capitalism or the hierarchical bureaucratic socialism of the Soviet Union. Cultural revolution referred not just to transformation at the level of "high" culture but, more important, to the transformation of everyday culture. It also required the elimination of institutional factors (all the way from bureaucratism to an undue emphasis on expertise to "bourgeois right" in economic remuneration) that stood in the way of developing a more egalitarian and just society.

These policies were enumerated in one official document after another from the late 1950s to the 1960s.[11] Taken together, they added up to the promise of an alternative mode of development—alternative both to capitalism and to Soviet-style socialism. In the circumstances of the period they made eminent good sense, and still do, especially if we look at what has happened under Mao's successors to Chinese "socialism," which, confirming the direst predictions of the period, has moved from reversion to capitalism to new class formations to the emergence of a hedonistic consumer culture—except for one thing: China and the Chinese in general have gotten richer, which everyone would seem to be enjoying tremendously. To recall these policies at the present, however, is not to fall in line with the ideological claims of the Cultural Revolution, as many were wont to do earlier. Some of the problems of the Cultural Revolution were evident even when it was an object of uncritical admiration; idol worship, distempered language, and wanton violence were all there to warn the observer that there was more (or, if you like, less) to the Cultural Revolution than revolutionary slogans. It was not that the evidence was not there; it was that at a time when revolution seemed to be the order of the day, the available evidence was easier to dismiss as silly, or marginal to the main business of revolution. Now that we have a much better grasp of what transpired at the ground level, it is possible and necessary to judge the intentions against the consequences.

"Delinking" from the capitalist world economy was never complete, and it was too short-lived to produce any significant results. If its goal was to create a well-rounded economy that answered the needs of the Chinese people rather than the distorting requisites of involvement in the world economy, too many other factors were involved—technical and political—to achieve that goal in such a short period. The policy was also intended to cow those in China who believed that economic and technological development required assistance from the outside; it may have been successful in this regard for a short period, but already by the 1970s the question was a moot one. If the idea that the Chinese could go it alone inspired enthusiasm and technical creativity for a short period, the obverse side was to encourage chauvinism, xenophobia, and self-righteousness that cut the Chinese off from the world intellectually and culturally—not just from the capitalist world but also from new ways of thinking about Marxism and revolution. Most seriously, China never delinked from the capitalist world-system ideologically; developmentalist assumptions that had their origins in capitalism (and were evident throughout in aspirations to surpass capitalist countries in production) were an important factor, I will suggest below, in undermining the promise of an alternative kind of socialism.

The question of social relations (or relations of production) was to prove to be even more problematic. While insistence on the need to pay close attention to social relations was both theoretically and politically justifiable, the Cultural Revolution leadership never came up with any sophisticated analysis of the question of social relations under socialism in general and in China in particular. Throughout, there was a tendency to reduce all social relations to class relations, which are but one manifestation of social relations in general. To make matters worse, the leadership was unable to provide a convincing class analysis of Chinese society that could serve as a guide to action, beyond clichés about socialist and capitalist roaders. The question of class was complicated in China by an interaction between prerevolutionary social and ideological relationships that persisted into the new regime, the new caste system of rankings imposed upon the population after 1949 in terms of their relationship to the revolution, and the structure of power created by the Communist regime itself. Given this situation, it was not at all clear against whom class struggle was to be conducted. As Richard Kraus observed in his study of this problem, for lack of clarity on the question, the concept of class became the site of the struggle that it was supposed to guide. How this worked out in practice has been demonstrated in another excellent study of the Cultural Revolution, Hong Yung Lee's *The Politics of the Chinese Cultural Revolution.* Depending on the winds of change, class could be defined economically, politically, organizationally, or ideologically. At its worst, class was reduced to a biological category in the so-called blood-line theory that rendered class into a matter of lineage.[12] Rather than guide a coherent struggle, class, like other things during the Cultural Revolution, became a tool to justify contingent power struggles. Under the circumstances, efforts to establish new production relations in other areas, such as new management practices, were also confounded by lack of clarity about what constituted proper socialist behavior and were immobilized by uncertainty about what might come next. Terms such as socialist and capitalist did not provide guidelines either, as they were reduced from concepts to handy labels, to be manipulated in power struggles even by those who had little idea as to what they meant.[13]

The question of property relations—in other words, the problem of collectivization—also needs to be recalled with a critical eye. While the formation of collective production units in agriculture and productive and living "units" (*danwei*) in urban areas from the late 1950s on was a necessary step toward socialism, under conditions of centralized power, they, too, played an ambiguous role. In his recent interesting study, *Policing and Punishment in China,* Michael Dutton observes sharply the coincidence of utopianism and social control in such units.[14] While this may be a problem of all communities, the problem is obviously exacerbated when the community is under the supervision of a power outside itself, which also raises questions about the claims during the Cultural Revolution to an alternative mode of development.

This is quite evident in the third aspect of the Cultural Revolution I listed above: self-reliance, which was key to the political, economic, and cultural goals of the Cultural Revolution. While certainly appealing as an idea, especially in its insistence on giving priority to public over private interest under conditions where the state reserved for itself the embodiment of the "public" and committed itself to a productionist ideology, self-reliance could also serve as a cover for exploiting the labor of the people. There is plentiful evidence of that also, even in work that is favorable to the Cultural Revolution. "Grasp revolution, promote production" was another common slogan of the Cultural Revolution, implying the instrumentalization of revolution in the cause of production. The other side of the coin was minimizing consumption in the cause of public commitment. In either case, putting the public interest ahead of private interests could easily be converted into sacrificing all individual and local interest in favor of a "public," which served as a euphemism for the state and the party. The claim that the state of the people cannot exploit the people is not very convincing, based as it is more on a "social imaginary" of the state than on actual relations between state and society.

Similar critiques may be offered with regard to problems of cultural revolution and the idea of continuing the revolution: theoretically convincing, but quite problematic in actuality. Cultural revolution, orchestrated from above, easily degenerated into cultural despotism. It silenced all alternative cultural activity in the realm of high culture. At the level of everyday life, the transformation of life habits was tied in so closely with Mao-worship that it converted the quest for self- and social improvement into a zealous bigotry that bore all the marks of a religious intolerance that could justify the worst acts of cruelty against opponents. The shifts in policy at the top, confounding the zeal that was prevalent initially, also bred cynicism, giving rise by the end of the Cultural Revolution to pervasive opportunism in the name of the revolution.

Finally, there is the question of continuing revolution, on which rest the claims of the Cultural Revolution to being a revolution. There was much about the Cultural Revolution that was indeed revolutionary in aspiration, but in light of what I have written above, its actualities must be qualified seriously. Did the Cultural Revolution, launched in the name of a struggle against capitalism and bureaucracy, have any serious vision of an alternative society—more specifically, a society without the party, which would imply also a society without "the dictatorship of the proletariat"? In Karl Marx's vision of postcapitalist society, there were two competing models for progress to socialism: the "dictatorship of the proletariat" model, and the commune model, inspired by the Paris Commune of 1871. The Paris Commune might have provided a genuine alternative to the dictatorship of the proletariat. But while there was discussion during the Cultural Revolution of the commune and the possibility of communal reorganization appeared in 1967, Mao himself was to back away from this alternative model and reaffirm his commitment to the dictatorship of the proletariat, which was to result over the ensuing decade in the restoration of party rule, and the punishment of those who had dared to voice opposition to the party. The memory of the Cultural Revolution as a revolution was tainted by the acts of its leadership before its opponents got around to questioning it.

William Hinton, the foremost chronicler of the Chinese revolution, has written that:

the Cultural Revolution that had seemed, from a distance, to be a watershed in history—a breakthrough that would enable people to shake up the superstructure of old China, all the inherited institutions and culture of an entrenched feudalism, and remold it into harmony with the new communal relations of production, a harmony that could propel production forward—now seemed to have degenerated into a most bizarre and Byzantine free-for-all, a no-holds-barred factional contest for power from top to bottom, where nothing mattered but getting the best of the opposition, and all means to that end seemed justified. If capitalism was an economic jungle, socialism, if that was what existed in China, looked like a political jungle.[15]

If the Cultural Revolution was based on questionable premises, betrayed its own goals, and visited untold suffering on the people, why bother, one might ask, to dwell on the intentions that underlay the Cultural Revolution or the ambiguities arising from the discrepancy between intention and result? Precisely because the explanations engendered by this attitude are quite problematic themselves. The intentions that inspired the Cultural Revolution are a matter of historical record and, for a while at least, inspired considerable enthusiasm; recalling them is a way not only to recover the historical record in China but also to confront the lineage of our own contemporary historical explanations. Unless it can be demonstrated that the policies in and of themselves inevitably led to the opposite of what they were intended to accomplish, it is necessary to explain the conditions that led to the consequences. The Cultural Revolution as here conceived had a history that was the product of the interaction between policy and circumstance, theory and practice, socialist goals and material conditions.

The question is not merely academic. Ignoring these intermediating factors and discrediting the intentions by holding them directly responsible for the consequences is a means to bury not just the Cultural Revolution but also the revolutionary problematic that inspired it in the first place. Ironically, those intermediating factors that may have done much to distort the initial aspirations of the Cultural Revolution are still in place, while the aspirations are systematically "forgotten." Before I return to a consideration of those factors, a few words may be in order here concerning the problems presented by contemporary representations of the Cultural Revolution.

THE PAST IN THE PRESENT: OUR WAYS OF SEEING CHINA

As I noted above, contemporary interpretations of the Cultural Revolution do not differ significantly from the initial responses to it in 1966, except that they have been enriched by the testimony of Chinese witnesses and victims. The testimony contributes to our understanding in significant ways, but the representations based on it are not without serious problems.

Most devastating may be that literature, popular and influential, that depicts a society so bizarre and corrupt at all levels that it becomes meaningless even to speak of problems of revolution.[16] In the name of capturing Chinese realities at the everyday level, this literature offers lurid tales of sexual perversion and cannibalism that serve well to sell books to a voyeuristic reading public but also dissolve serious political issues into Orientalist representations of a China immune to the ordinary (and normal) operations of politics. While in at least one case the veracity of such accounts has been challenged—also implicating scholars involved in the production of the account[17]—the problem with this literature in general is not veracity but its contribution to a discourse that renders irrelevant basic questions of historical explanation. If I may use an unkind analogy, to understand the Cultural Revolution (or Chinese politics) on the basis of such works is not very different from going to *People* magazine as a source for understanding American society and politics.

This literature also has confirmed a tendency, apparent since the mid-1980s, to use the depredations of the Cultural Revolution to discredit the Chinese revolution as a whole. The first work that I am aware of to make this connection explicitly was Anne Thurston's *Enemies of the People,* which attributed pervasive vindictiveness in individual behavior during the Cultural Revolution to a century of ethical degeneration brought about by the revolution.[18] This work was not alone; the enthusiasm over Deng Xiaoping's policies before the Tiananmen tragedy burst the bubble was accompanied by a feeling among many, specialists and nonspecialists alike, that China had returned to a normal path after more than a century of revolutionary deviation of which Mao and the Cultural Revolution had been culminations.

While it is quite legitimate and necessary to point to the connections between the Cultural Revolution and the revolutionary process that had brought the Communist Party to power, there are two problems with the way in which this connection is approached—indeed with the whole problematic of the Chinese revolution as it appears in these works. First, both the Cultural Revolution and the Chinese revolution are treated as if they were sui generis products of the internal dynamics and characteristics of Chinese society, without any reference to the global context of the revolution—and the problem of imperialism—which was of so much concern both to Chinese revolutionaries and to an earlier generation of scholars. Second, while China scholars have long argued (misleadingly, in my view) that socialism in China was little more than a euphemism for a national search for "wealth and power," when it comes to the depredations of the Cultural Revolution or its roots in the Chinese revolution, this connection is forgotten in a rush to lay the blame at the feet of socialism rather than a socialism contaminated by nationalism (although, to be fair, there have been those who suggest that such depredations may be explained in terms of "nasty" strains within China's cultural legacy, which contrasts remarkably with the praise bestowed on Chinese culture, also a product of the 1980s, when it comes to explaining capitalist development in Taiwan or Singapore).

While the attitudes above may be viewed as rehearsals of an earlier Orientalism that are effective in burying historical problems presented by the Cultural Revolution but too vague themselves in their culturalism to explain anything, more intriguing are explanations of the Cultural Revolution in terms of power relations that address questions of immediate context. How the structure of power established after 1949 may have been complicit in both the origins and the consequences of the Cultural Revolution is a fundamental question. It ought to be distinguished, however, from those views that reduce the question of power to personal power, that view the Cultural Revolution and its policies merely as a cover for factional power struggles, or the efforts of a waning Mao Zedong to recover the power he had lost after the Great Leap Forward. Mao may have lost prestige after the Great Leap Forward, so that others were not as prepared as before to follow his bidding, but there is little evidence that he lost the ability to coerce his opponents by force, if necessary (he did, after all, have Lin Biao and the military). This also raises the question of style, which has been an insistent question since the Cultural Revolution; in other words, if Mao was engaged in a Stalinist purge of his opponents, why did he not use Stalinist means rather than resorting to mass mobilization, which made considerable sense in terms of the legacy of the Chinese revolution? Finally, and most important, there is the question of policy. Politics—all politics—is about power, to be sure, but except in the most unscrupulous cases, the search for power is connected with certain policy positions. In the Cultural Revolution, too, there were policy positions; if they are denied now (in China and abroad), that may have more to do with the denial of historical logic to the Cultural Revolution, to an assumption that under such bizarre conditions of Oriental politics, ordinary assumptions of politics do not apply. As the quotation above from Hinton suggests, those bizarre conditions may have been a product, rather than the premise, of the Cultural Revolution; in other words, it is important once again to remember the historicity of the Cultural Revolution, that it assumed certain characteristics in its unfolding.

I will return to the question of power momentarily. But first it is necessary to confront one body of evidence against the Cultural Revolution that would seem to be irrefutable in its testimonial: the proliferating memory literature written by the victims of the Cultural Revolution. This body of literature, in what it has exposed of the workings of the Cultural Revolution at the ground level, would seem to leave no doubt that the policies of the Cultural Revolution were quite irrelevant to its workings, only providing a cover for petty struggles for power. While the emotive power of this literature is such that it seems obscene even to raise questions about it, we nevertheless need to make certain distinctions and point to certain ambiguities with regard to this literature as well.

First, there is the question of whose memories they are. One would not expect memoirs written by victims to convey anything but the most devastatingly negative portrayals of the Cultural Revolution. But what about other kinds of memoirs? In a recent discussion of this literature, Mobo Gao notes that the occasional memoir that offers a less condemnatory account of the Cultural Revolution is not well received.[19] One could go further and suggest that there has been a suppression of memories of the Cultural Revolution that, while recognizing its undesirable outcome, insist on accentuating the positive in terms of policy. One recent example is Qin Huailu's *Ninth Heaven to Ninth Hell,* a story of the Dazhai Brigade (a model of self-reliance during the Cultural Revolution) and its leader, Chen Yonggui.[20] A hero of the Cultural Revolution, Chen Yonggui was discredited subsequently through a systematic campaign. Likewise the Dazhai Brigade, earlier a model of collective agriculture, was to come under attack as soon as policies were adopted for the privatization of agriculture. Qin's book, which seeks to clear the names of Dazhai and Chen Yonggui against their detractors, was not allowed to be published in China and was smuggled out of the country for its English publication.[21] The case of Dazhai may be unusual (after all, it was the supreme agricultural model), but the case is an instance of the politics of memory in China and, therefore, abroad. Peasants, at least some peasants, remember Mao and the Cultural Revolution (though not Lin Biao, the Gang of Four, et cetera) differently than in the memoirs that have recently dominated our consciousness. Peasants in the Chinese countryside have converted Mao into a Buddha figure and have erected temples to him.[22] This is not to say that we should ignore the wrongs described by the victims of the Cultural Revolution but simply to note that historical assessment must come to terms with other kinds of memories as well. Even memories of intellectual victims of the Cultural Revolution are not free of ambiguities. Again I will take a recent example, Ma Bo's *Blood Red Sunset.*[23] This account of a young intellectual (son of the famous writer Yang Mo) rusticated in Inner Mongolia is a devastating account of the arbitrary and corrupt power of party cadres who could inflict harm on others with impunity, all the time mouthing the slogans of the Cultural Revolution. Ma Bo was victimized by such cadres and condemned for years to a horrendous life. At the same time, this is an unusually frank account that lets the reader know that, whether or not he deserved the fate he got, the author of the memoirs was capable himself of vile and corrupt behavior. His horrendous experience of punishment nevertheless leads to a personal transformation, so that the Ma Bo at the end of the account is a much more sympathetic person than the Ma Bo at the beginning, who starts his revolutionary activities in Inner Mongolia by the attempted murder of a "capitalist-roader" Mongolian herdsman and the actual murder of his dog. The reader of the account may draw his or her conclusions on how to respond ethically to a story such as this one; I will only note here that the account both proves the premises of the Cultural Revolution (class differences, urban-rural differences, hostilities between party and intellectuals, the corruption of the cadres) and the manner in which the Cultural Revolution itself was to become a source of intellectual, moral, and material corruption.[24]

Mobo Gao writes that "when a memoir is written at a time when the prevalent framework of discourse is different from that of the time when the memoir is written about, events and even feelings can be restructured without the writer's knowledge. It is true that personal suffering and violent brutality did occur during the Cultural Revolution. But explanations of why they occurred and how people felt about them can be restructured."[25] Much the same could be said of most writing on the Cultural Revolution in our day. One way of overcoming this problem, which is a general problem of history, is to judge the Cultural Revolution against its own claims, which also requires that we give credibility to the claims themselves rather than rendering them into verbal masks for something else. It is to this question that I return.

BACK TO AMBIGUITY: WHERE DID THE CULTURAL REVOLUTION GO WRONG?

The consequences of the Cultural Revolution were inevitable, I will suggest, but the inevitability was historical rather than implicit in the policies promoted. It is simply that given the ideological dispositions of the regime and the material structure of power it had put in place after 1949, those policies could not be realized and were likely to lead to the consequences they did. Mao's tragedy was that given the conflicting roles he assumed, he was bound almost of necessity to betray the revolution that he launched.

I suggested above that ideology (both in a narrow political sense and in the broadest sense that Karl Mannheim assigned to it, as life-outlook, or Weltanschauung), the legacy of Orientalism, and even market forces contribute to the making of contemporary representations of the Cultural Revolution. Even where there is agreement on the "factuality" of facts, which is not always the case, what significance we assign to competing facts and how we contextualize them remain problematic, and so do our evaluations.[26] I acknowledge readily that my own comments on the Cultural Revolution, including the insistence on ambivalence, are infused with ideological assumptions in both of the senses above. If I place a positive evaluation on the policies that informed the Cultural Revolution, it is because I think they had something important to say about socialism as it existed, about the necessity of socialism both as a critique of capitalism and as a source of alternative conceptualizations of human development. These same assumptions infuse my critical comments about the Cultural Revolution: about its developmentalist ideology and its reductionist assumptions about social relations, socialism, and capitalism; about its exploitation of the notion of "self-reliance"; about its chauvinistic nationalism; about its conceptions of cultural revolution and revolution. Some of these criticisms are informed by my own objections to nationalism or the fetishism of development, which are quite contrary to the assumptions and aspirations of many under capitalism or socialism as we have known it, in the First World or the Third World; they may indeed be most objectionable to those in the Third World, living under conditions of poverty, who see in national striving the way out of such poverty. Likewise my statements about self-reliance and culture, which may seem the most irrelevant to the majority peasant population in a country like China who have to work hard no matter what and who may not feel terribly deprived by not having access to other cultures (although they may feel different presently, now that television and Hollywood have entered the everyday lives of Chinese peasants.

With this in mind, let me offer a few considerations that I think are fundamental to the evaluation of the Cultural Revolution. First, the Cultural Revolution was doomed to failure because the policies that motivated it, if they were to be workable, required a social and political context different from the structure of power that had been put in place after 1949. The most important of these policies were legacies of the Chinese revolution. The assumption that these revolutionary policies could be kept alive under a postrevolutionary regime that had ensconced itself in power seems in hindsight somewhat anachronistic. If these policies were to be instituted, the post-1949 regime would have had to he transformed, which was not the intention of the Cultural Revolution and maybe was inconceivable given both the national and the international context. The Cultural Revolution has been attributed, among other things, to Mao's utopianism. It is possible to suggest from this perspective that Mao was insufficiently utopian, for he was unable or unwilling, because of his own ideological assumptions, to think beyond the "dictatorship of the proletariat" or the developmentalist nation-state. As a consequence, rather than challenge the existing structure of power as the Cultural Revolutionaries professed, Maoist policies ended up as instruments in a competition for the conquest of power within the existing structure, a competition that the Cultural Revolution did much to unleash.

Second, there was the power structure itself. This has, of course, been the intractable problem of all socialist regimes: a new power structure is necessary to the transformation of social relations, but how to render power subservient once again to the new social relations without opening the way to the resurgence of older social relations? The contradiction goes even deeper: with the overthrow of existing social relations, what is put in place is not new social relations but organized power; is it possible to return from a politics of organization to politics as the expression of social relations without jeopardizing the future of the revolution?

The power structure that was put in place after 1949 represented the invasion by the Communist Party of not only political but also social space; indeed, the distinction was abolished as society was reorganized according to a social imaginary that was an expression of the party's own power. Party omnipotence can be exaggerated; the new centralized, hierarchical bureaucracy that infiltrated society was subject, like all bureaucracies, to routinization and the slackening that attends it; the bureaucracy itself was not immune to infiltration and influence from below (expressed in continuing concern with localism). Still, it is difficult to ignore that, if we take into account the party and its subsidiary organizations, one in every ten Chinese (of all ages and genders) belonged to at least one organization. Furthermore, the designation of class ranks imposed upon society as a whole the party's political conceptualization of society, creating something akin to a caste system. If in ordinary times bureaucratic slackening and/or moderate policies could leave some social space outside of organized control, the party could always strike back, as it held in its hands the instruments of control and coercion; frequent mobilizations beginning shortly after 1949, whatever their other intentions, also served this purpose.

Even without the explicit or direct use of coercion, the power of the party was anchored in an ideology that made the party into a frame of reference in all activity. Three consequences of this power structure may be noteworthy. First, it abolished all "public" space outside of the party. Especially important with reference to Cultural Revolution policies was the abolition of local autonomy. The stress on the local remained throughout, and local initiative was recognized in terms of economic development; but, as Christine Wong writes of the rural industrialization program, "it was a program initiated from the top, which determined the scope and objectives of rural industrialization. The conflicting aims of local participation and central control interacted to produce a situation in which control often became divorced from responsibility, with unforeseen but extremely undesirable outcomes."[27] William Hinton spells out the political consequences of the abolition of the local:

Hemmed in by institutional feudalism at the top of the hierarchy, Mao failed to give effective support to the popular institutions of self-government sprouting at the base, the place where democracy, however limited, had the most chance of success. . . . higher bodies routinely usurped the sovereign power that should have resided in elected village congresses or revolutionary committees. . . . Nobody—not even Mao, apparently—was willing to trust villagers with substantive local power, and this made it all but impossible short of major, centrally led mass movements of the sort initiated from the Party center for people on the land to challenge the bureaucracy at all. Once the movements ebbed, traditional rule always reasserted itself.[28]

Second, a by-product of the continued invasion of the local from the top was to impose a bureaucratic uniformity on rural China, which led to the abolition in policy of differences among localities, a recognition that had been a strength of the Communist Party in revolutionary years and continued to receive emphasis in formal policy statements. Such a recognition would have done much to alleviate both the political and the economic despotism of the new structure of power. The third consequence of the new structure of power was its effect on individual personality and behavior. The structure created an urge to satisfy the power structure so as to be able to join it. Rather than nourish a cooperative culture, this led to behavior that oscillated between slavish compliance and aggressiveness, religious faith and cynicism, encouraging an almost irrational degree of competitiveness under the guise of public commitment.[29] The political structure, in other words, bred "nastiness."

The third consideration fundamental to the evaluation of the Cultural Revolution is the question of the challenge to the power structure in the name of Maoism. Given the problems of this structure and the obstacles it presented to socialism in any meaningful sense, the challenge was understandable, but what was the nature of the challenge itself? We know that this power structure, with all the tensions and resentments it contained, was the initial context for the Cultural Revolution. We also know that when this same power structure was threatened in the heat of the Cultural Revolution, Mao himself was to lead a quick movement to protect it. What was the challenge about, then? For all the documentation we have of rapid changes during the Cultural Revolution and the succession of power takeovers and declarations of new organizational forms, in the absence of any serious theoretical elaboration or articulated vision, it is difficult to say what the challenge amounted to. All we know is that against the Liu Shaoqi/Deng Xiaoping line of the early 1960s, which assigned to the party a supervisory-managerial role while opening up some social spaces outside of the party's daily intervention, Maoism proposed a more fundamentalist and thorough integration of politics and society, both from the top and the bottom, that presupposed greater participation in politics from the bottom but also opened up the possibility of a more thorough political infiltration of social space. Is it possible to suggest that if Maoism was utopian, it was a utopianism directed not against the existing power structure but a utopianization of that very structure, an experiment designed perhaps to fulfill the premises of that structure? There is some reason to think so, since when occasions arose during the Cultural Revolution of genuine challenge to the existing structure of power by the socially disaffected (including disaffected workers), as during the January Revolution in Shanghai in 1967 and the anarchistic *shengwulian* protests against the party later the same year, these alternatives were quickly rejected; there was, in other words, no apparent plan to transform the political organization in accordance with social demands. Political mobilization served under the circumstances to complete the unfinished task of party-state-society integration that disorganized the political organization but also, under the circumstances of power hierarchy and inequality, resulted inevitably in the abolition of all private social space, the terrorism of power, and the surfacing of divisions and resentment that had been barely contained so long as the political organization had retained some coherence. Frequent power takeovers by competing factions, and the declarations of new revolutionary forms of government that accompanied them, in practice added up to little more than occasions for factional revenge on opponents. It is noteworthy that these power takeovers, while they claimed local initiative, in actuality followed directives from the center. Putting "politics in command" may have inspired public commitment, individual initiative, and creativity; but in the end, rather than bring about the organic unity it was intended to achieve, it led to its opposite, exaggerating divisions. The politicization of everyday life "automatically raised every incident to a level of higher principle like 'class struggle.'"[30] As William Hinton writes of such "higher principles,"

> the most damaging excesses had their roots in Mao's constant reiteration of such slogans as "Never forget class struggle" and "Grasp class struggle, and all problems can be solved."
>
> While these calls laid bare the essence of the overall situation and defined the principal contradiction besetting society at each stage of development, they did little to illuminate most of the problems that came up from day to day. Cadres who treated all contradictions as class conflicts raised them artificially to absurd levels of antagonism, created "class enemies" where none existed, and ended up fighting battles that they never should have fought.[31]

Mao was only part of the problem. To use a distinction that the historian Harry Harootunian has employed with regard to the role of the Japanese emperor in politics, it is useful, I think, to distinguish Mao as a principal of politics from Mao as a principle of politics. Mao, of course, did serve as a political agent, playing a role in the initiation of the Cultural Revolution as well as intervening personally at crucial points. But more important may be the part that Mao played as a principle of politics. To most Chinese Mao was either a remote figure, an object of adulation, or a body of texts, most notably the "little red book," of little importance as a theoretical text but most significant as an inspirational one. As a principle of politics, Mao was open to interpretation, and many of the conflicts of the Cultural Revolution may be viewed also as conflicts over the interpretation of Mao. In this sense, while Maoism was offered in the Cultural Revolution as a challenge (and an alternative to the existing structure of power), in reality it was open to interpretation and appropriation by all sides, including the power structure that it purportedly challenged—which was possible because, while the texts invited "revolution," the revolution was premised on the preservation of the existing power structure. This is not to absolve Mao of responsibility, for in the end he turned to the support of that power structure when it was challenged. It does enable an explanation of the conflict conducted in the name of Mao Zedong. The reception of Mao, and the different uses to which Maoism was put during the Cultural Revolution, indicates the existence of deep social divisions and resentments that the Cultural Revolution did much to bring to the surface. Rather than resolve those divisions, the Cultural Revolution may have exacerbated them. In the end, it was to be a casualty itself of those divisions.

The fourth problem is an ideological one, what I will describe as "developmentalism." Developmentalism was not a peculiarity of Mao and the Cultural Revolution; it has its roots in a Marxism that accepted the premises of capitalism concerning human need, was perpetuated in the Soviet Union under Lenin and Stalin, and continues today in China under the post-Mao regime. It needs to be specified as a problem in connection with the Cultural Revolution because, I think, that it distorted policies of "self-reliance," greater popular initiative in development, balanced development, and even cultural policies. My premise here is that those policies could have led to positive outcomes only under conditions of local autonomy and decision making, which would have enabled a primary emphasis on the local community and the needs of the people as they perceived and defined them, and would have shifted emphasis to a negotiation of difference and inequality rather than their exaggeration—which was to undermine all sense of community. Culturally speaking, developmentalism, which is wedded to the idea of an inexorable move away from the past, rules out the possibility of drawing on the past as well as the present in defining the future.

The question here is not whether or not all development is undesirable, but rather what are the criteria for development. While the Cultural Revolution placed much verbal emphasis on the people, and Maoist economic policy was not without real benefits for the people, as Hinton, Bramall, Wong, and others have argued, the developmentalism that I am referring to here had its sources, on the one hand in a productionist interpretation of Marxism and on the other hand, in considerations of national wealth and power. This may not be a problem for the kind of "socialism" that has been pursued under Deng Xiaoping, but it does present a problem in light of the premise of Maoism that attention to relations of production should have priority over the forces of production in the creation of socialism. What exactly those relations of production should be was never spelled out clearly, but if local community and initiative were to be essential components of such new relations of production, as the Maoists intimated, subjecting the local community to central directives rather than guaranteeing it some kind of autonomy was not the best way to achieve that goal.

Finally, a problem that is often ignored in our day, even though it was central to earlier evaluations of the Cultural Revolution, is the problem of nationalism in relation to the global environment. As I have intimated already, considerations of national wealth and power did not disappear in the Cultural Revolutionary preoccupation with rejuvenating the revolution for socialism, but, if anything, assumed a more exaggerated, chauvinistic form. The Cultural Revolution, however, was launched at a time of genuine crisis in China's relationship to both the United States and the Soviet Union. Now that China has been incorporated into a capitalist world-system (although still not without friction), it is easy to "forget" that it was not Maoist paranoia but real and declared threats to China from both powers that played an important part in this crisis. The war mentality that this situation created was quite apparent during the Cultural Revolution in everything from economic policy to the language of politics.[32] Given the revolutionary tradition of the Communist Party, in which the language of politics had never been clearly distinguishable from the language of war, this may not seem very peculiar; but the sense of crisis created by the military threat from abroad certainly played a part in reinforcing the militarization of politics and the chauvinistic turn in Chinese nationalism. We may never know exactly what part these factors played in the initiation and the course of the Cultural Revolution, but it may be said with some confidence that they need to be factored into any consideration of how the goals of socialism were distorted by the sense of crisis that they expressed.

With an event as momentous as the Cultural Revolution, which touched the lives of all in China and destroyed many, it is easy to confound historical explanation with the justification for the movement. On the other hand, it is necessary also to consider the consequences of not making some effort at explanation. It is difficult to write about the Cultural Revolution because it was a traumatic event. It is also difficult not to write about it because it had a great deal to say, in both its promises and its betrayals, about the world in which we live. Distancing it to an alien time and space is not the best way to hear the messages it conveyed as one of the most important events of the twentieth century.

How does the historian confront historical trauma and still retain the will to historicize? The question forces a reminder that history ought not to be a positivistic undertaking that objectifies the past but at best a dialogue between the historian and those who lived the past, between the historian's construction of the past and the way that the past was or is constructed by those who lived it. If the historian has one obligation, it is to engage in a dialogue with as many memories as possible. What is inexcusable is to privilege some memories over others and, at worst, to render individual memories and experiences into a substitute for historical understanding.

In the case of events such as the Cultural Revolution or World War II, it is presently almost impossible to undertake this task of comprehensive dialogue, because some memories are silent while others are so traumatic as to make speech impossible. But there is another, more abstract, problem as well. The changes of the last decade have been so fundamental that the world of the Cultural Revolution seems to be a world quite distant in time from ours, that operated according to different rules than our world, so that the memories of individuals who lived through that world seem to be the only thing that connects them. With socialism seemingly a thing of the past, who cares about the Cultural Revolution's challenge to socialism? With China a playground for capitalism and former Red Guards turned into entrepreneurs in global capitalism, what meaning could "delinking" and "self-reliance" have? With peasants becoming millionaires, even if they are once again the object of scorn among intellectuals, why recall the ideals of collectivization? With national boundaries increasingly in question, what might have been the point about the Chinese revolution—or imperialism?

All these questions are in the air, even if they do not appear often as points of entry into discussions of the Cultural Revolution—or the Chinese revolution, for that matter. As all the questions that sought earlier to make sense of the Chinese or other revolutions fade into the past, all that remains in historical memory is the suffering of those who lived through those events, a suffering that seems all the more pointless because the events that caused the suffering have been deprived of meaning. Those events may be relegated safely to an oriental temporality and spatiality, denying their connections not just to our present but to their presents as well. In a historical perspective that takes them seriously as events in the history of modernity, however, the same events appear otherwise: as the constituents of a final effort—the most impressive of all such efforts—to create an alternative Third World modernity based on socialism.

In the temporal and spatial distancing of the Cultural Revolution lies a danger, I think, because this same distancing, in denying the modernity of the Cultural Revolution, suppresses the problems of modernity as well, which are still part of our present. In his discussion of the Holocaust, Zygmunt Bauman has argued that far from being a throwback to the past, the circumstances that led to the Holocaust were very much a part of the history of modernity.[33] Those who would speak of the Cultural Revolution as a holocaust might keep his reminder in mind. If the Cultural Revolution was indeed an event comparable to the Holocaust, the question of modernity was very much complicit in its outcome; the Chinese revolution itself was very much an assertion of Chinese modernity, and the Cultural Revolution was a phase of that process. In the discussion above, I have sought to bring out this aspect of the Cultural Revolution: how modernizationism economically, socially, politically, and culturally was very much on the agenda of the Cultural Revolution and distorted the aspiration to create an alternative modernity to produce the outcome it did.

There is widespread agreement on the outcome; after all, even Mao Zedong was in the end ambivalent about what he had set in motion. But the quest for an alternative modernity has not therefore ceased, because the problems of modernity which were part of the Cultural Revolution have not gone away in spite of brave declarations of "the end of history" that would have us wallow in the ravages of a capitalist modernity. And in this quest, the name of Mao Zedong keeps coming up one way or another, and so do the aspirations that inspired the Cultural Revolution. After being propelled with full force into global capitalism and consumerism in 1992, Chinese of all walks of life were suddenly gripped by a "Mao fever" in 1993 that, however distant in its consumerism from the political days of the Cultural Revolution, points at the least to the persistence of nostalgic memories that are not entirely innocent of political dissatisfactions with the present. The topography of the Chinese economy, at least partially responsible for the economic success of the last decade, bears upon it the imprint of Maoist policies of integrating industry and agriculture in a program of rural industrialization. Some analysts have observed also that earlier collectivization experiences have enabled the rural population in some areas to create new forms of cooperation on their own.[34] Wherever these experiences may lead in the end, they are indications that earlier aspirations to an alternative modernity have not been extinguished, and they have ties to historical memories of the Chinese revolution of a kind different from those that capture the headlines.

GLOBALISM, HISTORY, AND MEMORY

The Cultural Revolution in its consequences has done its share to discredit revolutions. I would like to suggest, however, that in order to comprehend their political ramifications, contemporary representations of the Cultural Revolution need to be viewed within the context of a general repudiation of revolutions. While Maoism was once perceived as an alternative to Stalinism, this distinction seems to have lost its significance when Maoism is portrayed as another version of Stalinism or Mao and Stalin are held forth as examples of tyranny along with the likes of Hitler.[35] It is not only socialist revolutions that are at issue. Critics of the Chinese revolution draw freely for inspiration on the work of François Furet. The criticism of the French Revolution has been quite significant in shaping contemporary attitudes toward revolution; unlike the criticism of socialist revolutions, which all along have been viewed with suspicion within the context of capitalist societies, criticism of the French Revolution is far more profound in its consequences, as it calls into question one of the founding moments of modernity, thereby casting doubt on all revolutions, regardless of political orientation, and the aspirations and visions that endowed revolutionary change with meaning.[36]

Condemnation of revolution is as old as the history of revolutions. Present-day critics of the French Revolution such as Furet recall in their criticism contemporaries of the revolution such as Alexis de Tocqueville.[37] Those who have suffered from revolutions, had their interests or ways of life threatened by them, or simply perceived in revolutions the breakdown of everyday human norms obviously have no reason to look upon revolutions with a friendly eye. While it may be possible historically to point to revolutionary traditions marked by the various revolutions of the last two centuries, it is necessary also to remember that, rather than follow a triumphal trajectory from one revolution to the next, revolution as an idea has suffered many ups and downs in its appeal and prestige.[38] There have been all along severe critics who could perceive in revolutions little more than sources of terror and totalitarianism. To pick a few especially memorable twentieth-century examples at random, one thinks readily of Pitirim Sorokin who, in his 1942 work, *Man and Society in Calamity,* included revolutions among calamities such as war, pestilence, and famine; of Hannah Arendt, who in her powerful *Origins of Totalitarianism* equated the experience of socialist revolutions with the devastation under Nazism; and in the case of the Chinese revolution, of works dating back to the 1950s such as Karl Wittfogel's *Oriental Despotism* or Robert J. Lifton's *Thought Reform and the Psychology of Totalism.* These scholarly condemnations of revolution may pale in the significance of their impact when placed alongside works of fiction or semifiction by George Orwell, Arthur Koestler, Eugene Zamiatin, et cetera, or, in the case of China, the popular blockbuster by Richard Condon, *The Manchurian Candidate,* and the movie based on it. There is little in contemporary condemnations of revolution that could surpass the powerful antirevolutionary message conveyed by these works.

What is most remarkable in our day, however, is the broad consensus over revolutions that could not be sustained even in the hottest days of the Cold

War, when revolutions, for all their flaws, seemed to be going concerns and could be called upon in critiques of capitalist society. The present consensus is made possible above all by the evidence of those who experienced revolutions firsthand and revolutionary leaderships that have renounced their pasts. At a time when history and memory diverge and conflict in so many ways, in the case of revolutions they would seem to confirm one another—which suggests, in the case of a recent event such as the Cultural Revolution, that there is also a great deal of forgetting at work, because only as late as two decades ago there was no shortage of memory or history to give an entirely different account of the event against its critics. Conversely, the repudiation of revolution has brought forth alternative memories. Memories of victimization and corruption that I discussed above have been supplemented in recent years by more triumphalist memories of survival, usually in the form of family narratives, and opposition.[39] When he wrote memorably in *The Unbearable Lightness of Being* that "the struggle against power is the struggle of memory against forgetting," Milan Kundera probably did not anticipate that his statement foreshadowed a surge of memory against Communist regimes from Eastern Europe to China that became part of the process of overthrowing and, in the case of China, transforming those regimes.[40]

The reversal in memory and forgetting is interesting, and may be revealing. Where under the Communist regimes memories were of survival and opposition in "the old society," now it is the revolution that had to be survived, and "the old society" has reappeared in a completely different, and favorable, light. The reversal in China began in the late 1970s with the retreat from revolution and the gradual incorporation into capitalism, which almost overnight turned former revolutionaries into conservatives and former "capitalist-roaders" into reformers. With antirevolutionary memory surging, history has not been far behind—especially history that seeks to authenticate itself through contact with the bearers of memory.[41] There is a tendency to deprive revolution of its social legitimation—its claim, in other words, that it was a product of social forces and gave voice to the aspirations of the oppressed in society. Revolution appears now as a political act that may even have gone against deepest social aspirations.[42] Alienation from revolution has also allowed a positive evaluation of the prerevolutionary period. As revolution is rendered into an enemy of economic and political progress, the former targets of revolution (and not just the Communist revolution) are restored into history as the bearers of progress whose promise was extinguished by revolution—not just the modern bourgeoisie, but even the gentry and landlords of the late Qing.[43] One beneficiary of this revision of prerevolutionary history is the idea of "civil society," which purportedly was in the process of formation when the victory of Communism put an end to it. Here, needless to say, history has moved beyond memory, because what is at issue is no longer just what revolutions did to people or what they failed to accomplish but the validity of the discourses that justified and guided revolutions.

It may be instructive to take a brief detour here to place the interplay of memory and history of revolutions within the broader problematic of memory and history that has become quite prominent over the last decade or so. The concern with memory and history would appear to have different sources in different contexts—the Holocaust in Germany; the Armenian massacres in Turkey for the Armenian population in the United States; the two-hundredth anniversary of the revolution in France; World War II in the United States, Japan, and China, et cetera.[44] It also appears prominently in the efforts of populations suppressed by hegemonic histories to recover their histories through memory, as in the case, for example, of indigenous peoples. In all cases, recovering lost or suppressed identities would seem to be an important concern. So is, however, settling accounts with the past. It may be an irony of our times that there is a proliferation of memory when forgetting is increasingly a condition of existence; it is as if the past must be remembered so as to complete the break with it. The proliferation of memory and its enhanced status, especially through its use in media like television, implies that memory may no longer be viewed merely as "the raw material of history."[45] Viewed with suspicion by scholars since the publication of Maurice Halbwachs's classic *The Collective Memory,* which underlined the constructedness and partialness of memory, memory has emerged as a competitor with history in opposition to the latter.[46] Memory may be both a beneficiary of loss of faith in abstract, hegemonic history and an element in its dissolution. Individual memories all along have been part of the materials out of which we have constructed history; the contradiction between history and memory may accordingly be viewed as part of a contradiction between history and the materials out of which we construct history. But with an increasingly pervasive feeling that history itself is little more than a construction that has served purposes of social and political hegemony, it has become increasingly difficult to sustain history's claims against memory—or, for that matter, literature. Evidence of historians' "forgetting" does not help much to instill confidence in history.

Pierre Nora writes that "the loss of a single explanatory principle, while casting us into a fragmented universe, has promoted every object—even the most humble, the most improbable, the most inaccessible—to the dignity of historical mystery. Since no one knows what the past will be made of next, anxiety turns everything into a trace, a possible indication, a hint of history that contaminates the innocence of all things."[47] On the other hand, the decline of the hegemony of the past has allowed for a proliferation of memory that talks back; not just recent memory, where it is most visible, but even distant forgotten memories that have returned to challenge history. The result is a multiplication of "private memories demanding their individual histories."[48] If history often has forgotten or suppressed memories not suitable to its purposes, memory often appears as if it is immune to the history or histories that constitute it. Ironically, the confrontation of memory and history seems also to promise abolishing the difference between the two. We may view the proliferation of memory as an indication of the impossibility of history. We may also view it as the proliferation of histories: many histories that do not cohere, and have no hope of doing so, which may be the price to be paid for "the democratization of social memory."[49] The proliferation of memory, or the fragmentation of history, has obvious political consequences. In Charles Maier's eloquent words, "the surfeit of memory is a sign not of historical confidence but of a retreat from transformative politics. It testifies to the loss of a future orientation, of progress toward civic enfranchisement and growing equality. It reflects a new focus on narrow ethnicity as a replacement for encompassing communities based on constitutions, legislation and widening attributes of citizenship."[50] The political consequences may be even more significant for revolutions, whether nationalist or socialist, that drew upon history for their justification and legitimation. While the fragmentation of history may be tied in with the ethnicization of politics that Maier speaks of, it also has a depoliticizing effect. As we find it increasingly difficult to speak of right or left in politics, it becomes impossible also to distinguish one kind of revolution from another, or even revolution from reaction. "Terror" or "genocide" takes over as the common element that marks all revolutions.[51]

To leave the matter here, however, is to leave unquestioned the power context for memory/history. The proliferation of memory may express a democratization of history, among other things, but it is also quite obvious that not all memory receives equal treatment, or even finds a voice. While it may be possible these days to whitewash Nazism or Japanese atrocities in East Asia, it is not possible to find many to speak for revolutions, or for them to get heard when they speak. I have given examples in the discussion above. Let me just add here that there are Chinese intellectuals who would reexamine and reevaluate the Cultural Revolution who hardly get a hearing, partly because of political restrictions but also because the very idea immediately invites condescension; I myself have been made into an "Orientalist" recently for speaking favorably of some legacies of the Cultural Revolution. For those new "democratic" Chinese intellectuals, nothing will do but total censorship of discussion. On the other hand, peasants in the countryside who seek to erect temples to the Mao they have deified are suppressed by the government, and if they find their way into discussion of contemporary politics and culture, they do so as curious throwbacks to a past best forgotten. Indeed, this seems to be the judgment these days on all who would speak favorably of revolutions: voices from the past obsessed with past problems; in the words of two labor activists, "overcoming alienation, exploitation, subordination—this is stuff of times past."[52]

A historian of Germany, Wolfgang Benz, has written in another context that "historians . . . enjoy especial success whenever the results of their research and their interpretations are in harmony with the longings, dreams and yearning for deliverance of the rulers and society of their times."[53] That the reconfiguration of memory is somehow bound up with the victory of the political right globally seems obvious. As I noted above, while the silencing of revolutionary memories may be a characteristic of our times, there is little that is new in the representation of revolutions, which is reminiscent above all not of liberal criticism of revolutions, marked by some ambivalence, but of conservative criticisms. The former, even where they did not approve of revolutions, still recognized some merit to them or at least viewed them in terms of social and political necessity, be it social oppression and exploitation, imperialism, or the pressures of modernity.[54] Conservative condemnation, however, has seen in revolutions nothing but perversions of humanity and politics by unscrupulous ideologues. The goal of conservative criticism, moreover, has been not only to condemn revolutions for their misdeeds but also to erase the political discourse of revolution. These are also the characteristics of contemporary condemnation of revolutions. Yet it is remarkable that such condemnation can assume an academic garb in portraying political questions as empirical ones, and get away with it. Few eyebrows seem to be raised over François Furet's frank acknowledgment of his politics in his interpretations of the French Revolution.[55] Since political considerations and ideology have been removed from history, the lifting of revolutions from their social and political context does not seem to raise too many questions either. A case in point is the recent preoccupation in Chinese historiography with the question of civil society. Whatever the merits of civil society as a political goal, its introduction into the historiography of prerevolutionary China obviously has something to do with postsocialist developments in Chinese society as well as a conservative reaffirmation of the virtues of classes that were in the past viewed as obstacles to China's development (not just by historians, but by generations of radical intellectuals). But these political questions do not seem to attract much attention. Neither does the historically quite significant question that the revolution, rather than the extinguishing of a burgeoning civil society (if that is what it was), was a product of the incapacity of civil society to enfranchise large social groups produced by a Chinese modernity.

To describe the recent reorientation of memory and history as part of a turn to the right may be accurate, but it is not sufficient in my view to explain the changes that seem to be at work, and itself needs explanation. While the preoccupation with memory would seem to have different sources in different contexts, the temporal coincidence is nevertheless intriguing. There may be a clue to it in Nora's reference to a connection between memory proliferation (or, as Maier puts it, "memory industry") and a "regime of discontinuity." There is good evidence to support the claim of many social scientists that we are in the midst of a break with the past—whether we conceive of it in terms of globalism versus modernity, postmodernism versus modernism, postcolonialism versus colonialism, or even postsocialism versus socialism. That the world is still structured by capitalism, perhaps to an unprecedented degree, does not negate the momentousness of the changes that have affected everything from economic and political structures to the structures of everyday life to the most basic cultural and ethical values. The kinds of collective resistance associated with revolutions no longer seem relevant under the circumstances. Even the social fractures that informed and dynamized revolutions are in the process of transformation, as class, gender, and community identities are overwhelmed by a search for primordial identities lodged above all in ethnicity and race. As Manuel Castells put it recently: "In a world of global flows of wealth, power and images, the search for identity, collective or individual, ascribed or constructed, becomes the fundamental source of social meaning. This is not a new trend, since identity, and particularly religious and ethnic identity, have been at the roots of meaning since the dawn of human society. Yet identity is becoming the main, and sometimes the only, source of meaning in a historical period characterized by widespread destructuring of organizations, delegitimation of institutions, fading away of major social movements, and ephemeral cultural expressions. People increasingly organize their meaning not around what they do but on the basis of what they are, or believe they are."[56] On the other hand, the transformations of the present have given rise to new problems that require new kinds of solutions.

I suggested above that there might be a contradiction presently between the proliferation of memory and forgetting as a condition of existence—which may not be too much of a contradiction, as remembering and forgetting may be but parts of the same process. Is forgetting anything but remembering differently? And what is its relationship to power? Certainly Germany and Japan, now that times have changed and with it their places in the world, seek to be remembered for other reasons than their Nazi or Fascist pasts. On the other hand, how else to remember failed revolutionary regimes but for their misdeeds, as both the structural conditions that produced them and the discourses that informed them are dissolved by the reconfiguration of the world? There is also an ethical question of the utmost importance: the question of divisiveness. While social division, too, may be a fact of life, who would want to further contribute to it by constantly drawing attention to it? Standing on the threshold of a new world that seems to be in the making, it seems both more plausible and ethically correct to reconcile, rather than to divide.

What we have witnessed over the last two decades is not the victory of the right but the disappearance of the left. Along with that, we have lost the ability, I think, to imagine an outside to capitalism, and alternatives to it. It is in this context that we need to ask what it means to forget revolutions. While the conditions of life have changed, they have transformed rather than abolished the problems that, in the past, revolutions set out to resolve. Of Sorokin's four calamities, only revolutions seem to have disappeared, for war, famine and pestilence are still with us. Social divisions, rather than disappear, proliferate and deepen. If we recall what revolutions stood for, it is not to bring back revolutions as they were but to recall the possibilities of alternatives to the present.

I think that revolutions in history need to be decentered so that we may perceive the past in new ways that may also suggest options for the present. The preoccupation in our day is to erase revolutions so as to bring forth histories that justify the present, whether we call it development or civil society. A radical decentering of revolutions, however, cannot dispense with the critique of the present. From that perspective, one of the more revealing aspects of current denunciations of revolution is their obliviousness to the way in which the revolutions of modernity, having internalized the ideologies of modernity, foreclosed alternatives to modernity, or suppressed alternative visions of modernity that challenged assumptions of economic developmentalism and parochial nationalism. Interestingly, these alternatives, too, have resurfaced with the waning of revolutions and enable critical perspectives not just on the past but on the present as well. It is important for any radical project to understand these alternatives in their relationship to the revolutions of the past—both the ways in which they continue the revolutionary tradition and the ways in which they break with the past. The revolutions of modernity have failed to achieve the goal of liberation they promised—although they did achieve a good bit otherwise—but they are as crucial today as at any time in the past to any discourse on liberation. That may be the reason that it is the discourse of revolution, and not just its misdeeds or failures, that is the ultimate target of the contemporary condemnation of revolutions. As Margaret Thatcher once expressed a wish to "bury socialism," the dominant culture of the present seeks to bury not just revolutions but what revolutions stood for and articulated; it is against this contemporary hegemony that the memory of revolutions must be sustained if there is to be any hope of envisioning the future differently. To quote Le Goff by way of summation, "Memory, on which history draws and which it nourishes in return, seeks to save the past in order to serve the present and the future. Let us act in such a way that collective memory may serve the liberation and not the enslavement of human beings."[57]

TWO LEGACIES

I began this discussion with a plea for recognition of the ambiguities of Mao and the Cultural Revolution. I will end with an illustration of this ambiguous legacy, in locations very far from China, that shows that the legacy is still alive and still very much ambiguous. Two radical movements in Latin America have in recent years evoked memories of Mao and the Cultural Revolution. The better known one is that of the Shining Path in Peru. The anthropologist Orin Starn writes of Abimael Guzman's Maoism:

> A final theme centers on violence. Guzman cited Mao to contend that "violence is a universal law . . . and without revolutionary violence one class cannot be substituted for another, an old order cannot be overthrown to create a new one." During the Cultural Revolution, the future rebel leader visited China at least three times. The Savonarolan fervency of the Gang of Four reappeared in Gonzalo Thought [the appellation used for Guzman's thought, similar to Mao Zedong Thought in an all-or-nothing vision of history as a ceaseless struggle between the "glorious forces of true revolutionaries" and "the miserable revisionism" of other Peruvian socialist parties. . . Opponents were "filthy," "parasitic," "cancerous," and "reptilian" in this social etiology of purity and danger, providing the ideological framework for the murder of hundreds of trade unionists, peasant activists, and neighborhood leaders from other political parties.[58]

The other movement is not one that claims an explicit relationship to Maoism or is widely known for such a connection. Its leaders, too, however, were products of the radical ferment of the 1960s and, according to one historian, were "Maoist in their underpinnings,"[59] although in this case their Maoism was articulated closely to local needs and culture, as Maoism theoretically should be. One of those leaders writes:

> Not everyone listens to the voices of hopelessness and resignation. Not everyone has jumped onto the bandwagon of despair. Most people continue on; they cannot hear the voice of the powerful and the fainthearted as they are deafened by the cry and the blood that death and misery shout in their ears. But in moments of rest, they hear another voice, not the one that comes from above, but rather the one that comes with the wind from below, and is born in the hearts of the indigenous people of the mountains, a voice that speaks of justice and liberty, a voice that speaks of socialism, a voice that speaks of hope . . . the only hope in this world. And the very oldest among the people in the villages tell of a man named Zapata who rose up for his own people and in a voice more like a song than a shout, said, "Land and Liberty."[60]

It is a long way from the shrill screams of the Cultural Revolution and Guzman to the gentle strains of the Zapatistas, from Mao's Faustian poetry to the earthbound aspirations of the Indians for whom Zapata spoke, but there is a grammar that they share: the grammar of an alternative modernity rooted in the welfare and the interests of the people. The self-restraint of the Zapatista language, which is imbedded in a deeper self-restraint of aspiration, may also help us grasp where Mao and the Cultural Revolution went wrong—and what we might remember or reject of their legacies.

NOTES

1. Charles Maier, "A Surfeit of Memory? Reflections on History, Melancholy and Denial," *History and Memory* 5, no. 2 (Fall/Winter 1993): 136–51, 136.

2. I owe the term to Pierre Nora, "Between Memory and History: Les Lieux de Mémoire," *Representations* 26 (Spring 1989): 7–25, 17.

3. For a critical discussion of the "linguistic turn" in connection with the French Revolution, see Roger Chartier, "Discourses and Practices: On the Origins of the French Revolution," in *On the Edge of the Cliff: History, Language, and Practices,* trans. Lydia G. Cochrane (Baltimore: Johns Hopkins University Press, 1997), 72–80.

4. Gilbert Rist, *The History of Development: From Western Origins to Global Faith,* trans. Patrick Camiller (London: Zed Books, 1997), esp. chaps. 8 and 9.

5. For the deployment of ambivalence in critiques of modernity, see Zygmunt Bauman, *Modernity and Ambivalence* (Ithaca, N.Y.: Cornell University Press, 1991); and Ulrich Beck, *The Reinvention of Politics: Rethinking Modernity in the Global Social Order* (Cambridge, England: Polity Press, 1997).

6. This was the view of a distinguished political scientist at the University of California at Berkeley, Chalmers Johnson. Asked to explain to the public this puzzling phenomenon of a regime launching a revolution against itself, he could see in the event only the final confirmation that Mao had gone irredeemably mad. That postrevolutionary interpretations have confirmed what he had to say does not, obviously, mean that he was correct in his diagnosis, but only the logic of a political science operating according to the conventional norms of power.

7. See, e.g., Chris Bramall, *In Praise of Maoist Economic Planning: Living Standards and Economic Development in Sichuan since 1931* (Oxford: Oxford University Press, 1993); and the essays in William A. Joseph, Christine P. W. Wong, and David Zweig, eds., *New Perspectives on the Cultural Revolution* (Cambridge: Harvard University Press, 1991).

8. This broad, twenty-year periodization of the Cultural Revolution is not mine alone but is implicit in the works of Roderick McFarquhar, Jean-Luc Domenach, Mark Selden, Karl Riskin, etc. These scholars all perceive significant changes in the 1956–1957 period that were to culminate in the Cultural Revolution. The best argument for this periodization, however, was provided by the Communist Party, which, in its policy reversals of 1978, declared a return to the contradictions in Chinese society as defined in the Eighth Party Congress of 1956: a contradiction between the people's needs (and the needs of an advanced social formation, socialism) and backward forces of production, rather than a contradiction between classes, which had been the line to emerge from the early 1960s.

9. Samir Amin has been the foremost theorist of "delinking." The Cultural Revolution

in China played a very important part in Amin's conceptualization of delinking, as well as the thinking on socialism of important world-system analysts such as Immanuel Wallerstein, Terence Hopkins, Giovanni Arrighi, etc. See Samir Amin, *Delinking: Towards a Polycentric World,* trans. Michael Wolfers (London: Zed Books, 1990). For Maoism in Amin's thinking, see his *Rereading the Postwar Period: An Intellectual Itinerary,* trans. Michael Wolfers (New York: Monthly Review Press, 1994). For the importance of the Cultural Revolution in worldwide thinking on development issues, see the (unsympathetic) account in Gilbert Rist, *History of Development.* For an argument that asserts the continued relevance of Maoism in the Third World, see W. F. Wertheim, Third World Whence and Wither? *Protective State versus Aggressive Market* (Amsterdam: Uitgeverij Spinhuis, 1997). For critical but sympathetic accounts from a contemporary perspective, see the essays in Arif Dirlik, Paul Healy, and Nick Knight, eds., *Critical Perspectives on Mao Zedong's Thought* (Atlantic Highlands, N.J.: Humanities Press, 1997).

10. Mao Tsetung, *A Critique of Soviet Economics,* trans. Moss Roberts, notes by Richard Levy (New York: Monthly Review Press, 1977).

11 Everything I have noted above, and more, is to be found in the excellent compilation of documents by Mark Selden, *The People's Republic of China: A Documentary History of Revolutionary Change* (New York: Monthly Review Press, 1979). Selden's introduction is exemplary of the interpretation placed on these policies at the time. See also the assessment by an economist, John Gurley, *China's Economy and the Maoist Strategy* (New York: Monthly Review Press, 1976).

12. Even though they were written without the benefit of the evidence that has become available since, the works by Kraus and Lee stand to this day as among the most astute analyses of the Cultural Revolution's ideology and reality. Richard Kraus, *Class Conflict in Chinese Socialism* (New York: Columbia University Press, 1981); and Hong Yung Lee, *The Politics of the Chinese Cultural Revolution: A Case Study* (Berkeley and Los Angeles: University of California Press, 1978). Another study of the time that was quite revealing of everyday realities and that compares favorably with the author's later writings, was Andrew Walder, *Chang Ch'un-ch'iao and Shanghai's January Revolution* (Ann Arbor: University of Michigan Center for Chinese Studies, 1978).

13. While by now there is a proliferation of studies and memoirs that impart a good idea of how these conflicts and manipulations worked at the local level, one study I would like to single out for its complex approach to the subject is Anita Chan, Richard Madsen, and Jonathan Unger, *Chen Village: The Recent History of a Peasant Community in China* (Berkeley and Los Angeles: University of California Press, 1984).

14. Michael Dutton, *Policing and Punishment in China: From Patriarchy to the "People"* (Cambridge: Cambridge University Press, 1992).

15. William Hinton, *Shenfan* (New York: Random House, 1983), 753.

16. I am referring here to works such as Nicholas Kristoff and Sheryl Wu Dunn, *China Wakes: The Struggle for the Soul of a Rising Power* (New York: Times Books, 1994); Li Zhisui, *The Private Life of Chairman Mao: The Memoirs of Mao's Personal Physician,* trans. H. C. Tai with Anne Thurston (New York: Random House, 1994); Harrison E. Salisbury, *The New Emperors: China in the Era of Mao and Deng* (New York: Little, Brown, 1992). These works, popular best sellers, also have been influential on academics, judging by some of the reviews they have received in the most prestigious publications.

17. I am referring here to a document circulated by the China Study Group in New York

concerning Li Zhisui's memoirs. The document also includes a statement of protest by those close to Mao concerning Li Zhisui's claims. According to this document, Li was himself quite upset by the preoccupation with Mao's sex life in reviews of his work.

18. Anne Thurston, *Enemies of the People* (New York: Alfred A. Knopf, 1987).

19. Mobo C. F. Gao, "Review Essay: Memoirs and Interpretation of the Cultural Revolution," *Bulletin of Concerned Asian Scholars* 27, no. 1 (1995): 49–57, 55. Gao notes in this regard Chen Xuezhao's *Surviving the Storm,* which refuses to denounce the Cultural Revolution. Informally, I know many people in China who, even though they too were victimized one way or another, refuse to engage in blanket condemnation of the Cultural Revolution.

20. Qin Huailu, *Ninth Heaven to Ninth Hell: The History of a Noble Chinese Experiment,* ed. William Hinton, trans. Dusanka Miscevic (New York: Barricade Books, 1995).

21. See the preface and the afterword by Hinton for the politics of the book. There have been other efforts in recent years to discredit "model workers" of earlier years, and usually there is sex involved somewhere along the line. In 1993, another model worker, Wang Guofan of Zunhua County (Hebei), was to come under attack, again with lurid tales of his misdoings. Wang was an example of the "baresticks" Mao lauded in 1955 in his collection *Socialist Upsurge in China's Countryside.* Indeed, a systematic study of the fate of earlier model workers might be quite revealing in terms of the politics of landownership in post-Mao China.

22. Thanks to a Chinese friend, Dr. Yu Keping, I have a photograph from a temple in Zhejiang where Mao occupies the seat of the Buddha, flanked by the "Boddhisatvas" Yang Kaihui (the first Mrs. Mao, killed in 1930) and Zhou Enlai. Early in 1995, party cadres in Hunan had to intervene to suspend the construction of a huge temple to Mao, once again to be built with peasant funds. The "Mao fever," which peaked in 1993 on the one-hundreth anniversary of Mao's birth, reveals also that these memories are not restricted to peasants but are pervasive among urban populations, including young intellectuals. In surveys, Mao still comes out ahead of all competitors as the greatest man of all time. Just recently it was reported that the city of Changsha in Hunan plans to construct a Mao square, surrounded by Mao's poetry in neon lights. See *South China Morning Post,* 13 January 1998.

23. Ma Bo, *Blood Red Sunset: A Memoir of the Cultural Revolution,* trans. Howard Goldblatt (New York: Viking Books, 1995).

24. In light of the preoccupation in this book with sexual corruption and the author's often expressed resentment that girls got a better deal by using their sexuality, it may be worth noting here that a different spin may be put on the issue of sexuality. At least for the girls, according to a Chinese woman friend who also spent these years in Inner Mongolia, the frontier provided possibilities of liberation (including sexual liberation) that were not available in a place like Beijing. This does not excuse the sexual dalliances of party cadres, but it suggests that the ethical atmosphere of the frontier may have made a difference.

25. Ma Bo, *Blood Red Sunset,* 51.

26. The post-Mao regime, if only out of concern for its own legitimacy, has been much readier than scholars abroad to recognize the problematic nature of the evaluations of Mao and the Cultural Revolution. For a remarkably honest recognition of these problems, as well as of history writing as a process of negotiation (both in terms of "facts" and politics), see Deng Xiaoping, "Remarks on Successive Drafts of the 'Resolution on Certain Questions in the History of our Party since the Founding of the People's Republic of China' (March

1980–June 1981)," in *Selected Works of Deng Xiaoping (1975–1982)* (Beijing: Foreign Languages Press, 1984), 276–96. The party leaders also know that much of the carnage during the Cultural Revolution was perpetrated by those in power, whose power would survive the Cultural Revolution, as Maurice Meisner has pointed out in a number of works.

27. William Hinton, "The Maoist 'Model' Reconsidered: Local Self-Reliance and the Financing of Rural Industrialization," in New Perspectives on the Cultural Revolution, Joseph, Wong, and Zweig, 183–96, 195.

28. Hinton, *Shenfan,* 766.

29. Anita Chan, *Children of Mao: Personality Development and Political Activism in the Red Guard Generation* (Seattle: University of Washington Press, 1985).

30. Qin Huailu, *Ninth Heaven,* 305.

31. Hinton, *Shenfan,* 765.

32. The importance of war preparation in determining economic policy has been analyzed cogently in Barry Naughton, "Industrial Policy during the Cultural Revolution: Military Preparation, Decentralization, and Leaps Forward," in *New Perspectives on the Cultural Revolution,* Joseph, Wong, and Zweig, 153–81.

33. Zygmunt Bauman, *Modernity and the Holocaust* (Ithaca, N.Y.: Cornell University Press, 1989).

34. Zhiyuan Cui has documented this phenomenon in many works. For an example, see "Particular, Universal, and Infinite: Transcending Western Centrism and Cultural Relativism in the Third World," in *The Idea of Progress Revisited,* ed. Leo Mark and Bruce Mazlish (Ann Arbor: University of Michigan Press). See also Dev Nathan and Govind Kelkar, "Collective Villages in the Chinese Market," pts. 1 and 2, *Economic and Political Weekly,* 3 May 1997, 951–63; 10 May 1997, 1037–47.

35. See, e.g., Daniel Chirot, *Modern Tyrants: The Power and Prevalence of Evil in Our Age* (New York: Free Press, 1994). For an eloquent criticism of such views, see Maurice Meisner, "Stalinism in the History of the Chinese Communist Party," in *Critical Perspectives,* Dirlik, Healy, and Knight, 184–206.

36. Edward Berenson, "The Social Interpretation of the French Revolution," in *Debating Revolutions,* ed. Nikkie R. Kiddie (New York: New York University Press, 1995), 85–111, 86 and 107 n. 5. "New" perspectives on the Chinese Revolution are offered in the special issue of *Modern China* 21, no. 1 (January 1995). The perspectives offered here indicate eloquently that changes in attitude toward the revolution may not be explained simply by recourse to new evidence; it is probably less accurate to say that new data have changed historians' interpretations than to say that historians, having changed, have begun to see data differently. Otherwise how to explain an observation in the special issue by a senior historian, an enthusiastic proponent of the Chinese Revolution in earlier days, that "the revolution was not a liberation but (foremost) was the replacement of one form of domination with another" (Joseph Esherick, "Ten Theses on the Chinese Revolution," 48)? It is hard to imagine that it would take a practicing historian thirty years to see the domination in the Communist regime! See also Marie-Claire Bergere, *The Golden Age of the Chinese Bourgeoisie, 1911–1937* (Cambridge: Cambridge University Press, 1989), for a more honest admission concerning change in outlook and its relationship to historical evaluation. For a repudiation of revolution by two distinguished Chinese intellectuals, who also point to connections between the French and the Chinese revolutions, see Li Zehou and Liu Zaifu, *Gaobie geming: huiwang ershi shiji Zhongguo* (Goodbye to revolution: Retrospect on twentieth-century

China) (Hong Kong: Cosmos Books, 1996), esp. 129–36, where the authors discuss, not the Communist revolution, but the nationalist revolution led by Sun Yat-sen and suggest that Sun's choice of the French over the English path to revolution was a mistake (131). The French Revolution's relationship to later socialist revolutions has been on the minds of both Marxist historians and contemporary conservative historians such as Furet and Simon Schama. See Berenson, "Social Interpretation," 92–93; and Michel Vovelle, "1789–1917: The Game of Analogies," in *The Terror,* ed. Keith M. Baker, vol. 4 of *The French Revolution and the Creation of Modern Political Culture* (Oxford: Pergamon Press, 1994), 349–78.

37. Patrick H. Hutton, History as an Art of Memory (Hanover, N.H.: University of Vermont Press, 1993), 144. See also Mona Ozouf, "The Terror after the Terror: An Immediate History," in *The Terror,* Baker, 3–39.

38. For fascinating illustrations, see Ronald Paulson, *Representations of Revolution, 1789–1820* (New Haven: Yale University Press, 1983).

39. I am referring here to such works as Jung Chang, *Wild Swans: Three Daughters of China* (New York: Simon & Schuster, 1991); and movies such as *Blue Kite* (Tian Zhuangzhuang, 1993) and *To Live* . For opposition narratives, see Rubie S. Watson, *Memory, History, and Opposition under State Socialism* (Santa Fe, N.M.: School of American Research, 1994), esp. Paul Pickowicz, "Memories of Revolution and Collectivization in China: The Unauthorized Reminiscences of a Rural Intellectual," 127–47. The family-narrative literature has also spilled over to the United States through the works of Amy Tan and others.

40. Watson, *Memory, History, and Opposition.* See also Kathleen E. Smith, *Remembering Stalin's Victims: Popular Memory and the End of the USSR* (Ithaca, N.Y.: Cornell University Press, 1996).

41. See Pickowicz, "Memories of Revolution," n. 35, where the author begins his discussion by stating that "between 1978 and 1987 I traveled five times to Raoyang county" (128). The number of trips to the source also appears prominently in Edward Friedman, Paul Pickowicz, and Mark Selden, *Chinese Village, Socialist State* (New Haven: Yale University Press, 1991). Here, too, there is an interesting parallel to earlier, highly positive accounts of the revolution. For an example, see Committee of Concerned Asian Scholars, *China: Inside the People's Republic* (New York: Bantam Books, 1972), which is an account of the first trip to China by a group of American scholars in 1971 (Pickowicz was a member of that group).

42. This is the argument, for the post-1949 period, offered by Friedman, Pickowicz, and Selden. See also Ralph Thaxton, *Salt of the Earth* (New Haven: Yale University Press, 1997). For a broader judgment along similar lines, see Joseph Esherick, "Ten Theses on the Chinese Revolution," *Modern China* 21, no. 1 (January 1995): 45–76. This also has been the major thrust of revisions of the French Revolution by Furet and others. See Berenson, "Social Interpretation." The strong anti-Marxist thrust in such interpretations is rather transparent not only in the rejection of a social foundation to revolutions but also in the repudiation or downplaying of the issue of class. For an explicit example of the latter, see Elizabeth Perry, ed., *Putting Class in Its Place: Worker Identities in East Asia* (Berkeley: University of California Institute of East Asian Studies, 1996). It is ironic that social history, which was long tied to radical causes, should now find service in the repudiation of radical possibilities. Social history has fallen upon hard times. For a fascinating discussion of how a depoliticized social history has been used by some German historians to deflect attention from Nazism,

see Mary Nolan, "The Historikerstkeit and Social History," in *Reworking the Past: Hitler, the Holocaust, and the Historians' Debate*, ed. Peter Baldwin (Boston: Beacon Press, 1990), 224–48.

43. For a work that acknowledges an explicit connection between the waning of revolution and its own undertaking, see Bergere, Golden Age of the Chinese Bourgeoisie. For the origins of a "public sphere" with the late Qing gentry, see Mary Backus Rankin, *Elite Activism and Political Transformation in China, 1865–1911* (Stanford, Calif.: Stanford University Press, 1986). The confusion of "the public sphere" with "civil society" is most readily apparent in the recent writings of Prasenjit Duara, who has discovered "civil society" in the Chinese idea of *fengjian* (commonly, "feudalism"), and in the activities of late Qing gentry. For Duara, it is nationalism that aborted the rise of civil society in China. The nostalgia for the past appears in accompaniment to the repudiation of revolution. For a critique, see chap. 1. For a debate on civil society in China, see the special issue of *Modern China*. For a critique of the ways in which the idea of civil society is deployed in the historiography of China, see Arif Dirlik, "Civil Society/Public Sphere in China," in *Zhongguo shehui kexue jikan* (*Chinese Social Sciences Quarterly*) 3 (1994) (English and Chinese).

44. For an overview of debates over the Holocaust, see Baldwin, *Reworking the Past*. A work that reconciles with some success history and memory in the case of the Armenian massacres, see Donald E. Miller and Lorna Touryan Miller, *Survivors: An Oral History of the Armenian Genocide* (Berkeley and Los Angeles: University of California Press, 1993). For World War II, see Takashi Fujitani, Geoff White, and Lisa Yoneyama, eds., *Perilous Memories: The Asia-Pacific Wars* (Durham, N.C.: Duke University Press, in press).

45. Jacques Le Goff, *History and Memory*, trans. Steven Rendall and Elizabeth Claman (New York: Columbia University Press, 1992), xi.

46. Maurice Halbwachs, *The Collective Memory*, trans. Francis J. Ditter and Vida Yazdi Ditter (New York: Harper & Row, 1980) (original French edition, 1950). See also Maurice Halbwachs, *On Collective Memory*, ed., trans., and with an introduction by Lewis A. Coser (Chicago: University of Chicago Press, 1992), esp. Coser's introduction, which also refers to the disorientation caused among Russian and East European populations by the necessity of forgetting the past (and remembering it differently), 21–22.

47. Nora, "Between Memory and History," 17.

48. Nora, "Between Memory and History," 15.

49. Le Goff, *History and Memory*, 99.

50. Maier, "A Surfeit of Memory?" 150.

51. Robert Melson, Revolution and Genocide: On the Origins of the Armenian Genocide and the Holocaust (Chicago: University of Chicago Press, 1992), for an example. The substance of Melson's study inquires into the relationships between the Young Turk revolution of 1908 and Hitler's revolution and between the Armenian massacres and the Holocaust. The validity of his comparison may be questionable, but what is interesting is what is encompassed by the term "revolution." His final comparative chapter casts the net even farther by bringing in statism and the Khmer Rouge, among others. Interestingly, Melson has nothing to say about the Cultural Revolution, which others have dubbed a "holocaust," presumably because his analysis of genocide rightly gives considerable weight to intention along with structural factors.

Terror itself is depoliticizing in focusing attention on criminality and mindless evil. We have had an interesting example of this effect recently. On 9 January 1998, the *New York*

Times carried three stories, one on Theodore Kaczynski ("Unabom Chaos Grows on Talk of Suicide Try,"sec. A, p. 1), one on Ramzi Ahmed Yousef ("the mastermind" of the World Trade Center bombing) ("Mastermind Gets Life for Bombing of Trade Center," sec. A, p. 1), and one on the Denver trial of Terry Nichols and Timothy McVeigh ("Joint Trial to be Sought in Oklahoma in Bomb Case," sec. A, p. 14). The lineup is interesting in the diversity of political positions. Kaczynski's actions draw upon a left-wing eco-anarchist legacy, Nichols and McVeigh represent right-wing responses to recent changes in U.S. society, and Yousef is in the line of Arab nationalist violence against the United States. Yet the politics was clear only in the case of Yousef, who, much like nineteenth- and twentieth-century militant political terrorists, declared that he was "a terrorist, and . . . proud of it," for the United States and Israel left no option for Arabs but terrorism (for which the presiding judge called him "an apostle of evil"). Kaczynski obviously agonized about his status but in the end gave in to pressures to declare him "mentally defective," much like rebels against the Russian czars or the Soviet state—which, however, did not spare him the same depiction as an incarnation of evil. Nichols and McVeigh, on the other hand, seem not to have made much of their politics in getting the best deal they could get, and there was little question among their victims, and many others as well, that they, too, were evil persons. The question is, what might be made of this coincidence by the reader of the *Times* that day, especially since another story the paper carried that day was the degeneration of violence in Algeria to killing for the sake of killing? On the other hand, the paper had little to say about the state terrorism in Chiapas, Mexico, where forty-five people (mostly women and children) associated with the Chiapas uprising were killed by military or paramilitary forces.

52. Gerard Greenfield and Apo Leong, "China's Communist Capitalism: The Real World of Market Socialism," *The Socialist Register 1997,* ed. Leo Panitch (London: Merlin Press, 1997): 96–122, 96.

53. Wolfgang Benz, "Warding Off the Past: Is This a Problem Only for Historians and Moralists?" in *Reworking the Past,* Baldwin, 196–213, 196.

54. Sorokin, while he viewed revolutions as calamities, nevertheless accorded them a progressive role in history. In the China field, scholars such as John King Fairbank, Joseph Levenson, and Benjamin Schwartz sought to come to terms with the Chinese revolution in different ways. While they were attacked by a younger generation for not being sufficiently prorevolutionary, their ambivalence made for an open-mindedness that is missing from their erstwhile critics, who have now mostly turned antirevolutionary. A remarkable contemporary example of such ambivalence is Melson's *Revolution and Genocide,* cited above. Having argued that revolutions create conditions for, and sometimes result in, genocide, Melson concludes by stating that "it is distinctly not my purpose to debunk the revolutionary tradition and to throw my lot in with its detractors. Though the human costs of revolutions were always high, in many important instances their results were indeed to uplift the poor, educate the illiterate, open up the social structure to merit, broaden liberty and participation, strengthen the state against foreign exploitation, and help to adapt society and economy to modernization and industrialization" (259).

55. Hutton, *History as an Art of Memory,* 144–45.

56. Manuel Castells, *The Rise of the Network Society,* vol. 1 of *The Information Age: Economy, Society, and Culture* (Malden, Mass.: Blackwell, 1997), 3.

57. Le Goff, *History and Memory,* 99.

58. Orin Starn, "Maoism in the Andes: The Communist Party of Peru—Shining Path and the Refusal of History," in *Critical Perspectives,* Dirlik, Healy, and Knight.

59. John Ross, *Rebellion from the Roots: Indian Uprising in Chiapas* (Monroe, Maine: Common Courage Press, 1995), 280. See also 274–75 for the origins.

60. Subcomandante Marcos, quoted in Alexander Cockburn, "Jerry Garcia and El Sup," *Nation,* 28 August–4 September 1995, 192.

3

IS THERE HISTORY AFTER EUROCENTRISM?

GLOBALISM, POSTCOLONIALISM, AND

THE DISAVOWAL OF HISTORY

Ours would seem to be another age of paradoxes. Localization accompanies globalization, cultural homogenization is challenged by insistence on cultural heterogeneity, denationalization is more than matched by ethnicization. Capitalism at its moment of victory over socialism finds itself wondering about different cultures of capitalism at odds with one another. There is a preoccupation with history when history seems to be increasingly irrelevant to understanding the present. Worked over by postmodernism, among other things, the past itself seems to be up for grabs, will say anything we want it to say.

It is another one of these paradoxes that I take up below: the paradox of Eurocentrism. The repudiation of Eurocentrism in intellectual and cultural life seems to be such an obvious necessity that it may seem odd to speak of it as a paradox. Yet a good case can be made that Eurocentrism, too, has come under scrutiny and criticism at the very moment of its victory globally. Whether we see in the present the ultimate victory or the impending demise of Eurocentrism depends on what we understand by it and where we locate it. The widespread assumption in our day that Eurocentrism may be spoken or written away, I suggest below, rests on a reductionist culturalist understanding of Eurocentrism. Rendering Eurocentrism into a cultural phenomenon that leaves unquestioned other locations for it distracts attention from crucial ways in which Eurocentrism may be a determinant of a present that claims liberation from the hold on it of the past. What is at issue is modernity, with all its complex constituents, of which Eurocentrism was the formative moment. Just as modernity is incomprehensible without reference to Eurocentrism, Eurocentrism as a concept is specifiable only within the context of modernity. Rather than define Eurocentrism from the outset, therefore, I seek below to contextualize it in order to restore to it—and the many arguments against it—some sense of historicity.

If Eurocentrism is crucial to thinking modernity, we need to raise the question of whether or not it may be repudiated without a simultaneous disavowal of history. The question necessitates confrontation of Eurocentrism as a historical phenomenon against the background of other "centrisms"; in other words, the ways in which Euro-American production, dissemination, and domination of modernity differs in its values and processes from earlier forms of domination such as, say, "Sinocentrism." It is also necessary, in assessing Eurocentrism as a historical problem, to take account of earlier critiques of Eurocentrism. This latter is crucial especially to accounting for the historicity of contemporary critiques of Eurocentrism, in terms of both their relationship to the past and their relationship to contemporary configurations of power.

I suggest by way of conclusion that a radical critique of Eurocentrism must rest on a radical critique of the whole project of modernity understood in terms of the life-world that is cultural and material at once. Modernity in our day is not just Euro-American but is dispersed globally, if not equally or uniformly, in transnational structures of various kinds, in ideologies of development, and the practices of everyday life. It does not just emanate from Euro-America understood geographically, nor are its agencies necessarily Euro-American in origin. A radical critique of Eurocentrism, in other words, must confront contemporary questions of globalism and postcolonialism and return analysis to the locations of contemporary struggles over the life-world. I should note here that the critique of Eurocentrism is a diffuse characteristic of all kinds of critiques of power in our day, from feminist to racial critiques. On occasion, it seems as if the problems of the world would be solved if somehow we got rid of Eurocentrism. This, of course, is silly. It not only misses much about Eurocentrism, it ignores even more about the rest of the world. Not the least of what it ignores is that while the agencies that are located in Euro-America may be the promoters of Eurocentrism, they are by now not the only ones, and possibly not the most important ones. Eurocentrism may not be global destiny, but it is a problem that needs to be confronted by any serious thinking about global destinies. These problems are too serious to be left in the hands of elites to whom Eurocentrism is an issue of identity in intraelite struggles for power.

EUROCENTRISM: WHAT AND WHERE?

At one level, the question of what Eurocentrism is and where it is located is sufficiently straightforward. Eurocentrism is crucial to understanding the spatialities and temporalities of modernity, not just in Euro-America but globally, from at least the late nineteenth century. The spatial conceptualizations around which we have organized history, from nations to areas to continents and oceans to the Third World and beyond, are in a fundamental sense implicated in a Eurocentric modernity. Even more powerful may be the reworking of temporalities by a Eurocentric conceptualization of the world, where the particular historical trajectory of Euro-American societies was to end up as a teleology worldwide in marking time. This was enunciated "theoretically" in the social sciences by the discourse of modernization, in its bourgeois as well as its Marxist formulations. History itself, as Nicholas Dirks puts it succinctly, is "a sign of the modern."[1] For the last century, but especially since World War II, Eurocentrism has been the informing principle in our constructions of history; not just in Euro-American historiography, but in the spatial and temporal assumptions of dominant historiographies worldwide. Euro-Americans conquered the world; renamed places; rearranged economies, societies, and politics; and erased or drove to the margins premodern ways of knowing space, time, and many other things. In the process, they universalized history in their own self-image in an unprecedented manner. Crucial to this self-image was the establishment by the European Enlightenment of a paradigm of the rational humanist subject as the subject of history, armed with reason and science, conquering time and space in the name of universal reason, reorganizing societies to bring them within the realm of rationality, and subjugating alternative historical trajectories to produce a universal history ever moving forward to fulfill the demands of human progress. The paradigm rendered the Euro-American experience of history into the fate of humankind, which then could serve as the rationalization for the pain let loose upon the world by its transformative aspirations.

Let us ignore for the moment an immediate objection to such an account of Eurocentrism: that it recapitulates an ideological Eurocentrism worthy of a most unreconstructed Eurocentrist. There is no recognition in this account of the incoherence of Eurocentrism as a historical phenomenon, because it is oblivious to the historicity of Eurocentrism, as well as to the contradictions that both dynamized its history and limited its claims. I will return to those questions in the next section. The immediate issue here is where to locate Eurocentrism.

Culture and discourse would seem to be the most popular choices of location in contemporary answers to Eurocentrism, represented most prominently by postcolonialism and globalism.[2] While quite different, and perhaps even antithetical, in their appreciation of the relationship of the present world situation to the past, postcolonialism and globalism would seem to be at one in their attitudes toward the location of Eurocentrism, or a Eurocentric modernity, which may account for their confounding by some cultural critics. The differences are deeply methodological and historical. Methodologically speaking, postcolonialism in its most popular forms (in the United States, at least) eschews questions of the structurations of the world in terms of "foundational categories" and stresses local encounters in the formation of identities; it is in many ways driven by a radical methodological individualism and situationist in its historical explanations. Globalism, on the other hand, draws attention to the structurations of the world by forces that operate at the highest level of abstraction and, in some of its versions, find in such abstraction the reaffirmation of the scientistic promises of social theory. Equally interesting may be their differences in the relationships they posit between the present and the past. Armed with the insights of the present, postcolonialists proceed to reinterpret the past with those very same insights. In this perspective, Eurocentrism, rather than shape history, appears to have been an ideological cover thrown over the past to disguise the complexity of local interactions; postcolonialism then offers a way to discover the past in its true complexity, more often than not expressed in the idea of "hybridity." In contrast to this presentist colonization of the past, globalism proclaims a "rupture" between a "present condition of globality and its many possible pasts."[3] It is a consciousness of totality that must be distinguished from similar consciousnesses of earlier periods; what it does, however, is to deny to Eurocentrism its claims to the creation of such a totality ("its many pasts") and opens up the possibility that the Others of Euro-America may have been partners in its creation.

While I have no wish to reduce intellectual orientations that claim no coherence for themselves to one or another of their articulations, the differences to which I point above may be illustrated through two statements by those who have gained some reputation as spokespeople of postcolonialism and globalism.[4] The editors of several influential volumes on postcolonial criticism write that

> European imperialism took various forms in different times and places and proceeded both through conscious planning and contingent occurrences. As a result of this complex development something occurred for which the plan of imperial expansion had not bargained: the immensely prestigious and powerful imperial culture found itself appropriated in projects of counter-colonial resistance which drew upon the many indigenous and local hybrid processes of self-determination to defy, erode and sometimes supplant the prodigious power of imperial cultural knowledge. Post-colonial literatures are a result of this interaction between imperial culture and the complex of indigenous cultural practices. As a consequence, postcolonial theory has existed for a long time before that particular name was used to describe it.[5]

Postcolonialism, then, is merely the current expression of forms of knowledge that have been around for a long time, except that there was no consciousness of it earlier. That those who are convinced of the discursive construction of knowledge should be oblivious to the positivistic implications of such an assertion is nothing short of remarkable.

By contrast, advocates of globalism leave no doubt about the break they seek to accomplish between the present and the past, including a break between a present condition and the factors that may have brought about such a condition. Roland Robertson, an enthusiastic advocate of globalization of social theory, writes:

> I argue that systematic comprehension of the macrostructuration of world order is essential to the viability of any form of contemporary theory and that such comprehension must involve *analytical separation of the factors which have facilitated the shift towards a single world—e.g., the spread of capitalism, western imperialism and the development of a global media system—from the general and global agency-structure (and/or culture) theme.* While the empirical relationship between the two sets of issues is of great importance (and, of course, complex), conflation of them leads us into all sorts of difficulties and inhibits our ability to come to terms with *the basic and shifting terms* of the contemporary world order.[6]

The projects of postcolonialism and globalism are prima facie antithetical: the one repudiating all structurations but the local, the other aiming to uncover global structures; the one situationally historicist, the other seeing in complex empirical relations an obstacle to the formulation of grand theories; the one reenvisioning the past, the other proclaiming a break with it.

And yet they stand to one another in the relationship of the local to the global and share a desire to break down the boundaries (or structures) that may intervene between the two. In the phraseology of one author who seeks to reconcile postcolonialism and globalism:

> [O]ne essential, underlying truth must be pointed out. Most of these peripheral postmodern effects and claims I have been recording stem directly from decomposition, under the contemporary phase of globalization, of the two fundamental assumptions of the three worlds theory. . . . The cultural borders authorized/enforced under that theory yield to perception of cultural interpenetration and transgression as the normal state in both the demystified past and the avant-garde present. And the evolutionary timeline along which the three worlds theory ranks cultures is cut up into discontinuously segmented, free-floating "realities," with even more transgressive an effect, making the primitive postmodern, and startlingly juxtaposing, not only different cultures and lifestyles, but even distinct epochs.[7]

In reading this statement, we need to remember that the "three worlds theory" was imbedded in the Eurocentric mapping of the world. For the immediate purposes here, Buell brings together postcolonialism and globalism in such a way as to articulate their common points in spite of the differences that I have stressed above: there is an assumption in both cases that culture is the site on which Eurocentrism needs to be challenged, and a disavowal of history in spite of differences toward the relationship between the present and the past. While postcolonialists make no secret of the prominence they assign to culture in their stress on identity formations and negotiations, someone like Roland Robertson is equally anxious in his discussion of globalization to separate the "agency-structure (and/or culture) theme" from the forces that account for the emergence of globalization in the first place.[8] It may be that for globalists no less than for postcolonialists, cultural boundaries are easier to negotiate than the boundaries of economic, social, and political power, which "inhibit" coming "to terms with the basic and shifting terms of the contemporary world order."

It may not be too surprising, in light of the culturalism implicit in such declarations not just of the autonomy but of the priority of culture, that postcolonialism and globalism also share a disavowal of history. Anthony Smith observes that there is something "timeless about the concept of a global culture," which, "widely diffused in space . . . is cut off from any past."[9] Timelessness is clearly visible in the statement from Buell, which reorders many pasts into some kind of postmodern pastiche. It is equally visible in the statement from Ashcroft, Griffiths, and Tiffin, for whom the past was not in any way significantly different from the present but did not know it until the present articulated for it its potential consciousness.

The question at issue here should be obvious by now. Can Eurocentrism be grasped in its significance without reference to the structures of power that it implies? Conversely, can the present, and its many claims against and over the past, be understood in its full historicity without reference to the past perspectives it seeks to erase, either through colonization or through assertions of rupture with the past? Both questions require consideration of Eurocentrism as a historical phenomenon, its formations, and the agencies that have enabled it to serve as a formative moment in not just a Euro-American but also a global modernity.[10]

EUROCENTRISM IN THE PERSPECTIVE OF HISTORY

The argument I offer here may be stated simply: Eurocentrism as a historical phenomenon is not to be understood without reference to the structures of power Euro-America produced over the last five centuries, which in turn produced Eurocentrism, globalized its effects, and universalized its historical claims. Those structures of power include the economic (capitalism, capitalist property relations, markets and modes of production, imperialism, et cetera), the political (a system of nation-states and the nation-form—most important, new organizations to handle problems presented by such a reordering of the world, new legal forms, et cetera), the social (production of classes, genders, races, ethnicities, and religious forms as well as the push toward individual-based social forms), and cultural (including new conceptions of space and time, new ideas of the good life, and a new developmentalist conception of the life-world). The list is woefully inadequate, and the categorizations themselves are admittedly problematic, but it suffices to indicate the intractability of the problem of Eurocentrism, which is my major purpose here. A culturalist appreciation of Eurocentrism that proceeds from a quite productive assertion of the autonomy of culture to an obscurantist isolation of culture and discourses from questions of political economy, and even renders culture into a privileged site that has priority over other aspects of life, may end up only with a dehistoricized, desocialized understanding of Eurocentrism that does not even come close to acknowledging the problems it presents. Does capitalism, regardless of the possibility of "different cultures of capitalism," nevertheless serve as an agent not just of new economic forms but also of certain fundamental values emanating from Euro-America? Does nationalism, as Partha Chatterjee argues, have imbedded in its "thematic" the most fundamental assumptions of a Euro-American Orientalism?[11] Does the very existence of certain forms of media, even apart from their content, introduce new values into everyday life globally? What may be said of "material" agencies as the carriers of Eurocentrism may be observed in reverse of the ways in which cultural constructs of Eurocentrism may acquire the power of material forces. Does it matter at some point that the current mapping of the world was a Euro-American construct, when that mapping is internalized by others and shapes the goals and boundaries of life activity? Especially important in this regard is the ideology of developmentalism, on which I will say more below.

There seems to be some anxiety in contemporary thinking that to raise anew the question of these structures is to open the way to some kind of "functionalism" that once again reduces social phenomena to a few of their elements.[12] Let us leave aside the point that culturalist functionalism may be as much a functionalism as any other. To recognize a multiplicity of phenomena that coincide historically and appear in structural and structuring relationships of one kind or another requires neither that we reduce those phenomena to one or more of their number nor that we ignore the relationships of contradiction between them that in effect serve to undermine efforts to functionalize the structure. In fact, it is these relationships, in their totality and particularity as well as their functionality and contradictoriness, that enable a coherent grasp of differences in history—not self-referential, localized differences that "result in an utter particularism in which history becomes a meaningless jumble of stories with no connection to each other,"[13] as in much of the postcolonial alternative, or deterritorialized totalities that have no clear spatial and temporal referents, as in the globalist alternatives.

The complexity of Eurocentrism becomes even more daunting if we note that Eurocentrism, as we have it now, is hardly a Euro-American phenomenon. Much of what we associate with Eurocentrism is now internal to societies worldwide, so that to speak of "Europe and its Others" itself appears as an oxy-moronic distraction. Legacies of Euro-America are everywhere, from global structures to daily economic practices, from state formations to household practices, from ideologies of development to cultures of consumption, from feminism to the centering in politics of race and ethnicity. Ashis Nandy, like Frantz Fanon in an earlier day, locates them in the psyches of "Europe's Others."[14] They are also in the ways we think the world, from theorizations about society to thinking about history. Even where claims are made these days to premodern, and therefore pre-"historical," ways of knowing, they fail to convince because their own efforts to refute a modernist historicism are conditioned by a self-consciousness about their own historicity. And how would we write the world without the legacies of Eurocentric mappings? Writing the world, no less than anti-Eurocentrism itself, may be incomprehensible without reference to those same legacies. If today we may find it impossible to think the world without reference to classes, genders, et cetera, premoderns (and maybe even pre-postmoderns) would have been surprised that identities are negotiable, as one negotiates commodities in the marketplace.

The recognition of the pervasiveness of Eurocentrism in its various dimensions in many ways reveals the limitations of a preoccupation with "Europe and its Others." That juxtaposition may still make sense with reference to the past, when a separation could be assumed between Europeans and others that would play an important part both in the construction of Others and in the construction of Eurocentrism. At the present, when more than ever the Others are most visible in their relocations to older colonial centers, they have, so to speak, come home. As a Euro-American modernity long has been internalized in the rest of the world, the rest of the world has now entered the interior of Euro-America physically and intellectually—which, not surprisingly, is also the prime location for the concern with Eurocentrism. Preoccupation with "Europe and its Others" seems under the circumstances to be a distraction from the confrontation of the victory of Eurocentrism, which is evident above all in the rendering of Euro-America and its many products into objects of desire globally. The contemporary concern with Eurocentric constructions of the Other, interestingly (and with some irony) seems to provide endless occasion for speaking about Euro-America, perpetuating the Eurocentrism it would formally repudiate—which may be the form this desire takes among intellectuals. At the risk of simple-minded psychologizing, anti-Eurocentrism strikes me above all as the mirror image of this desire, not so much as a negative compensation for it but rather as a demand for admission of non-Euro-American cultural elements into the interior of a world that has been shaped already by its historical legacy in a Eurocentric modernity. What, after all, is multiculturalism, which calls for the recognition of cultural relics or heritages without challenging the structures of power that are the products of Euro-American domination of the world and are imbued through and through with its values? These same circumstances may have something to tell us about why globalism and postcolonialism, in their very contradictoriness, have caught the imagination of many as ways to deal with such a contemporary situation—even though in their different ways they may evade the most fundamental and pressing question: whether or not there is an outside to Eurocentrism in a world that has been worked over by the forces of modernity.

If Eurocentrism understood as a cultural phenomenon is insufficient as a critique of Euro-American domination of the world, which was hardly just a "discursive" domination but has been imbedded in structures of power, the power of Eurocentrism itself is not to be grasped without reference to these same structures. This is not to say that culture and discourses are insignificant, but only to reiterate that they are insufficient as explanations of the world; the separation of culture and discourse into realms apart from the material is itself very modern. For the same reason, to argue for a reconnection of culture and discourse to the materiality of everyday life is not to argue for a return to an earlier privileging of political economy but, rather, to open up new ways of thinking the connection under contemporary circumstances—which implies also rethinking the connections that were repudiated under the regime of modernity. Eurocentric modernity then appears as one way of connecting modes of living and cultures, rather than as establishing a "scientific," and therefore forever valid, causal relationship between the two. The problem, as a historical problem, then is to inquire why Eurocentric ways of representing this relationship have acquired such power. Eurocentrists may suggest that it is the power of Euro-American cultures. I would like to suggest here that it is power, which has little to do with culture, that then dynamizes the claims of culture. The issue here is not one of ethical judgment or choice. The issue, rather, is ethical domination. And cultural domination is hardly its own justification. Neither Eurocentrism nor the contemporary challenges to it may be understood without reference to elements outside of the strictly cultural—which, needless to say, raises significant questions about what we mean by the cultural.

To recognize Eurocentrism as a historical phenomenon, it is necessary to view it within the context of other instances of domination, of which Eurocentrism was neither the first instance nor is likely to be the last. Such a historical perspective may also provide clues for a more thoroughgoing critique of power and domination than is currently available.

Eurocentrism is a complex term that disguises all manner of struggles within Euro-America over the meanings of "Europe" and "modernity," but, most important, that Eurocentrism was the product of a historical process, if not itself a historical process, that is inextricable from the invention of Europe's

Others. While at the level of power there may be little question that by the end of the nineteenth century Euro-Americans had more or less conquered the whole world and proceeded to produce ideological legitimations for the conquest, as a cultural orientation Eurocentrism itself is a hindsight invention of the Europe/Other binary, not the other way around.[15] Clichés about Enlightenment rationalism, unilinear histories, et cetera, that are quite common these days in the critiques of Eurocentrism overlook the ways in which historical processes mediated the understanding of such ideological products within a Euro-American context. Euro-America itself is still within this historical process of invention. Globalism, explicitly, and postcolonialism, inadvertently, may well be constituents of this process in its contemporary phase.

I have observed elsewhere that without the power of capitalism and all the structural innovations that accompanied it in political, social, and cultural organization, Eurocentrism might have been just another ethnocentrism. It is rather remarkable in an age of proliferating ethnocentrisms such as ours that so little attention should be paid to ethnocentrism not just as a legacy of Eurocentrism (although that may have contributed to it in significant ways) but also as a condition of the world at the origins of modernity, more often than not expressing the centrality in a variety of "world-systems" of the cultural assumptions of those who dominated those world-systems. This may be stating the obvious, but it needs to be stated nevertheless, since considerations of political correctness have led to a shyness about criticism of ethnocentrisms other than the Euro-American (or blatantly murderous expressions of it in places like Bosnia, Rwanda, or Turkey). Spheres of cultural hegemony that more or less coincided with economic and political domination have been present all along, defining a "Chinese" world, an "Islamic" world, "Arabic" and "Indic" worlds, et cetera. In spite of real or imagined hegemonies over vast territories, however, none of these worlds was in the end able to match Eurocentrism in reach or transformative power. The statement may seem foolhardy when the end of history is not yet in sight; what seems safe to say is that if these other cultural hegemonies are ever globalized and universalized in the same manner as Eurocentrism, it will be on the basis of a world globalized and universalized through Eurocentrism and in their articulations to this new world. There are presently efforts to discover an early "modernity" in East and Southeast Asia, but it did not occur to anyone in those regions to even raise the question of modernity until modernity had been established as a principle of history. Similarly, East Asian societies may claim a "Confucian" heritage that explains their recent success in capitalism, but this Confucian heritage is one that has been reinterpreted by the very requirements of capitalism.

Eurocentrism is the one centrism that historically has encompassed the globe and reached levels of life that were not even of much concern to its competitors; it revolutionized lives around the globe, relocated societies in new spaces, and transformed their historical trajectories—to the point where it makes no sense to speak of history without reference to Eurocentrism. There may have been no shortage of "cultural hybridities" earlier; what is interesting and compelling about Eurocentrism is that by the time its globalizing aspirations neared (for they could never be reached) their geographical boundaries, Eurocentrism was to become a constituent of most people's hybridities—which is not to be said of any of the other centrisms, which were regionally limited and historically unstable.

The question is, then, what accounts for this power? The Eurocentric answer is clear enough: the superiority of Euro-American values. It is an answer that is convincing only to Eurocentrists themselves. It is also the cultural level at which most critiques of Eurocentrism proceed, and run into dead ends. The problem with the culturalist critique of Eurocentrism is not only that it provides no explanation for the hegemony of Eurocentrism, in contrast to other centrisms, but that it is also for the same reason incapable of addressing normative questions of value. The values of the dominant (such as human rights) are not prima facie undesirable because of the fact of domination, just as the values of the dominated are not to be legitimated simply by recourse to arguments of cultural difference. If capitalism is as much an agent of Eurocentrism as the advocacy of human rights, it does not make much sense to laud the entry into capitalism of other societies while also collaborating in their abuse of human rights on the grounds of cultural difference. The conflict between history and value is nowhere better illustrated than in the historicist (culturalist) affirmations of difference, which then proceed nevertheless to discover in these different societies civil societies, et cetera, without any awareness that these societies might be products of Eurocentric teleologies, imbedded in the very terms themselves, that contradict the notions of difference.

I suggest here that such contradictions are products of the isolation of cultural questions from those of political economy. Eurocentrism was globalized not because of any inherent virtue of Euro-American values but because those values were stamped on activities of various kinds that insinuated themselves into existing practices (such as trade), proved to be welcome to certain groups in non-Euro-American societies, or, when there was resistance to them, were enforced on the world by the power of arms. In other words, the globalization and universalization of Eurocentrism would have been inconceivable without the dynamism it acquired through capitalism, imperialism, and cultural domination.

It is remarkable, then, that there should be a tendency in various realms of intellectual activity in recent years to erase the role of capitalism in history on the grounds that it is a perpetuation of Eurocentrism to speak of capitalism as the formative moment of modern history. We may suggest to the contrary that without an account of the relationship between Eurocentrism and the enormous power of capitalism that enabled Euro-American expansion, the criticism of Eurocentrism may not only perpetuate Eurocentrism in new guises but also disguise the ways in which globalism itself is imbued with a Eurocentric worldview. The preoccupation with Eurocentrism pervades not just cultural studies but also the rewriting of history, most visibly in efforts to produce a new "world history" that is immune to the Eurocentrism of past histories. These efforts overlook the fact that the urge to world history may itself be a Euro-American preoccupation that perpetuates earlier hegemonies in a new guise. I am quite sympathetic to the epistemological concerns of world-history proponents— namely, to overcome the restrictions of nation-based histories. There is also nothing objectionable about "putting Europe in its place" historically. On the other hand, the representation as Eurocentrism of emphasis on the historical role of modern capitalism promises not only to erase the distinctiveness of modern history but also to eliminate the capitalist mode of production as a distinct mode with its own forms of production and consumption, oppression and exploitation, and ideology. This is the case with Andre Gunder Frank's "5,000 year world-system," which, in the name of erasing Eurocentrism, universalizes and naturalizes capitalist development in much the same fashion as classical economics; that is, by making it into the fate of humankind rather than the conjunctural product of a particular history. Gunder Frank also does not explain why a China- or Asia-centered history constitutes more of a world history than a Euro-American-centered one. Most seriously, the naturalization of capitalism historically also undermines the possibility of perceiving other alternatives in history, as the only alternatives it allows are alternative capitalisms.[16]

Even more revealing of the hegemonic implications of a globalized world history is a recent report on the status of world-history writing in China that observes ironically (and to the astonishment of its author) that contrary to what one might expect (we are not told who shares in the expectation—presumably all "Westerners"), Chinese historians continue to write modern world history around the history of capitalism and, it follows for the author, a Eurocentric paradigm. To the author, of course, this is a product of the continued domination of Chinese historical thinking by the "ideological framework" of "a European-centered, Marxist-imbued world history."[17] The irony that Chinese should perpetuate Eurocentrism when Euro-Americans have already liberated their thinking from it escapes the author. So does the patronizing conclusion that this is the result of the domination of Chinese thinking by ideology (in contrast, presumably, to *our* scientific approaches), which perpetuates the hegemonic attitudes of an earlier day. No wonder that the author can also state that the large place given to Chinese history (autonomously of world history) in school curricula issues "from an ethnocentric view not unfamiliar to Western historians. China's self-perception as *Zhongguo*, or the 'Central Kingdom,' is well-known."[18] Not only does the author erase Chinese historians as contemporaries instead of questioning her own version of world history, but she also proceeds to erase Chinese history by falling back upon the authority of long-standing clichés in the "Western" historiography of China. Aside from the fact that this Chinese "self-perception" has its own history, other societies, too, teach their national histories separately from world history and give them a large place. This has more to do with nationalist education in the modern world than some Chinese "ethnocentrism." The questions of whose ethnocentrism and whose ideology jump to mind immediately, but those questions may not be as important as the underlying hegemonic assumptions in much of the discussion on globalization, including the globalization of history. World history as an undertaking is not to be held responsible for this kind of obscurantism, but its possible hegemonic implications are a reminder nevertheless of the need for intellectual vigilance in an undertaking that is highly vulnerable to producing the opposite of what it intends. One necessary caution is to distinguish Eurocentrism from recognition of the historical role that Euro-America, empowered by capitalism, played in the shaping of the modern world.

One of the most remarkable pieties of our times is that to speak of oppression is to erase the subjectivities of the oppressed; this piety does not seem to recognize that not to speak of oppression but still operate within the teleologies of modernist categories is to return the responsibility for oppression to its victims.[19] Alternatively, it is to make a mockery of any notion of resistance to oppression by identifying resistance with any kind of deviation from "normalcy." The result, in either case, is the evasion of any significant, and historically determined, notion of politics by turning all such encounters into instances of cultural politics. What is also remarkable is the resonance between the political conclusions of contemporary culturalism and the culturalism of an earlier modernizationism: what is at issue is not politics or political economy but culture.

A blatant example of the dangers implicit in the new culturalism is provided by Samuel Huntington's vision of "the clash of civilizations."[20] Huntington's views on "civilizations," his approach to the question of culture, and the conclusions he draws are diametrically opposed to those of postcolonialism and globalism. He reifies civilizations into culturally homogeneous and spatially mappable entities, insists on drawing impassable boundaries between them, and proposes a fortress Euro-America to defend Western civilization against the intrusion of unmodernizable and unassimilable Others. What is remarkable about his views is his disavowal of the "West's" involvement in other civilization areas. His is a conception of the contemporary world that divides the world into several "civilization" areas, where each hegemonic power should be responsible for the achievement of order in its area. Huntington sustains this remarkable view of the world by refraining from serious analysis of the structures of political economy (he does not even say if fortress Euro-America is to withdraw its transnational corporations from the rest of the world); by taking out of the definition of culture any element of material culture; by confounding ethnicity, culture, race, and civilization; by questioning the significance of the nation; by erasing the legacies of colonialism and insisting that whatever has happened in other societies has happened as a consequence of their indigenous values and cultures; and, at the most general level, by disavowing history. His divisions of the world are a far cry from the insistence in globalism and postcolonial criticism on the abolition of boundaries, rejection of cultural reification, and negotiation of cultural identity. On the other hand, his reinstatement of the power of indigenous "cultures," understood not in terms of nations but "civilizations," his erasure of colonialism and reinstatement of persistent native subjectivities, his obliviousness to questions of political economy, and his disavowal of modernity's history resonate with globalist and postcolonial arguments. This is to suggest, not that they are therefore identical or even operate out of the same paradigm (Huntington's is a paradigm of top-down order), but that they are contemporaneous. There may be a world of difference between the bounded ethnocentrism of Huntington's vision of the world and the multiculturalist pluralisms of globalism and postcolonialism, but they are at one in foregrounding ethnicity to mystify the transnational structures of unequal power that are their context.

Recognition of Eurocentrism as a historical phenomenon that differs from other centrisms in terms of the totalizing structures that served as its agencies returns us to the question that I raised above. If Eurocentrism globalized a certain ethnocentrism and rendered it into a universal paradigm, is there then an outside to Eurocentrism? An outside to Eurocentrism may be found in places untouched and marginalized by it, which are fewer by the day, or it may be found in its contradictions, which proliferate daily. The universalization of Eurocentrism must itself be understood in terms of the ways in which Euro-American values were interpellated into the structures of societies worldwide, transforming their political, social, and economic relations but not homogenizing them or assimilating them to the structures and values of Eurocentrism. Questions of homogenization versus heterogenization, sameness versus difference, assimilation versus differentiation are misleading in many ways, for they confound what are historical processes with the apportionments of identity into ahistorical, static categories. As I understand it here, the universalization of Eurocentric practices and values through the Euro-American conquest of the world implies merely the dislodging of societies from their historical trajectories before Europe onto new trajectories, without any implication of uniformity, for the very universalization of Eurocentrism has bred new kinds of struggles over history, which continue in the present. It also implies, however, at least in my understanding, that these struggles took place increasingly on terrains that, however different from one another, now included Euro-American power of one kind or another as their dynamic constituents. That, I believe, distinguishes what we might want to describe as a modernity defined by Euro-America from earlier forms of domination, which were regionally, politically, and socially limited by the technological, organizational, and ideological limits of domination. Sinocentrism, however effective in East and Southeast Asia, was nevertheless limited to those regions.

Eurocentrism, as compared to earlier "centrisms," is universal in three senses. First, it is the omnipresence globally of the institutions and cultures of a a Euro-American modernity. While the effects of this modernity may not be uniformly or equally visible on all the surface implied by "global," it is nevertheless everywhere forcing widely different peoples into parallel historical trajectories (which, I stress, does not imply identity). Second, it is universal in the sense that Eurocentrism may be diffused through the agencies of non-Euro-Americans, which underlines the importance of a structural appreciation of Eurocentrism. And, finally, while Eurocentrism may not be universal in the sense that it permits no outside, it is nevertheless the case that it has become increasingly impossible to imagine outsides to it, if by outside we understand places outside of the reach of Euro-American practices. It is not that there are no outsides but that those outsides must of necessity be conceived of as post-Eurocentric, as products of contradictions generated by the dialectic between a globalizing Euro-America and places that struggle against such globalization. What this implies is a common history that of necessity provides the point of departure even for imagining outsides or alternatives to Eurocentrism. Eurocentrism, in other words, is not to be challenged by questioning the values that emanate from Euro-America. It requires challenging values and structures that are already part of a global legacy.

In a world that operates, not according to the norms of functionalism, but rather of contradictions, the globalization of Eurocentrism inevitably brings multifaceted contradictions into the very interior of a Eurocentric world, undermining at every moment the integrity of that world, beginning with the notion of Eurocentrism itself. The contemporary critique of Eurocentrism is driven, I have argued elsewhere, not by victimization by Eurocentrism but by empowerment within it. Foremost among the critics of Eurocentrism in our day are not those who are marginalized by Eurocentrism or left out of its structures of power but those who claim "hybridities" that give access to both Eurocentrism and to its Others—probably more of the former than the latter. If Orientalism was a product of Euro-Americans located in "contact zones" outside of

Euro-America, on the margins of non-Euro-American societies, anti-Eurocentrism is a product of contact zones located at the hearts of Euro-America or in transnational structures and circuits of power. As contact zones earlier presented Euro-Americans with a choice between civilizing mission and dissolution into "barbarism," the new contact zones present intellectuals of Third World origin with a choice between "bridging" cultures, which, given the persistent inequalities between societies, may mean further invasion of the rest of the world by the structures of power over which Euro-America continues to preside, or burning the bridges, so that alternatives might be thinkable to a Eurocentric vision of human futures.

The contrast between building bridges and burning bridges offers a convenient way of identifying differences between contemporary and past radicalisms in their attitudes toward Eurocentrism. As late as the 1960s and the 1970s, radical evaluations of Eurocentrism insisted on intimate ties between questions of cultural domination and political economy, more often than not encompassed by the term "imperialism." Third World national liberation struggles, synthesizing in locally particular ways goals of national independence and socialized economies, sought to "delink" national economies from the global markets of capitalism, to reorganize those economies in accordance with local needs, and to achieve "cultural revolutions" against Euro-American cultures of capitalism that would create citizenries responsive to national needs. In First World social sciences, insistence on considerations of political economy became the means to challenge the culturalism of modernization discourses that blamed "backwardness" on the native traditions and cultures of Third World societies.

From a contemporary perspective, both these earlier radical movements and their articulations in new social science theorizations (such as "world-system analysis") appear, contrary to their claims, to have been dominated by the master narratives and "foundational" assumptions of Eurocentrism. And to a large extent, this is plausible. In spite of the revolt against capitalism, national liberation movements for the most part remained wedded to the developmentalism of Euro-American modernity. They also remained within the spatial webs of Eurocentrism in taking for granted the spatial arrangements of modernity, most prominently the idea of a Third World itself. The nation-form was taken for granted, with the consequence that the nation was rendered into the location for culture, ignoring the fact that the idea of a national culture could be realized only through the colonization of diverse local cultures.[21]

Other aspects of contemporary critiques of the radical assumptions of an earlier day seem a great deal more problematic, and may have more to say about the present than the past. The charge of essentialism is a favorite weapon in the arsenal of postcolonialism. It has been brought to bear on ideas of the Third

World, Third World nationalism, et cetera, which says less about the historical unfolding of these ideas than about efforts to create straw targets against which to validate postcolonialism. While "Third World" may have carried essentialist connotations in modernization discourse, this was hardly the way it was understood by the Third Worlders, to whom "Third World" connoted anything but the identity of the societies so described; rather, Third Worldness was a condition of national situations, contingent upon relationships between capitalist and noncapitalist societies. In revolutionary nationalisms, national cultures were not the givens of some tradition or other but were conceived of as cultures yet to be created through national struggles for liberation. Foundational categories were anything but foundational; I have described elsewhere how, in the context of a guerrilla revolution in China, for instance, there was considerable attention given to the overdetermined and locally contingent nature of social categories, especially of class.[22] That these revolutions worked from a Euro-American spatiality means only that present realities provided the point of departure for thinking alternatives to them. Most bizarre is the idea, rather common these days, that to speak of oppression and imperialism as determinants of these revolutions is to ignore or suppress the subjectivities of the oppressed,[23] when these movements themselves represented nothing short of the reassertion of native subjectivities and sought to create new revolutionary subjectivities. What this silly charge elides are questions of whose subjectivities are at issue and what kinds of subjectivities we are talking about.

Questions of this nature imply that there is much to be gained from viewing the present in the perspective of the past. The world has changed, indeed, and the radicalism represented by immediate postcolonial struggles in the Third World truly appear in the present to belong to a distant past, no longer relevant to a contemporary politics. The question is how the world has changed: whether what we witness in the present is a rupture with the past or a reconfiguration of the relationships of power that have facilitated the globalization of earlier forms of power, while eliminating earlier forms of resistance to it. New economic, political, social, and cultural spaces are now in the process of production. Do these new spaces mean that the earlier spatializations of the globe are no longer relevant, or are they superimposed on those earlier spaces to provide more complicated arrangements of domination? There are now assertions of temporalities (including reassertions of traditions). Does that mean that the temporalities of Eurocentrism have disappeared? Consumerism, culture industries, the production of signs seem to have moved to the forefront of economies, replacing political by discursive economies—at least for those situated in postmodernist First Worlds. Does that mean that production and political economy are no longer relevant? The diffusion of markets and market mentalities have rendered the production of cultures and identities into a matter of negotiation. Does that mean that there are no longer inequalities in the market place? The list could go on, but it will suffice.

That these questions are missing from much of the contemporary discussion of globalism and postcolonialism may not be too surprising, because for all their claims to radicalism and significant differences between them, both globalism and postcolonialism represent accommodations to contemporary configurations of power in which they are complicit. This is quite evident in the case of globalism, which is promoted by capital and its institutions, for whom globalization is anything but a matter of culture. In this perspective, globalism is little more than a recognition that capital is no longer just Euro-American, that there are successful participants in it who hail from other locations, and that other than Euro-American cultures must be incorporated into the structures and operations of capital because transnationalism itself implies the interiorization of difference—so long as they recognize the primacy of those structures in the first place.[24] In social science theory, or history for that matter, these Others must be recognized in the fullness of their "traditions" and indigenous subjectivities, which are denied in discourses of imperialism and oppression. Never mind that social science theory, into which differences are interpellated, itself represents a kind of thinking about the world grounded in Eurocentric structures of power. Hence it becomes possible to speak of different "civil societies," grounded in different social configurations, as if the term "civil society" were innocent in its political implications. And, of course, "rational choice theory" represents a transcending of cultural differences in its "scientificity," as if science as a mode of comprehending the world had nothing to do with culture. One foundation representative remarks in support of globalization that "Western theories" are not "for the rest of the world to adopt."[25] There is no indication in the statement that "Western" itself might be redundant, as it may be implicit already in the term "theory."

Unlike globalization, which is founded in the developmentalist assumptions of capitalism, postcolonialism seems to me to be more of an accommodation with a current structure of power than an apology for it. In an earlier essay, I suggested that the present situation is better described as postrevolutionary rather than postcolonial because while the immediate response to postcoloniality as historical phenomenon was revolution, contemporary postcolonialism eschews revolutionary options for accommodation to the capitalist world-system. The postcolonial rush to culture is an escape not only from the structures of political economy but, more important, from revolutionary radicalisms of the past, which are now denied not only contemporary relevance but even past significance.

Postcolonialism's complicity with contemporary configurations of power rests in its explicit repudiation of structures and "foundational" categories, which obviate the need to address the question of structured power in considerations of change, but also in its culturalism. Localized encounters and identity politics seem to serve in postcolonialism not as a refinement of, but as a substitute for, structured inequalities and struggles against it. More significant may be the rereading of the past with such a "methodology," which also serves to erase the memory of more radical struggles for culture and identity and renders localism into a metanarrative that postcolonialism supposedly repudiates. What is remarkable about postcolonialism methodologically and conceptually is that for all its objections to "essentialism," it is based on presumptions of essentialized identities, which are implicit in notions of "hybridity," "third space," et cetera. Repudiation of foundational categories also relieves it of the obligation to confront "differences" along the fault lines of classes, genders, races, et cetera, which all become subject to negotiations of one kind or another. Postcolonialism, repudiating Eurocentric spatializations, ironically also returns us to pre–World War II spaces, where spaces established by colonial empires are acknowledged on unguarded occasions to provide spaces for theorizing about culture and identities.[26] Most important, however, may be that in its repudiation of the structures of political economy in the name of discourses and culture, postcolonialism returns us past an earlier concern with political economy to the culturalism of modernization discourse. Its own discourse on culture is quite different, needless to say, from the spaceless and timeless cultures presumed by modernization discourse, but it is at one with the latter in elevating culture to primacy in social and cultural theory.

The parallel has interesting implications. Culturalism in modernization discourse served to conceal inequalities in the realms of economy and politics and to shift the blame for problems in development from the dominant to the dominated—all the time assuming a certain teleology of development. Postcolonialism eschews teleology, and it eschews fixed, essentialized notions of culture. But what are we to make of its isolation of questions of culture from those of political economy? Does it also serve as some kind of a cover for inequalities and oppressions that are no less a characteristic of the present than they were of the past? Postcolonialism itself does not provide an answer to these questions, because it refuses to address them in the first place. Clearly, the present represents not a rupture with the past but its reconfiguration. If the transnationalization, and transnational domination, of capital is one prominent feature of the contemporary world situation, another is the transnationalization of the class structures associated with capitalist domination. Postcolonialism, as Aijaz Ahmad observes, may be a "matter of class."[27] But it is not *just* a matter of class. It is also a matter of a class relocated to the centers of capital, in the new contact zones to which I referred above, which serve as sites of negotiation—"in the belly of the beast," as Gayatri Spivak once put it. Spivak knows better than to say that this is the whole story, but for most postcolonialists who do not share in her radicalism, that does seem to be the whole story. The "contact zones" at the heart of Euro-America provide locations where cultural difference may be asserted while sharing in the powers of the center, in which culture serves as a means of evading questions of inequality and oppression in interclass relations but is a useful means to identity in intraclass negotiations for power. Contact zones located on the boundaries of societies of the "Other" produced earlier Orientalisms; contact zones at the core produce "self-Orientalizations."[28] Unlike the former, which distanced societies from one another, the latter produces multiculturalist redefinitions of global power—as is indicated in the idea of "ethnoscapes" or the stipulation of diasporic identities, regardless of place, class, gender, et cetera. Interestingly, it is a new generation of Third Worlders, firmly established in the structures of Eurocentric power, who now speak for the societies from which they hail, while those back at home are condemned to inaudibility—or parochialism.

The refusal to situate theory with respect to the structures of power also has significant political implications. Culturalism of the contemporary variety also makes it impossible to evaluate cultures in terms of their political implications. It is a commonplace these days that there is no longer a "right" or a "left," or conservatives or radicals. This may be an improvement over an earlier modernization discourse, which classified people outside of Europe according to where they stood vis-à-vis the values of Europe and the United States, so that any defense of native culture, for example, immediately led to the label "conservative," while liberals and radicals derived their standing similarly from their willingness to assimilate Eurocentric conceptualizations of culture and politics. On the other hand, acquiescence in a contemporary cultural relativism—such as in "multiculturalism"—rules out political judgment except on the most contingent basis, which is one reason for the recent call by Slavoj Zizek for a renewal of Eurocentrism.[29] Zizek credits Eurocentrism as a source of universalisms that are crucial to radical politics. While there is much to be said for his argument, the plea nevertheless begs the question of what the agency and content of a contemporary universalism might be.

HISTORY AFTER EUROCENTRISM

Much of what I have observed above may seem to have little to do with history as a discipline, for historians have been notably absent from recent discussions over history as epistemology. It is probably not too much of an exaggeration to suggest that a crisis of historical consciousness is one of the markers of life at the end of the twentieth century. The crisis refers to the ways in which we think the relationship between the present and the past, and, therefore, the relevance and validity of anything we may have to say about the past. A sense of a break not just with the immediate past but with the whole history of modernity calls into question anything history might offer to an understanding of the present. Historians might have a significant part to play in reasserting the significance of past perspectives in a critical appreciation of the present, but they seem to have adjusted with remarkable speed to the contemporary rewriting of the past. It is a professional disease of historians, especially of positivist historians, and a limitation on their imagination, that they may blame everything on the limitations of archives. A conviction that the only obstacle to truth lies in the limitations of archives helps historians avoid the challenges of historical crises by falling back on archival limitations. If things did not go the way a previous generation of historians had indicated, or if the problems of a previous generation no longer seem relevant, the historian can always claim that it was not in the archives.

In my own field of modern Chinese history, changes in China call for an urgent consideration of historical paradigms and an evaluation of competing paradigms. Two generations of historians of China (in China and abroad) have taken revolution to be the paradigm around which to write modern Chinese history. That paradigm now lies in ruins, not because the paradigm itself was wrong necessarily, but because the revolution is a thing of the past in a China where leaders may pay lip service to the revolution in their very unrevolutionary and unsocialist turn to incorporation into capitalism. Rather than observe the turn critically, historians have been quick to deny that there was a revolution, claiming that what had been considered a revolution was really nothing more than the perpetuation of backwardness and that it was the archives that were responsible for their failure to foresee the fate of the revolution. The denial of revolution, not surprisingly, is accompanied by a shift of attention to pasts that may be more consonant with the self-images of the present. The question here is not just one of ideology in history; it is also a question of bad history that refuses to acknowledge the ways in which the revolutionary past, having failed to achieve its putative goals, nevertheless served to shape the present.[30]

A reasonable alternative to this rapid adjustment to the present that also requires a disavowal of the past (both the past in actuality and the past in historiography) might be to acknowledge the crisis and turn to a revaluation of the past, not by an abandonment of the paradigm of revolution, but by inquiring into the meaning of revolution.[31] Radical historiography does not consist of the abandonment, or rewriting, of the past every time a new historical situation presents itself—in which case it cannot overcome a continuing adjustment to the present, which is hardly a claim to radicalism, as it makes it impossible to differentiate what is radical from what is mimicry of the demands of power.

Rather, it is informed by a principled defense of autonomous political positions that question ever shifting claims to reality, not by denying reality, but by critically evaluating its claims on the past and the present. If the past has no relevance to understanding the present but is merely a plaything at the hands of the present, there would seem to be little meaning even to claim validity for history as epistemology or, for that matter, to any truth imbedded in the archives of the past—which is the conclusion indicated by a radical postmodernism.

The proposition that "history is a sign of the modern" would suggest only to the most naive that the moment we have gone "postmodern," we may therefore abandon history. The posts of our age, to those who would read them with some sense of reality, should suggest that what comes after bears upon it the imprint of what went on before and that we are not as free as we might think of the legacies we have consigned to the past—which, for all his obscurantism, is the point that Huntington makes forcefully. The same goes for postrevolutionary and for what has been my primary concern in this discussion, post-Eurocentric. Our conceptions of the world face the predicament of turning into ideologies the moment that they forget their own historicities. And awareness of historicity requires attention both to transformations and to the presence of the past in such transformations.

To clarify further what I am suggesting here, it may be useful to contrast my critique of Eurocentrism with that of the historian of India Dipesh Chakrabarty.[32] At least in his more theoretical writings, Chakrabarty shares many of the arguments advanced here: most fundamentally, that Eurocentrism is everywhere, including the very writing of history (and, I might add, geography). He is also unwilling, unlike in some more atavistic versions of anti-Eurocentrism, to repudiate either the legacy of the Enlightenment or that of the nation in the writing of history (indeed, he sees the nation as the location for historical consciousness, which is threatened by the consumerism of capital). Finally, he is quite willing to speak of history in relationship to the cultures of capitalism. Against this seemingly invincible hegemony of history (read Eurocentrism), Chakrabarty, in a stance very similar to the one here, finds in "fragmentary and episodic . . . knowledge-forms" a promise of a more democratic knowledge.[33]

On the other hand, it is not clear from Chakrabarty's arguments whether or not his own project includes anything beyond challenging Eurocentric "knowledge-forms" or "provincializing Europe." Judging by his argument, the "fragmentary and episodic . . . knowledge-forms" he speaks of are intended mainly to undermine Eurocentric claims to universality and not to privilege the lives, or modes of living, that produce those knowledge-forms. In the same vein, Chakrabarty has little to say on questions of development, capitalism, et cetera, except as they relate to colonialism's knowledge. It is not very surprising, therefore, that under his editorship the journal *Subaltern Studies* has shifted its priorities from its originary concern to give a voice to the "subalterns" to "deconstructing" colonial representations of India and the Third World.[34] By contrast, my argument here is intended to redirect attention from "culture" to "structures," or at the least, culture in relationship to the structures of political economy. The difference, I think, is a crucial one: if Eurocentrism resides ultimately in the structures of everyday life as they are shaped by capital, it is those structures that must be transformed in order also to challenge Eurocentrism. "Knowledge-forms" are crucial, but not as an end in themselves; they are most important for showing the way to different kinds of living. The project implied here is quite different from the postcolonial, multiculturalist thrust of Chakrabarty's culturalist critique.

To affirm the historical role Eurocentrism has played in shaping the contemporary world is not to endow it with some normative power but to recognize the ways in which it continues to be an intimate part of the shaping of the world that is not going to disappear with willful acts of its cultural negation. One aspect of Eurocentrism, which infused both earlier revolutionary ideologies and the accommodationist alternatives of the present, seems to me to be especially important, perhaps more important for the historian than for others because it is complicit in our imagination of temporalities: developmentalism. The notion that development is as natural to humanity as air and water is one that is deeply imbedded in our consciousness, and yet development as an idea is a relatively recent one in human history. As Arturo Escobar has argued forcefully in a number of writings, development as a discourse is imbedded not just in the realm of ideology, but in institutional structures that are fundamental to the globalization of capital.[35]

If globalism is a way of promoting these structures by rendering their claims into scientific truths, postcolonialism serves as their alibi by not acknowledging their presence. Historians meanwhile continue to write history as if attaining the goals of development were the measure against which the past may be evaluated. That, I think, is the most eloquent testimonial to the implication of our times in the continuing hegemony of capital, for which the disavowal of an earlier past serves as disguise. It also indicates where the tasks may be located for a radical agenda appropriate to the present: in questioning contemporary dehistoricizations of the present and the past and returning inquiry to the search for alternatives to developmentalism. However we may conceive such alternatives, they are likely to be post-Eurocentric, recognizing that any radical alternatives to modernity's forms of domination must confront not just the cultures but also the structures of modernity. At any rate, it seems to me that we need a reaffirmation of history and historicity at this moment of crisis in historical consciousness, *especially* because history seems to be irrelevant—either because of its renunciation at the centers of power where a postmodernism declares a rupture with the past, unable to decide whether such a rupture constitutes a celebration or denunciation of capitalism; or contradictorily, because of an affirmation of premodernity among those who were the objects of modernity, who proclaim in order to recover their own subjectivities that modernity made no difference after all. A historical epistemology will not resolve the contradiction or provide a guide to the future, but it might serve at least to clarify the ways in which the present uses and abuses the past and serve as a reminder of our own historicity—why we say and do things differently than they were said or done in the past. Ours is an age when there is once again an inflation of claims to critical consciousness. These claims are based often on an expanded consciousness of space. We need to remind ourselves, every time we speak of the constructedness of some space or other, that it may be impossible, for that very reason, to think of spaces without at the same time thinking of the times that produced those spaces.

NOTES

This chapter originally appeared as "Is There History after Eurocentrism? Globalism, Postcolonialism, and the Disavowal of History," *Cultural Critique* 42 (Spring 1999): 1–34, The author gratefully acknowledges the permission of this publication to reprint the article here.

1. Nicholas Dirks, "History as a Sign of the Modern," *Public Culture* 2, no. 2 (1990): 25–32.

2. This is not to say that culture and discourse are the popular choices *only* for postcolonialism and globalism. What I describe here as a new culturalism is characteristic of contemporary critical thought in general and has its origins in the turn from the 1970s to culture and discourse in varieties of poststructuralism, postmodernism, cultural studies, feminism, etc.

3. Michael Geyer and Charles Bright, "World History in a Global Age," *American Historical Review* (October 1995): 1034–60, 1042.

4. As I have remarked elsewhere, postcolonial criticism covers a wide political (and, therefore, intellectual) range: from the Marxist feminism of Gayatri Spivak to the near-libertarianism of Homi Bhabha and, more recently, Stuart Hall. That it is the more libertarian versions of postcolonial criticism that have caught the imagination of post-Reagan, post-Thatcher scholars in the United States and the United Kingdom may not be very surprising, as it points merely to the importance of context in the reception of ideas. The same may be said of globalism, which also covers a wide range of intellectual and political orientations: from leftists who look to a cosmopolitan world to rational-choice political scientists who would make sure that cosmopolitanism lives up to the demands of scientific ways of knowing the world—read Euro-American hegemony. The problem is not quite novel. Capital has long sought globalization. So have leftists, but not quite in the same way. What seems to be different about our times is the willingness of leftists to buy into the visions of globalization offered by capital.

5. Bill Ashcroft, Gareth Griffiths, and Helen Tiffin, eds., *The Post-Colonial Studies Reader* (London: Routledge, 1995), 1 (emphasis in original). I have offered more sustained critiques of the problems of postcolonialism elsewhere and draw upon those earlier critiques in much of the discussion below. These critiques may be found in Arif Dirlik, *The Postcolonial Aura: Third World Criticism in the Age of Global Capitalism* (Boulder, Colo.: Westview Press, 1997). Of special interest from the perspective of questions of history may be the introduction ("Postcoloniality and the Perspective of History"), "Three Worlds or One, or Many: The Reconfiguration of Global Relations Under Contemporary Capitalism," and "Postcolonial or Postrevolutionary: The Problem of History in Postcolonial Criticism."

6. Roland Robertson, "Mapping the Global Condition: Globalization as the Central Concept," in *Global Culture: Nationalism, Globalization, and Modernity,* ed. Mike Featherstone (London: Sage Publications, 1994), 15–29, 23 (emphasis mine in the longer section) For a somewhat more elaborate critique, see Arif Dirlik, "Globalization, Areas, Places," Center for Asian Studies–Amsterdam Working Papers (1997).

7. Frederick Buell, *National Culture and the New Global System* (Baltimore: Johns Hopkins University Press, 1994), 336–37.

8. For an even more uncompromising argument for the priority of culture, see Rob Boyne, "Culture and the World-System," in *Global Culture,* Featherstone, 57–62, where Boyne attacks Immanuel Wallerstein for speaking of culture in conjunction with economic and political analysis.

9. Anthony D. Smith, "Towards a Global Culture?" in *Global Culture,* Featherstone, 171–91, 177.

10. That we should be more attentive to modernity rather than Eurocentrism is a view that I share with John Tomlinson, *Cultural Imperialism* (Baltimore: Johns Hopkins University Press, 1991). I do not, however, share Tomlinson's conclusion that Euro-American agency may be taken out of the picture by such a shift of attention.

11. Partha Chatterjee, *Nationalist Thought and the Colonial World: A Derivative Discourse* (Minneapolis: University of Minnesota Press, 1993).

12. In a rather ill conceived essay, Stuart Hall brings a charge of "primitive" as well as "primeval" "functionalism" against this author (along with Robert Young). See Stuart Hall, "When Was 'The Postcolonial'? Thinking at the Limit," in *The Postcolonial Question: Common Skies, Divided Horizons,* ed. Iain Chambers and Lidia Curti (New York: Routledge, 1996). The charge does not call for comment, except to note that it is rather below the potential of such a distinguished cultural critic, to whose formulations I would myself acknowledge a debt. Rather than concerning methodological problems of culturalism and functionalism, Hall's attack may have something to do with the post-Thatcherite turn in British Marxism. For this turn, see Chantal Mouffe, "The End of Politics and the Rise of the Radical Right," *Dissent*: 498–502.

13. Ken Armitage, "The 'Asiatic'/Tributary Mode of Production: State and Class in Chinese History" (Ph.D. diss., Griffith University [Australia], 1997), 3.

14. Ashis Nandy, *The Intimate Enemy* (Oxford: Oxford University Press, 1983).

15. This is analyzed with brilliant pithiness by Samir Amin in his essay *Eurocentrism* (New York: Monthly Review Press, 1989). Historians of Europe have also demonstrated that Europe and "nations" within Europe were products of an internal colonization that paralleled the "European" colonization of the world. For Europe, see F. Braudel, *Civilization and Capitalism, Fifteenth to Eighteenth. Century,* trans. Sian Reynolds, 3 vols. (New

York: Harper & Row, 1984), esp. vol. 3, *The Perspective of the World.* For an outstanding study of internal colonization in the creation of nations, see Eugen Weber, *Peasants into Frenchmen: The Modernization of Rural France, 1870–1914* (Stanford, Calif.: Stanford University Press, 1976). Societies such as the United States, Canada, and Australia, themselves colonial creations, interestingly provide the most explicit examples of such colonization in the creation of modern nation-states.

16. Andre Gunder Frank, *ReOrient: Global Economy in the Asian Age* (Berkeley and Los Angeles: University of California Press, 1998), esp. chap. 1.

17. Dorothea A. L. Martin, "World History in China," *World History Bulletin* 14, no. 1 (Spring 1998): 6–8, 6.

18. Martin, "World History," 8.

19. I am referring here to certain kinds of writing that assume categorical teleologies and then proceed to judge other peoples for having failed to live up to them. An example of this kind of teleology, on the issue of class, is Dipesh Chakrabarty, *Rethinking Working Class History* (Princeton, N.J.: Princeton University Press, 1989). Equally prominent are writings on feminism. There has been an almost concerted writing attacking the condition of women in China, which not only ignores what Chinese women might or might not want but also has encouraged attacks on the socialist program for women, which has certainly accomplished a great deal for women. It is interesting that feminists who attack the socialist program for what it has failed to achieve are often oblivious to what socialism has achieved, because it has not achieved what they think ought to have been achieved. This is not to say that women's questions should be reduced to what is of concern to women under socialism, but that women under socialism or under precapitalism may have a great deal to teach women who have discovered their "womanness" under capitalism and, regardless of what they may claim, are conditioned in their feminism by the mode of production that is their context.

20. Samuel P. Huntington, "The Clash of Civilizations?" *Foreign Affairs* (Summer 1992): 22–49; and Samuel P. Huntington, *The Clash of Civilizations and the Remaking of World Order* (New York: Simon & Schuster, 1996).

21. It needs to be emphasized here that while contemporary theory has problematized the nation-form, contemporary political reality points in an opposite direction. The nation persists, minus its earlier revolutionary vision. If anything, nationalism in our day has taken the form of virulent nativism.

22. Arif Dirlik, *After the Revolution: Waking to Global Capitalism* (Hanover, N.H.: University Press of New England, 1994), chap. 2; and Arif Dirlik, "Mao Zedong and 'Chinese Marxism,'" in *Companion Encyclopedia of Asian Philosophy,* ed. B. Carr and I. Mahalingam (London: Routledge, 1997), 593–619.

23. Buell, *National Culture and the New Global System,* provides an egregious example of this tendency. The volume opens with an attack on Herbert Schiller for his views on cultural imperialism.

24. It is necessary to point out that the idea of "different cultures of capitalism," which acquired currency with the globalization of capital, is a rather tentative one. The recent crisis in Asian capitalisms and the measures imposed for its solution suggest the persistence of a struggle over the form of capitalism. The core capitalist state, the United States, unquestionably exerts hegemonic pressures to reorganize other capitalisms around its own model. For a discussion that calls into question Asian capitalism, see Wang Ruisheng, "Yazhou jiazhi

yu jinyong weiji" (Asian values and the financial crisis), *Zhexue yanjiu* (Philosophical research), no. 4 (1998): 23–30.

25. Quoted in Jacob Heilbrunn, "The News from Everywhere: Does Global Thinking Threaten Local Knowledge? The Social Science Research Council Debates the Future of Area Studies," *Lingua Franca* (May/June 1996): 49–56, 54–55.

26. Stephen Slemon, "Unsettling the Empire: Resistance Theory for the Second World," in *Post-Colonial Studies Reader,* Ashcroft, Griffiths, and Tiffin, 104–10, where Slemon suggests that postcolonialism may be most relevant to societies of the British Commonwealth.

27. Aijaz Ahmad, "The Politics of Literary Postcoloniality," *Race and Class* 36, no.3 (1995): 1–20, 16.

28. I am referring here to the reification of cultures at the level of diasporas, an egregious example being the idea of a "cultural China." For an extended discussion, see Arif Dirlik, "Confucius on the Borderlands: Global Capitalism and the Reinvention of Confucianism," *Boundary 2* 22, no. 3 (Fall 1995): 229–73. Attention to diasporas points to a second aspect of the part culture may play in intra-elite struggles. Preoccupation with Eurocentrism occludes the struggles among "native" elites over the definition of cultural identity. As diasporic populations may be denied their cultural "authenticity" by those in the societies of departure, the repudiation of "authenticity" and the reaffirmation of "hybridity" provide obvious strategies in countering such denial.

29. Slavoj Zizek, "A Leftist Plea for 'Eurocentrism,'" *Critical Inquiry* 24 (Summer 1998): 988–1009.

30. These questions are discussed at length in Arif Dirlik, "Reversals, Ironies, Hegemonies: Notes on the Contemporary Historiography of Modern China," *Modern China* 22, no. 3 (July 1996): 243–84.

31. For a gender-based argument that advocates adjustment to contemporary struggles while insisting on the immediate relevance of the past to the structuring of the present, see Vinay Bahl, "Cultural Imperialism and Women's Movements: Thinking Globally," *Gender and History* 9, no. 1 (April 1997): 1–14.

32. Some of Dipesh Chakrabarty's relevant writings are "Postcoloniality and the Artifice of History: Who Speaks for 'Indian' Pasts?" *Representations* 37 (1992): 1–26; "History as Critique and Critique(s) of History," *Economic and Political Weekly* (September 14, 1991): 2162–66; "Radical Histories and the Question of Enlightenment Rationalism: Some Recent Critiques of *Subaltern Studies*," *Economic and Political Weekly*, 8 April 1995, 751–59.

33. Chakrabarty, "Radical Histories," 757.

34. I owe some of these insights to Vinay Bahl, "Subaltern Studies Historiography," in *History after the Three Worlds,* ed. Arif Dirlik, Vinay Bahl, and Peter Gran (Lanham, Md.: Rowman & Littlefield, forthcoming).

35. See esp. Arturo Escobar, *Encountering Development: The Making and Unmaking of the Third World* (Princeton, N.J.: Princeton University Press, 1994). What kind of radical historical agenda this may call for is discussed in Dirlik, "Reversals, Ironies, Hegemonies"; and Arif Dirlik, "Place-Based Imagination: Globalism and the Politics of Place," *Review* 22, no. 2 (1999): 151–87.

4

THEORY, HISTORY, CULTURE:

CULTURAL IDENTITY AND THE POLITICS OF THEORY

IN TWENTIETH-CENTURY CHINA

Viewing the question of theory in twentieth-century China from a vantage point at century's end presents an interesting problem. Theories of society, politics, and culture imported from Euro-America, which are the theories under consideration here, have played an important part in Chinese politics for over a century. In their utilization of these theories to unlock the secrets of Chinese society and to guide it toward a new future, Chinese intellectuals, especially radical intellectuals, displayed the same confidence in the universalist claims of theory as the European and American thinkers who originally had formulated the various theories they drew upon. Their undertakings were to have momentous historical consequences.[1]

In spite of brave assertions to the contrary and the seeming invasion of politics and all areas of knowledge by theory at century's end, it seems to me that what is missing at the present moment is this faith in theory to do the job of guiding the present into the future—in China or the world at large. Theory has lost its innocence as its universalist claims have been deconstructed in one intellectual realm after another (including the natural sciences) to expose the hegemonies built into all theories. Skepticism toward the claims of theories to be informed by a rational grasp of the world that transcends the constraints of culture or history has also deprived theory of the role assigned to it earlier as a means to human transformation and liberation—which appears now as a cover for different, particularly modern, forms of domination. The consequences have been especially devastating for those theories, such as Marxism, that took human liberation as their explicit goal. The failure of these theories in practice to deliver on their promises has played no little part in generating skepticism toward the universalist claims of theory. But the skepticism is a more general one that calls into question all theories of modernity, including those that seek to universalize the claims of capitalism or the nation-state. More than ever, perhaps, theory serves the purposes of social and human engineering to overcome the contradictions that threaten existing arrangements of power. Few may take at face value the pretensions that social engineering is free of political and ideological motivation; but the recognition only confirms the conviction that the answer to the deployment of theory in social engineering is to be found not in the formulation of alternative theories but in escape from theory.

The role theory played in the century-long revolution in China, and in the fate of the revolution, is quite relevant to understanding this transformation in attitudes toward theory in general. So are the issues of history, culture, and theory that were brought forth in the course of the Chinese revolution. It is these issues that I take up in this chapter. The question of theory in twentieth-century China has many facets to it. One could speak to the changing political circumstances that invited theory after theory into Chinese political life; one could speak to the reversal in the histories of theories whereby the most recently popular theories in Euro-America found their way into Chinese thinking, to be traced back to their origins with progressive advances in their appreciation; one could speak to the relationship between the unfolding of problems in Chinese society and the successive appearance of theories of the state, of culture, of political economy and social theory, back to cultural theory; one could speak to the embroilment of theory in the relationship between war, revolution, and culture; one could speak to the invasion of Chinese thought by theories of feminism, postmodernism, postcolonialism, et cetera

I would like to focus in this discussion on one particular dimension of the question of theory that I think has been a lasting preoccupation of Chinese intellectuals: the relationship between theory and cultural identity.

In China, as in other societies that have experienced modernity as Euro-American colonialism or domination, theory has been called into question for the cultural assumptions that inform it: whether or not a theory that has been formulated out of one cultural situation may be applicable, in other words, to another, completely different cultural situation. In some ways this is one aspect of a general problem presented by theory, especially to historians who have always been suspicious of the erasure by theoretical generalization of the complexities of history. There is also the problem of the historicity of theory: that theories, while they aspire to overcome history by pointing to transhistorical generalizations, are limited in their statements by the historical circumstances that produced them. Thinkers from Marx to Weber have acknowledged that theories were as good as the histories that informed them, even if they were driven ultimately by universalist aspirations. The question of the applicability of theory across cultural boundaries is in some ways an instance of these broader problems.[2] The historicizing of theory finds a logical conclusion in the breakdown of assumptions of universality for theory, as is visible in recent tendencies to identify theory with national cultures—as in U.S. theory, German theory, French theory, et cetera.[3]

The additional dimension raised by the question of culture in contexts such as the Chinese, however, goes beyond problems of history in theory, for what it suggests is the quite important question of the entanglement of theory in cultural imperialism, or at the very least, of the distortion or erasure of the characteristics of one culture by their subjection to the cultural assumptions built into theories formulated under alien cultural circumstances. That such transposition of theory has taken place under circumstances of unequal power adds to the significance of the question. The questions of culture in theory raised under such circumstances have become an important issue at century's end in postmodernist or postcolonialist questionings of theory.

To complicate matters further, the questioning of theory is accompanied by equally fundamental questionings of culture and history that problematize historical or cultural readings of theory that have been informed in the past by the location of culture and history in the nation. Indeed, it is the coincidence of questions pertaining to theory with those on history and culture that may distinguish our times from earlier questionings of theory, that deprive questionings of theory of their anchoring in history and culture. The repudiation of earlier assumptions concerning the coincidence of culture with identifiable national boundaries—in other words, assumptions of national cultural homogeneity—also calls into question notions of "cultural imperialism," as it is no longer quite evident whose culture we speak of at either the sending or the receiving end of imperialism.[4] Theory here appears as a problem not just in its entanglement in relations of domination between nations but more immediately in its implication in relations of domination within nations.

History presents equally troubling questions. As in the cases both of theory and culture, the universalist assumptions of historical thinking have been called into question on the grounds that history as it has been practiced over the last century has been complicit in relations of domination within and between nations. This is apparent, as in the case of theory, not only in the breakdown of historical practice into national traditions but also in the repudiation of the nation as the unit of history, which erases the complexity of the histories encompassed in national histories. On the other hand, even more fundamental challenges to history have been voiced by postcolonial intellectuals who argue that history, as a cultural artifact of Euro-American modernity, not only has been used to justify colonialism and domination but also, even more fundamentally, to erase by its teleologies alternative ways of thinking about the past.[5]

Theory, history, and culture, then, appear in contemporary thinking in immensely complicated relationships. The relationships are, on the one hand, deconstructive, with theory deconstructing the claims of culture and history, history deconstructing the claims of theory and culture, and culture deconstructing the claims of history and theory. On the other hand, theory, history, and culture also appear in their complicity in relations of domination between and within nations, where theory reinforces the claims of history and culture, history reinforces the claims of theory and culture, with culture performing the same task for history and theory. In either case, what these intellectual developments have brought forth with uncompromising insistence is that it is no longer possible to think of any of these concepts outside of politics, or more specifically, the politics of modernity. The "repudiation of metanarratives," which for Jean-François Lyotard represents the fundamental intellectual characteristic of "the postmodern condition," holds equally for contemporary attitudes toward theory, history, and culture.[6]

Chinese attitudes toward the relationship between theory and cultural identity have ranged from outright rejection of foreign theories in the name of cultural integrity to the erasure of all considerations of culture in the name of theory, as exemplified most prominently in two movements that are also revealing of the political and ideological orientations that shaped those attitudes: the New Life Movement of the 1930s, and the Cultural Revolution of the 1960s. More interesting in their intellectual implications, however, are those efforts to reconcile theory and culture—what has been called "sinicization" or "sinification" of theory.

I will examine below two such efforts that are widely different in political context and intention, which in spite of their differences are revealing of some of the problems involved—problems, I should note, that anticipate contemporary problems of theory, history, and culture. One is the "sinicization of Marxism" (*Makesi zhuyide Zhongguohua*) undertaken by Communists during the Yan'an Period, credited to Mao Zedong but more likely the product of the joint effort of party intellectuals clustered around Mao.[7] The other is a discussion in the early 1980s by Chinese social scientists of the possibilities of "sinicizing sociology" (*shehuixue Zhongguohua*),[8] which its participants described as a "sinicization movement" in sociology. In juxtaposing these quite different instances of the confrontation between theory and cultural identity, my goal is, on the one hand, to point to concerns in Chinese thinking that cut across temporal and political divides and, on the other hand, to show that these concerns themselves are historical, subject in their articulation to changing historical circumstances.

In his famous essay "On New Democracy," Mao wrote:

> In applying Marxism to China, Chinese communists must fully and properly integrate the universal truth of Marxism with the concrete practise of the Chinese revolution or, in other words, the universal truth of Marxism must be combined with specific national characteristics and acquire a definite national form.[9]

"On New Democracy" was the crowning achievement of the "sinicization of Marxism," or perhaps even the intended goal to achieve that was the motivation underlying it. "New Democracy" referred to an economic and political formation (a mixed economy to facilitate economic development and an alliance across classes—under Communist leadership—in the pursuit of national liberation) suitable to China's immediate needs; but more significantly it also represented the insertion of a new stage in historical progress (between capitalism and socialism or, possibly, as a parallel to them) appropriate to all societies placed similarly to China in the world. Its premises were: (a) that the Chinese revolution was part of a global revolution against capitalism; (b) that it was, however, a revolution against capitalism in a "semi-feudal and semi-colonial" society to which national liberation was a crucial task; and (c) that it was also a national revolution, a revolution to create a new nation and a new culture that would be radically different from both the culture inherited from the past and the culture imported from abroad—including the culture implied by a universal Marxism. It is important to note, however, that even at the moment of asserting the importance of the nation in the midst of war and a rephrasing of the goals of a Communist revolution that made the latter sound like an updated version of Sun Zhongshan's Three People's Principles (*sanmin zhuyi*), which was not quite unintentional, Mao should reaffirm the universal claims of Marxist theory.

Chinese students of Mao's thought, following his example, have conventionally described the "sinicization of Marxism" as "the integration of the universal principles of Marxism with the concrete practise of the Chinese Revolution."[10] This seemingly straightforward formulation conceals the complexity of, not to say the contradictions presented by, the procedures of integrating universal principles (or theory) with revolutionary practice under particular circumstances. Stuart Schram has described sinicization as "a complex and ambiguous" idea,[11] which is evident in the conflicting interpretations to which sinicization has been subject. At one extreme, sinicization appears simply as the "application" (*yunyong*) of Marxism to the revolution in China, with no implications for theory; this would seem to be confirmed by Mao's own metaphors in later years of Chinese society as the "target" for the "arrow" of Marxist theory, or a "blank sheet" upon which theory could write its own agenda. At the other extreme it represents the absorption of Marxism into a Chinese national or cultural space, irrevocably alienated from its origins in Europe. In between are interpretations that hold that while sinicization left Marxism untouched at its basics, it brought to Marxism a Chinese "air" or "style."[12]

It is arguable that Mao's Marxism accommodated all of these different senses of sinicization. In the end, "the sinicization of Marxism" did not achieve an "integration of the universal truth of Marxism with the concrete practice of the Chinese revolution," if by that we understand a seamless synthesis that dissolved Marxism into China's circumstances or integrated China's peculiarities into the existing conceptual framework of Marxist theory. Mao's Marxism did not consist of merely applying Marxism to China's circumstances (which suggests too passive a role for what is Chinese in it, which is contrary to his insistence on the project of sinicization in the first place), or of just developing it (which, while arguable, is misleading to the extent that it suggests the absence of any disjuncture between Mao's Marxism and Marxism in general). The very tortured way in which Mao presented the project of sinicization may offer the most persuasive clue that the sinicization of Marxism entailed an effort to "integrate" what might not be integratable in the above sense of the term. It is worth quoting at some length the passage in which Mao used the term "sinicization" for the first time (which is also one of the fullest descriptions of what he meant by it of which I am aware) to convey a sense of the reasoning that, rather than argue out the logic of the project it presupposes, seeks instead to suppress the contradictions of the project by the force of its metaphors:

> Another task of study is to study our historical legacy, and to evaluate it critically using Marxist methods. A great nation such as ours with several thousand years of history has its own developmental laws, its own national characteristics, its own precious things. . . . The China of today is a development out of historical China. We are Marxist historicists; we may not chop up history. We must evaluate it from Confucius to Sun Zhongshan, assume this precious legacy, and derive from it a method to guide the present movement. . . . Communists are Marxist internationalists, but Marxism must be realized through national forms. There is no such thing as abstract Marxism, there is only concrete Marxism. The so-called concrete Marxism is Marxism that has taken national form; we need to apply Marxism to concrete struggle in the concrete environment of China, we should not employ it in the abstract. Communists who are part of the great Chinese nation, and are to this nation as flesh and blood, are only abstract and empty Marxists if they talk about Marxism apart from China's special characteristics. Hence the sinicization of Marxism, imbuing every manifestation of Marxism with China's special characteristics, that is to say applying it in accordance with Chinese characteristics, is something every Party member must seek to understand and resolve. We must discard foreign eight-legged essays, we must stop singing abstract and empty tunes, we must give rest to dogmatism, and substitute in their place Chinese airs that the common people love to see and hear. To separate internationalist content and national form reveals a total lack of understanding of internationalism.[13]

The tortuousness of this passage is partly a consequence of its politics. Raymond Wylie has suggested that the project of sinicization was part of intraparty politics, whereby Mao asserted his leadership against his Soviet-trained rivals, who were more adept at Marxist texts than he; and one can almost hear in this passage Mao's efforts to best his rivals by resorting to "the Chinese airs that the common people love to see and hear," not to speak of his reference to "foreign eight-legged essays."[14] But this is taking too narrow a view of the politics involved. By the time we reach the essay "On New Democracy," slightly over a year later, the politics also included, as I have already suggested, the project of capturing for the Communist Party the mantle of Sun Zhongshan's *sanmin zhuyi*. Even that, however, does not go far enough in capturing the political stakes involved because it still remains within the realm of the strictly political, ignoring the issues raised by "cultural politics." The intellectuals surrounding Mao had been involved in the mid-1930s in the politics of culture, which were of urgent concern to Chinese intellectuals during that decade. Too much pre-occupation with the myth of the May Fourth Movement in the historiography of modern China has distracted attention from the fact that by far the most interesting and sophisticated discussions of culture were conducted in the 1930s, when Chinese intellectuals confronted the cultures of modernity, including Marxism, with serious questionings.[15] It is possible even to assert that the discussion of culture as a problem achieved an unprecedented maturity in these years, when the concept of culture itself became the object of inquiry. Communist intellectuals were fervent participants in the discussions.

Even more fundamental were the questions raised by a Communist movement that had been forced into the countryside out of necessity, that had to confront differences within Chinese society—not only urban-rural differences, but also differences between one locality and another. The problem to a significant extent was empirical, the empirical complexities of an agrarian society that could not be contained easily in the categories of a theory formulated out of the characteristics of urban industrial society, and a politically and cultural-ly quite different one at that. The categories of Marxism such as class had to be drastically modified to account for other categories (such as gender or ethnici-ty) or contingent factors of concrete localities, if they were to serve the cause of revolution rather than throw obstacles in its way. Dogmatic loyalty to the cat-egories of theory ignored the fact that in reality attitudes toward the revolution were shaped not just by class interests but also by the whole web of social and political relationships that defined social and political location. The categories concealed, in other words, the fact that political and social orientations were "overdetermined" by the conjuncture of a multiplicity of social relations, of the past and the present, and of material circumstances and intangible cultural legacies. Mao's recognition of these problems is evident in his own well-known on-the-spot investigations of local situations.[16] If recognition of the historicity (in both a temporal and a spatial sense) of categories was necessary to revolu-tionary survival, however, it also created a predicament for revolutionary tele-ology. The "confrontation with the concrete," which brought the messiness of everyday life into theory, also threatened to fragment theory and its categories into so many empirical contingencies, depriving theory of its ability not only to make sense of the immediate environment but also to guide the revolution into the future. If theory must be historicized to guide practice, history had to be overcome by the theory.

The problems presented by revolution in the countryside were not only empirical "sociological" problems but were also deeply cultural. If Communism was to be "indigenized," the Communists had to learn to speak the languages of the many cultures they encountered. The sinicization of Marxism ultimately had to vernacularize the very language of theory without losing sight of the theory itself, because, as Mao insisted, following Lenin, there could be no revolutionary practice without a revolutionary theory. The contradictions presented by this task should be obvious. Theory was intended to unlock the secrets of social situations that in their very complexity revealed the limitations of theory; on the other hand, theory was to be articulated in many local languages without losing the integrity of its own language, which was almost unavoidable unless it was policed through organizational discipline. This discipline would oversee the absorption of local dialects into theory, to guarantee that the confrontation between theory and culture led, not to the dissipation of theory, but to a theory enriched by the confrontation and broader in its ability to account for the cultural diversity of its environment. The cultural confrontation between Western theory and Chinese culture was to be played out at many levels, not just at the level of an abstract national culture but also at the level of the many local cultures that constituted the national culture but also suppressed its abstraction.

The sinicization of Marxism is best grasped, I suggest, as the creation of a vernacular Marxism in the course of revolutionary praxis. We may recall that the appearance of a concern among Marxist intellectuals with language as a problem in revolution followed on the heels of Communist retreat to the countryside, which required new modes of communication and cultural activity to mobilize the party's rural constituencies.[17] The sinicization of Marxism was the culmination of these new requirements, recast in the language of "national form" in response to rising nationalist sentiment through the 1930s. Mao's Marxism may be viewed at two different levels. First, at the national level, he sought to "naturalize" Marxism by arguing that while Marxism as theory might have been formulated abroad, it was as natural an expression of Chinese society and history as it was of any other society in the world, and in fact that the universal principles of Marxism could only be confirmed through their different embodiments in different historical situations. At the same time, he rephrased Marxism in a Chinese language, almost literally, so that his discussions of Marxism, richly dressed in their allusions to historical events and parables, might have been incomprehensible to a foreign Marxist while they would have been readily comprehensible to his various audiences in China, intellectual or otherwise; to use his own metaphor, he endowed Marxism with "Chinese airs."[18] We must not overlook, however, the fact that translation is not a one-way process; Marxism may have acquired new characteristics as it was translated into a Chinese idiom, but that also brought the worldviews imbedded in Marxist concepts into the language of translation, also transforming it in the process. What made Mao's Marxism authentically radical (and not just an excuse for nationalism) was not his nationalization of Marxism, which, after all, his far less radical successors share with him, but his localizing of Marxism *within* the nation at the level of everyday life—indigenizing it, in other words, to the point where Marxism appeared as a natural growth from Chinese soil. In the same issue of *Chinese Culture* where Mao published "On New Democracy," Ai Siqi, one of Mao's close collaborators in the project of "sinicization," wrote in an essay that:

> Marxism is a universal truth (*yibande zhengquexing*) not only because it is a scientific theory and method, but because it is the compass of the revolutionary struggle of the proletariat. . . . That is to say, every country or nation that has a proletariat or a proletarian movement has the possibility (*keneng xing*) and necessity (*biran xing*) of giving rise to and developing Marxism. Marxism can be sinicized (*Zhongguohua*) because China has produced a Marxist movement in actuality (*shiji*); Chinese Marxism has a foundation in the internal development of Chinese economy and society, has internal sources, it is not a surface phenomenon. . . . The Chinese proletariat has a high level or organization and self-awareness, has its own strong party, has twenty years of experience in struggle, has model achievements in the national and democratic struggle. Hence there is Chinese Marxism. If Marxism is a foreign import, our answer is that Marxism gives practise (*shijian*) the primary place. If people wonder whether or not China has its own Marxism, we must first ask whether or not the Chinese proletariat and its party have moved the heavens and shaken the earth, impelled the masses of the Chinese nation to progressive undertakings. The Chinese proletariat has accomplished this. Moreover, it has on this basis of practise developed Marxist theory. . . . These are the real writings of Chinese Marxism, the texts (*shujue*) of Chinese Marxism. . . . Marxism cannot but assume different forms depending on the different conditions of development of each nation; it cannot assume an international form globally. Presently, Marxism must be realized through national forms (*minzu xingshi*). There is no such thing as an abstract Marxism, there is only concrete Marxism. The so-called concrete Marxism is Marxism that has taken national form.[19]

The Marxism that Chinese Communists inherited was a Marxism that had already been deterritorialized from its original terrain in European history. Ai's statement metonymically recognizes the difference of Chinese Marxism from an international Marxism, but in the process it also restates the relationship between Chinese and European (or any other) Marxism as a part-part relationship within a Marxism that as a whole has now been removed from any territorial associations. Synecdochically, he reterritorializes Marxism upon a Chinese terrain by asserting that Chinese Marxism is "intrinsically" as representative of a whole Marxism as any other. In this simultaneous recognition of a global Marxist discourse as a pervasive unity and the discursive appropriation of Marxism in Chinese terrain is expressed the fundamental essence and the contradictoriness of the structure of Mao's Marxism and the procedure of sinicization of which it was the product.

Mao did not come to Marxism as "a blank sheet of paper," and there are tantalizing traces in his thinking of various traditions in Chinese thought.[20] Recognition of these traces, however, is quite a different matter from assigning to them a determining power, which in the end serves only to capture him in a Chinese cultural space, without having to account for what that space might contain. Mao's dialectic, with its insistence on everything containing everything else, is often reminiscent more of certain currents in Buddhism and Daoism than the dialectic of Hegel and Marx—especially with its refusal to recognize an end to history. It is important to recognize nevertheless that these traces are mediated by, and refracted through, the problematic of revolution not just as a political but also as a cultural problem. This is to deny neither Mao's nationalism nor the legacies of the past that may have entered his thinking as formative moments; but it is to foreground the revolutionary activity that guided both his nationalism and his appropriation of historical legacies to that end. It is also to stress the contradictions (in the sense both of unity and opposition) between theory and history, the past and the present, and between narrowly national and broadly national liberationist goals.

I suggested above that the sinicization of Marxism is traceable to the social and cultural problems presented to theory by guerrilla warfare in the countryside from the early 1930s, and that it was recast within the problematic of the nation only later in the decade, in response to the demands of the anti-Japanese War. It is appropriate at this point to draw attention to a problem in this whole idea of the "nationalization" of Marxism, which may shed further light on Mao's relationship to the Chinese historical legacy. In the discussion above, I have employed the term "sinicization" even though it is quite misleading in its implications. The terms "sinicization" and "sinification" suggest the assimilation of others to Chinese ways, biasing interpretation to a culturalism that has long been nourished by dehistoricized notions of Chineseness, with a long-established tradition that swallows up all challengers in a Chinese cultural space. It is important to underline that unlike other terms, such as *tonghua* (making same) or *Hanhua* (making Han) that the Latinized "sinicization" has been used to translate in the historical literature, the term employed in the case of the "sinicization of Marxism" is *Zhongguohua*, literally "making Chinese," with the clear implication of "nationalization." Marxism, in other words, was not being brought simply into a Chinese cultural but a Chinese national space, with significant implications, because it is quite clear from the texts discussed above that *Zhongguohua*, while it referred to an existing Chinese national space, also implied that the culture defining this national space was in the process of creation. When Mao stated in "On New Democracy" that the new Chinese culture must be national, popular, and scientific (the latter a stand-in for Marxism), he obviously was referring, not to the textual traditions of Confucianism or other aspects of high culture that earlier had been the referent for sinicization, but to the culture of the people at large, as it would be transformed by Marxism. The concept of nation involved here is not a culturalist but a historical one, the nation as ongoing historical creation in which theory, history, and culture, as I have discussed them above, would all be participants. What is at issue here is not assimilation of the Other to the culture of the self, but the transformation of the self in the process, launching a new historical trajectory, the point of departure for which is the concrete present, in which the past and the West (in the forms of capitalism and Communism) are copresent in a contradictory relationship (that, if I may refer to the analysis at the beginning, coexist in a deconstructive as well as a constructive relationship).

The same contradictoriness applies to the status of imported theory in its relationship to indigenized practice. The urge to bring concretely Chinese circumstances, a Chinese "structure of feeling," or a Chinese voice into theory is expressed in the procedures of sinicization in the elevation of "practice" to an equal status with theory, as stated clearly in the quotation from Ai Siqi, where the practice of revolution serves as "texts" of Chinese Marxism, equal in their claims to the literal texts of theory. Theory provided new insights into Chinese society and new ways of grasping its workings, but it did not provide either a thoroughgoing analysis or a clear-cut guide to praxis; on the other hand, praxis, which revealed the limitations of theory, nevertheless could not do without theory that provided it with its teleology, a teleology that was not just ideological but bound up with China's placement in the world of capitalism. Here theory and practice appear once again in a contradictory relationship, which for its resolution requires the presence of the interpreting agent to read any particular situation with the aid of both history and theory. Historicized to account for concrete circumstances, theory can no longer be taken as the formulation of universal laws, which could anticipate the consequences of its application, but as a tool of interpretation, a hermeneutic instrument that was itself subject to reinterpretation at all times in its confrontation with practice. Statements about the universal claims of Marxism to the contrary, we are all aware of the priority Mao assigned to practice, which has made his Marxism suspect but which was in fact a consequence of his very Marxism as a revolutionary operating in circumstances that had not been anticipated in theory, who had to deal with theory not only as an abstract problem but as a social and cultural problem as well—at its most basic, as a problem of language. Teleology in Mao's Marxism is not a theoretical teleology but a teleology that is willed by the interpreting agent, who holds on to the promise of theory while abandoning the faith that theory in fact offers any such promise.

The "sinicization of sociology" (or, more literally, making sociology Chinese, *shehuixue Zhongguohua*), initiated by intellectuals in Taiwan around 1980 but bringing together sociologists from Hong Kong, Singapore, the People's Republic of China, and the United States, shared with its Communist predecessor little more than an urge to bring a Chinese voice into theory, this time sociological theory.[21] It had none of the urgency of a revolutionary struggle or the political stakes that involved getting the better of political rivals of one kind or another. It was, moreover, an undertaking of scholars who viewed it more as a proposition to be considered than a task to be accomplished at all costs, or one that required the suppression of opposing voices. It is remarkable, then, that it should have encountered problems of reconciling culture and theory that are quite similar to the ones discussed above. Part of the answer may be that the sociologists who were involved faced questions of translating universal theory into everyday practice that were not dissimilar to those faced by their Communist predecessors except in their politics. Unlike, say, historians, they were intensely aware as professionals of the universal demands of theory and sensitive to the problems of encompassing diverse social and cultural realities in one grand theory.[22] This time around, however, the discussion was carried out under vastly different circumstances of what it meant to be Chinese and an ideological and analytical openness that shed light on the earlier effort discussed above. On the other hand, this discussion, too, suppressed contradictions that were brought forth by the confrontation of theory with culture, which come into relief against the backdrop of its predecessor.

That the political stakes involved in the earlier discussion were absent from this later one does not mean, therefore, that there were no politics. The politics of culture in theory was still there, voiced with even greater sophistication than would have been possible for Chinese intellectuals in the 1930s. While the practical problems of the sociologist were one element in the calls for sinicization, the political conjuncture of the late 1970s and early 1980s played an even more important role. Accounts of the emergence of the problem by the participants point to the "maturing" of sociology in Taiwan in generating practical questions of research and theory. These practical questions derived their urgency, however, from changes in the politics of identity in East Asia that accompanied the reopening of the People's Republic of China, the withdrawal of U.S. recognition from Taiwan, and the flourishing of East Asian economies that not only brought forth new social problems but also brought scholars from various Chinese societies into closer contact with one another. The reopening of China meant in this case the reopening of China to sociology, which had been closed out since the early 1950s by the monopoly of state-sponsored Marxist ideology. Sociologists of Chinese origin who were invited to help reestablish sociology became more aware in the process of the special needs of Chinese society and the insistence of People's Republic of China sociologists on the necessity of "Chinese characteristics" (which included the continued centrality of Marxism). The withdrawal of U.S. recognition from Taiwan made Taiwanese sociologists more aware of the need for "self-reliance," which was reinforced by a growing awareness of a specifically Taiwan identity that appeared in the 1970s, accompanying rapid economic growth that brought forth new social problems but also the beginnings of democratization.[23]

We may add here two further considerations. First is the newfound empowerment of Chinese societies in East Asia with economic development, which may have contributed to the self-assertiveness implicit in calls for sinicization. Xiao Xinhuang, for instance, applies "world-system analysis" to argue that Chinese sociology suffered from a peripheralness vis-à-vis the U.S. core that paralleled the economic relationships between the capitalist core and the East Asian periphery; sinicization represented the self-assertion of the periphery. How this came about requires further consideration, as the self-assertion of sociologists coincided temporally with the Confucian revival that got under way these same years and overlapped with the "movement" in sociology. Second, self-conscious or not, there is some parallel between Chinese intellectuals' self-assertions against U.S. domination of sociology and the growing protests in the realm of culture against the complicity of disciplines such as history, anthropology, and sociology, not to speak of area studies scholarship, in U.S. domination of the world, which has since then issued in the cultural deconstructionism of postcolonial criticism. The parallel needs to be taken seriously, especially since the younger generation of Chinese sociologists involved in the sinicization movement, like the other intellectuals of Third World origins involved in postcolonial criticism, had been educated in the United States (and Great Britain) in the 1960s and 1970s. The volume to issue from U.S. scholars is almost inescapably a product of the 1970s in its attentiveness to issues of world-system analysis, feminist concerns, et cetera.[24] The references to "borderlands" sociologists and "borderlands" sociology may indicate further affinities with postcolonial discussions getting under way at this time—ironic in a movement to nationalize sociology, but also indicative of the problems it faced.[25]

According to Lin Nan, whose essay led the volume of U.S. sociologists' contributions to the discussion, the sinicization of sociology was intended "to blend (*rongna*) Chinese social and cultural characteristics and national character into sociology."[26] It was different from the creation of a "Chinese sociology," with scholarly and professional goals, or the application of sociology to Chinese society. The level of sinicization was to be determined "by the extent to which sociology acquired Chinese social and cultural characteristics and a Chinese national character." But "sinicization was an undertaking that transcended regional and national boundaries; social and cultural characteristics and national character entailed structures, relations between the group and individual, and different layers in society, which could all be blended into theory and method."[27] As examples of Chinese social and cultural characteristics that sinicization might entail, Lin specified family and kinship relations, centralized power that affected relations of hierarchy at all levels, the value systems and practices that bolstered the system, the consequences for society of a unified script—factors involved in China's development in an East Asia context that might offer views on development different from, say, world-system analysis. Bringing forth new kinds of evidence in these areas, and reformulating theory on that basis, might, according to Lin, effect a theoretical revolution that might resolve the "paradigm crisis" in sociology. This required, he suggested, following Thomas Kuhn, a community of scholars working to this end—which was an opportunity for Chinese scholars.

While Lin's discussion stressed structural factors, other contributors to the volume, especially those working with specific areas such as social psychology, alienation, women's sociology, et cetera, placed greater emphasis on everyday values that needed to be brought into the process of sinicization. Taiwanese sociologists in particular, according to Xiao, who conducted surveys among them, thought it was necessary to bring into consideration Chinese ethical values as well as the concepts in which those values were imbedded; such as the "transmission of the Dao" (*daotong*), humaneness (*ren*), Heaven (*tian*), propriety (*li*), *yinyang*, et cetera.[28]

In either case, however, whether dealing with structures or cultural values, scholars involved in the discussion for the most part agreed that the goal of sinicization was not to divide Chinese sociology from the world but to enrich sociology worldwide. According to Xiao's survey, scholars in Taiwan were divided almost evenly on the question of whether it was desirable to create a national sociology.[29] Hong Kong and Singapore sociologists for the most part were not interested at all in the question of sinicization. U.S. scholars, on the other hand, viewed sinicization as a form of "indigenization" (*bentuhua*) that was little more than a means in the long run to "globalization" (*quanqiuhua*). The most adamant about sinicization were scholars from the People's Republic, who displayed a chauvinistic (*shawenzhuyi*) attitude even toward their Chinese compatriots in their affirmation of Chinese characteristics.[30]

In this case, too, in other words, sinicization covered a broad ground: from the transformation of Chinese society through theory to the outright rejection of national differences in theory (which perceived difference only as a matter of the circumstances to which theory was applied); to the opportunistic uses of theory for national ends (*yang wei zhong yong*, making the foreign serve the Chinese) at the hand of mainland scholars, who saw no further cultural significance in theory; to the conviction especially of U.S. sociologists that theoretical formulations to emerge from sinicization would produce a paradigm revolution in sociology. With the possible exception of mainland scholars, sinicization meant to Chinese sociologists not the capturing of sociology in a Chinese national space but the bringing into sociology of Chinese voices, sentiments, and the social and cultural characteristics of Chinese society in order to create a more cosmopolitan and globalized sociology—to use a word that has become popular since then, a multicultural and multiculturalist socialism. They were anti-Eurocentric in a sense, since they knew that sociology bore upon it the stamp of its origins in nineteenth-century industrial Europe, but their specific focus was on the contemporary hegemony of U.S. sociology, which provoked national claims on sociology in Europe as well. Even in the case of People's Republic of China sociologists with their "chauvinism," we need to recall that the national characteristics they claimed also included as a formative moment the legacy of the "sinicization of Marxism." There were other Chinese sociologists, referred to by Xiao, who may have perceived a possible contradiction between sinicization and the universal claims of sociology, but this was largely muted, especially for U.S. sociologists who referred to themselves as border sociologists, who were outsiders as such to the workings of sociology in the People's Republic of China and Taiwan, and whose identification was primarily with their professional bases in the United States.

The contradictions presented by sinicization, ironically, arose more from a conflict between concretely Chinese and broadly universalist theory than from the problems Chinese societies presented to the project of "indigenization." The differences in historical context between this discussion and the earlier, Maoist, project of the sinicization of Marxism are nowhere more evident than in the meaning of "Chineseness." Mao's vernacularization of Marxism, I suggested above, proceeded at two levels: the national level and the level of everyday life, which presented a much more complex picture of Chinese culture than the level of the nation. These internal differences, however, could be interpellated into one national culture in the process of formation.

The situation in 1980 was vastly different, as war, revolution, colonialism, and migration had by then created vastly different Chinese societies that called into question the very notion of Chineseness. The different implications of indigenization (in addition to *Zhongguohua; quyuhua,* or regionalization; and *difanghua,* or localization, all of which are encountered in the discussions) could hardly be contained in one conception of a Chinese nation or culture shared by all the participants.[31] Strangely enough, a general discussion of the problems of sinicization, such as that offered by Lin Nan, did not even refer to the question, possibly because his self-image as an "outsider" made him reluctant to take up an in issue of great sensitivity. It was brought up by Xiao Xinhuang, who referred in his concluding essay in the volume to "four Chinas," differences among which needed to be respected.[32] The question came up also in Xiao's discussion of sociology in Taiwan, in a discussion of national minorities in China addressing issues of assimilation, and in the discussion of women's sociology, referred to above, where the author suggested that differences between the People's Republic of China, Hong Kong, and Taiwan provided an opportunity for comparing women's status in Chinese societies with their status in different economic systems.[33] The only discussion to meet it head on was a discussion on alienation by Ma Liqin. What he had to say is worth quoting at some length:

> In determining the objectives of research, we must use a definition of "China" that is open-minded and broad. What is the "China" in the term sinicization (*Zhongguo-hua*)? The China here needs to be taken as China in a broad sense, including Taiwan, the People's Republic of China, Hong Kong, Singapore, and all the societies of Chinese Overseas. This broad understanding of China has great significance for research into alienation. First, [the idea of] China must take as its main assumption Chinese, and Chinese cultural life; so that wherever there are Chinese and Chinese culture there is Chinese society, and wherever there is Chinese society there is China. This way, we are not limited by politics and its territorialities. . . . Secondly, giving priority to Chinese society over the state in defining China, we have [an idea of China] that is richer in its dynamism, transformations and variety.[34]

Ma concluded his essay by observing that to make China more dynamic and democratic, it might be better to help Chinese understand the workings of society—in other words, to emphasize "the sociologization of China" (*Zhongguo shehuxuehua*).[35]

What do these two instances of sinicization have to tell us about the more general problem of the confrontation of theory with cultural identity? The most obvious, and the most fundamental, answer is that sinicization is not a transparent term but is subject to different interpretations under different circumstances and in accordance with different political motivations. This also renders highly problematic the idea of the cultural transformation of theory (conceived itself as culturally bound) that is implied by the term. Culture and theory, too, are subject to historical change in the problems they present and in the different ways in which they are understood at different times. The question involves both the changing fortunes of theory and the way in which theory and culture are deployed in describing the interaction between the two, as well as the outcomes that may be expected from their confrontation.

It is possible, as Lin Nan suggested, that the confrontation of theory with a Chinese social and cultural situation may reveal sufficient anomaly to force a "paradigm change"; in other words, produce a richer, more all-encompassing theory. The sinicization of sociological theory, which one author described as a "long and arduous process,"[36] may yet issue in such a paradigm change, but that I think is a moot question. The evidence of the sinicization of Marxism would suggest that the confrontation of theory with an anomalous situation is just as likely to lead to the fragmentation of theory as to its enrichment—which may in fact generate new theories, but to the detriment of the universalistic claims of theory. This is also suggested by developments in postmodern and postcolonial criticism that have called into question theoretical claims to universality as well as the relationship between theory, culture, and history. I would like to reflect here on the politics of theory that may lead us to one or another conclusion.

There is little reason, other than a privileging of the Chinese-Western or Chinese-U.S. relationship, why such confrontation of theory with its cultural others should be restricted to sinicization—in other words, to a *Chinese* confrontation of theory. Social and political theories of various kinds originating in Europe and North America have already undergone significant transformation or breakdown in their confrontation with non-Western societies, including China; examples range from the appearance of Marxism-Leninism early in the century, to the emergence of "dependency theory" and "world-system analysis" in the 1970s, to contemporary questionings of development and globalization in which there are visible traces of the legacy of the Chinese revolution. Indeed, the movement to sinicize sociological theory may be viewed as one instance of proliferating cultural contradictions between Euro-American and postcolonial societies that account for the current problems of culture, theory, and history.

Why sinicization should be endowed with a privileged status in these contradictions is an important question, as it is also bound up with the particular mode in which it was expressed in the discussion of the 1980s. We have little prima facie reason to assume that sinicization must issue in an enrichment of theory rather than its breakdown; that, having indigenized theory in Chinese circumstances, it will then return to theory to render it more global and enhance its claims to universality. Placing it against the backdrop of the earlier effort to sinicize Marxism may be quite revealing in this regard.

It is difficult to argue that the sinicization of Marxism produced a new theory, one that could dislodge or transcend the universalist claims of Marxism. The idea of New Democracy was a genuine innovation in the Marxist conceptualization of historical stages on the way to Communism and would have

some appeal in Third World societies placed similarly to China.[37] Mao's vernacularization of Marxism gave his Marxism a populist cast that may account
for the appeal of his Marxism in the revolt of the 1960s against not just capitalism but also Soviet-style Marxism.[38] His rendering of Marxism into a
hermeneutic implicitly challenged the scientistic assumptions of theory and
suggested that Marxism might be applicable under a diversity of social circumstances that opened up new frontiers for revolutionary activity, even if it also
introduced a serious problem into Marxism in divorcing political action from
its social moorings in the theory.

On the other hand, if these innovations make it possible to speak of a Chinese Marxism, this Marxism remained as a special national case of Marxism
that retained its status as a general theory. Nor did Maoists suggest at any one
point that questioning the status of Marxism was their goal. Mao's "populism"
was contained ultimately by his insistence on the ultimate priority of class.
Having historicized Marxism in the name of the exigencies of revolutionary
practice, Chinese Marxism nevertheless reasserted the universal scientific claims
of theory, evident most readily in a refusal to question the teleology of theory
even when most evidence pointed to the absence of such a teleology in the
workings of Chinese society. This may not be surprising, given that the leadership role assumed by the Communist Party in China could be justified only by
this teleology; what is important is that considerations of party power also limited the extent to which theory could be deconstructed through the agencies of
history and culture.

Sinicization of Marxism may have achieved an "integration of universal theory with the concrete circumstances of Chinese society" in the practice of revolution; what it produced at the level of theory was not a new theory but a
predicament for it: the predicament of the dissipation of theory into so many
national and local situations. This dissipation was far more fundamental in its
implications than the production of a new theory, for it questioned the fundamental assumptions that made universalistic theory possible. Some theorists of
Western Marxism have credited the French Marxist Louis Althusser with breaking down "the ontological and epistemological foundations of western thinking—destabilizing the oppositional hierarchies of positivity/negation, necessi-
ty/contingency, importance/inconsequence, reality/representation."[39] What
these theorists often ignore is the direct debt Althusser acknowledged to Mao's
Marxism for inspiring his work.[40] The sinicization of Marxism would have far-
reaching consequences, through the influence of Althusser, for the breakdown
of theory globally.

While Mao and his colleagues continued to insist on the priority of theory,
in their elevation of practice to the level of theory, they created at least the possibility that theory was open to endless interpretation. Perhaps more signifi-

cantly, sinicization insisted on the importance of introducing a Chinese voice into theory that would have lasting consequences. As a reflection on Chinese society through the language of Marxism, and a simultaneous reflection on Marxism through the social and cultural circumstances (and even the language) of Chinese society, Mao's Marxism may be viewed best as what Jürgen Habermas has described as a "practical discourse."[41] The notion of practical discourse recognizes Mao (and the Chinese practitioners of Marxism) as the subjects who reflect on Marxism; their relationship to a global Marxism then appears not as a subject-object relationship but as an intersubjective one. Thus, theory may retain its universality, but it is made available to interpretation by the revolutionary subject. Teleology could contain the dissipation of theory; on the other hand, there is no reason why teleology itself could not be appropriated for a nationalized Marxism. Is it in the end a Chinese-style Communism, as Maoists called it in the heyday of their power, or socialism with Chinese characteristics, as Mao's successors prefer? In sinicization were the seeds of the disintegration of socialism into so many historical trajectories, which in subsequent years were to sprout into as many different socialisms as there were socialist nations.

As Mao and his colleagues tried to contain the dissipation of theory into local theories by reaffirming its claims to universal truth, the sinicization of sociology in many ways sought to do the same by reaffirming the ultimate validity of the theoretical universals of sociology, which would be enriched in its global claims through the very process of indigenization. For those who saw globalization as the goal of sinicization, sinicization represented no more than "a process and method."[42] Ma Liqin adds that sinicization represents "a transitional necessity in the process of 'developing Chinese sociology,' and a method to that end."[43] What is recognized in either case is the dual goal of sinicization: to bring sociology into a national cultural space, where it is to be domesticated to lose its foreignness, and return it a universal sociology to introduce to it a Chinese voice to make it more cosmopolitan. The whole procedure is not dissimilar to the Communist undertaking of sinicization, which sought to make Marxism less foreign in China while insisting on a Chinese voice at the global level. The difference is mainly in political goals and reference; this time around not to an international "brotherhood" of revolutionaries but to an international profession.

Unlike the Communists devoted to the goal of national liberation, concerned about the hegemony over national culture of a universalist theory, in this case the loyalties were more ambiguous. I am referring here both to ambiguities created by simultaneous loyalty to the global and the local and to the problems presented by difficulties of defining the Chinese nation, and a national culture, in a situation of global dispersal of Chinese populations. Unlike in the case of the Maoists who could suppress the cultural diversity of China with the rhetoric of national unity (and still did in the discussion of the sinicization of sociology), by the 1980s it was impossible to suppress the contradictions presented to the Chinese cultural idea of the coexistence of a multiplicity of Chinese societies with different historical trajectories—a situation that has gotten more serious since then. In such a situation, it was hardly possible to speak of "indigenization" as if that could be equated with the nation. The idea of a Chinese culture then appears more than ever as a "strategy of containment," where the myth of cultural unity may be sustained in the evidence of history.

The problems presented by the fragmentation of Chineseness were compounded by the different relationships of the various Chinese societies to their global environment, especially the hegemonic center in the United States. The conflicts referred to above over the issue of sinicization were bound up with these relationships. The contradictions are most readily visible in the case of Chinese-American sociologists, with their self-identifications as "border" intellectuals (a common metaphor of postcolonial criticism) who were at once "outsiders" to Chinese and American societies and, from a different perspective, insiders to both. But they are also visible in the differences claimed by sociologists from different Chinese societies, with People's Republic of China sociologists most adamant about their distance from the global hegemonic center.

These differences also cast in a different light the interpretation of sinicization as a process of indigenization with ultimate globalization as its goal. Why indigenization should lead to globalization rather than fragmentation, as in the case of Mao's Marxism (or other postcolonial fragmentations of theory) is not self-evident. I suggested above that while the sinicization of sociology may be viewed as one instance of postcolonial challenges to Euro-American or American centrism, it was also empowered in the case of Chinese societies by the immense prestige that accrued to them with successful performance in the global capitalist economy. If Chineseness was privileged in the discussions of sinicization, this empowerment had much to do with it, as it did with the Confucian revival at the time. In other words, what is at issue here is not just a traditional sinocentrism but a development on the global scene. To the extent that globalization refers to a rearrangement of global hegemony by admitting into it the resurgent economic powers of East Asia, it is easy enough to accord to sinicization a privileged place that sets it apart from other postcolonial encounters with theory: it promised further globalization and the consolidation of hegemony, not its fragmentation through indigenization. The hegemonic partnership suggested here, however, is a fragile one, made possible by suppressing the contradictions in its assumptions as well as its contradictions to a larger global environment. This has become evident since then in the assertion of "Asian values" against the cultural assumptions guiding "Western" theory. The preoccupation with Asian values appeared about the same time as the effort to sinicize sociology, and overlapped with those efforts. In spite of the effort of scholars to contain a possible contradiction between the two by a globalized, albeit still monistic, theory, the contradictions created by the intrusion of culture into theory are readily visible in conservative as well as radical attempts to find alternatives to Euro- or America-centric interpretations of Asian societies.

It may make sense, when there is so much shared culture, to speak of a globalized theory that is multivocal rather than parochially universalistic. But such efforts may ignore the contradictions built into the very undertaking at the risk of falling into ideological wishful thinking. The contradictions involved are not just contradictions between Chinese societies and U.S. theories, or between these societies themselves. They also invite consideration of contradictions presented by the global context of sinicization: other societies that demand voices in this multivocality. Having been sinicized and globalized, is theory then going to be also Indianized, Islamicized, et cetera? Can the unity still be maintained if other cultural voices are to be brought into it?

And what is the culture that is to be brought into theory? As I noted above, the so-called Western theory that is to be confronted with Chinese culture has already been transformed by its many confrontations with other societies and is now practically in a state of breakdown, challenged most radically by voices from within or, more accurately, no longer sure of what is within and what is without. Much the same may be said of "Chinese culture," which is already a product, and has been for some time, of the internalization of a century of confrontation with Euro-America. This is evident most readily once again in the case of the People's Republic of China, whose spokespeople guilelessly speak of a Chinese culture of which Marxism is an integral part, even though it is now supplemented by a born-again Confucianism that the revolution sought to eradicate for nearly a century—which is an indication not of the subjugation of history by culture but, as the pairing indicates, of the appropriation of cultural legacies in accordance with contemporary needs. And where do we locate Chinese culture, or an inside or outside to it, when the very notion of a Chinese nation has become deeply problematic?

That a notion of "culture" repeatedly finds its way into the consideration of theory (among other things), it seems to me, is itself evidence of the fragility of arguments that take globalization as their premise, because it is the process of globalization that itself renews the reification of culture in the problems of power and identity that it presents. As globalization is accompanied by fragmentation at different levels, as is frequently noted these days, culture is brought back into defining political authenticity and identity, even though few agree on what culture may mean, except as a means to policing boundaries of identity when all other social forces threaten to abolish it. And there is no reason why theory, rather than serve the purposes of communication across boundaries, should not be broken down along the lines of these policed cultural boundaries, as it has along fissures of race, gender, and ethnicity.

It might make sense, under the circumstances, to shift the grounds of the discussion to history. I do not mean by history here a culturalism that parades in the guise of historicism, that subjects history to the prerogatives of an unchanging cultural continuity that is more imagined than real. Nor do I mean history in any reified modernist sense that entraps the present in the past and colonizes the future with the present, which itself has become highly problematic. What I have in mind is history in the sense of historicity, which accounts for temporal and spatial divisions, and is the overdetermined product of the conjuncture of forces that go into the making of everyday existence, of which the repertory of the past is only one moment, albeit an important one.

Theory and culture are both products of historical conjunctures, as historical conjunctures contain theories and cultures as their determining moments. That a thoroughgoing historicization of theory and culture introduces a deep uncertainty into the meaning of either of these terms makes it unlikely that it may find easy acceptance among political ideologues, professionals devoted to the discovery of laws governing human behavior, or the everyday subjects of history who need some measure of stable meaning just to live. For as the assumption of cultural unity gives some meaning to social existence, theories about culture and history serve to order that existence. But we need to recognize also that human activity and the way human beings endow their activities with everyday meaning are part of the process that produces new theories, cultures, and histories that resist the classifications that are demanded by a political or professional urge to theorize life so as to bring to it an intellectual order that it may not have. The point is not just to create new theories that substitute new universalisms for old, satisfy abstract national or cultural desires, or entrap theorization in pasts of its own creation that promise little more than the perpetuation of human oppression in novel forms. The point is to create theories that point to possibilities suppressed in theories of order, so as to enable humane relations that give new meaning to human existence. Where in the repertory of past and present human existence the inspiration for such creativity comes from is at best a secondary consideration.

NOTES

1. An explanation is necessary concerning various problems associated with the concept of theory: what is understood by theory here and the even more complicated question, in light of the question of culture raised in this chapter, of whether or not theory means the

same thing in the two contexts at issue here, the "Western" and the Chinese. Theory has been subject to diverse interpretations even in Western thinking, even within the same field. In his classic work published first in 1906, *The Aim and Structure of Physical Theory*, Pierre Duhem defined physical theory as "a system of mathematical propositions, deduced from a smaller number of principles, which aim to represent as simply, as completely, and as exactly as possible a set of experimental laws." (Pierre Duhem, *The Aim and Structure of Physical Theory*, trans. Philip P. Wiener [New York: Atheneum, 1962], 19.) Duhem insisted that theory was a representation and "not an explanation." His discussion acknowledged not only the possibility of different conceptualizations of theory in different fields but also, even more interestingly, national cultural differences of style in representations of theory itself (most importantly in his case between the English and the French/German approaches).

There is no need here to belabor the even more vexing problems presented by theory as in social, political, and cultural theory, where normative and ideological elements are almost an inevitable part in the constitution of theory. I think that most of us working in these fields understand theory to mean the formulation of abstract relationships that seek to make sense of diverse historical phenomena; and that more often than not these relationships are expressed as relationships between concepts, derived from experience or experiment, that are themselves generalized representations of individual phenomena that lend themselves to generalization nevertheless in their apparent regularity. The grand theories or metanarratives associated with the names of K. Marx and M. Weber or, more recently, of world-system analysis, are of this type. For historians, however, theory may simply mean the use of abstract concepts such as class and gender in organizing and/or explaining historical data. Theory mediates the relationship between the particular and the general; it suggests patterns to the relationship, but it is different from laws in being open (at least theoretically) to other possibilities of interpretation. Regardless of the ultimate truth claims for theories sometimes made by their proponents, theories are inevitably limited in their claims, as they have no way to foreclose the simultaneous existence of competing theories; for the concepts that inform any one theory foreground certain aspects of reality over others, which means that they leave room for other concepts that reveal reality differently.

Theorization—the activity of producing theories—therefore is an interpretive act in its choice of concepts, and their relationships, to represent reality. The choices are political because they have political consequences even where they are not intended politically. Theory is also historical in the sense that it is in no position to anticipate the changing meanings attributed to concepts in different historical contexts, the changing relationships between concepts, and the very question of the relevance of concepts to changing social realities. It may be possible in the physical sciences to judge the validity of competing theories by making them serve as "prophets" (in Duhem's terminology), to "tell us the results of an experiment before it has occurred" (Duhem, *Physical Theory*, 27). Social theories may aim at similar prophecy, but in their case the prophecy is mediated by history, which rules out the regularity to be found in nature (although historicity often needs to be considered in the natural sciences as well). It is not that there is no regularity in human behavior or relationships but that, more often than not, such regularity may be established only at the cost of the denial of difference. An example is the concept of class. There is little question that the concept of class opened up new lines of inquiry into social relations that had been hidden from view earlier. It is easy enough for those opposed to class analysis to point to its inability to account for social organization or political behavior, since the concept of class, like all concepts of social representation, is fuzzy along the edges because it is overdetermined—intermediated, in other words, by other social relationships. However, we need also to ask if the realities represented by the concept of class have equal saliency at all times, as in our day, for instance, when it is overshadowed by concepts of gender and race. The effort to render class relationships into a "natural" condition of humanity, as under Communist regimes, on the other hand, required the classification of all individuals into class categories, which rendered a concept with liberating intentions into an intellectual and social prison house. Theorization in social and cultural studies, if it is to avoid such imprisonment, must recognize of necessity that social and cultural theories are loaded with uncertainties and ideological implications, subject to the meanings attributed to them under different circumstances.

Theorization as interpretive activity is built into the very term. The American literary scholar Wlad Godzich, tracing the etymology of "theory," observes that the Greek *theorein*, meaning "to see, to behold," referred to the adjudication of complex situations by the *theoros*, who were appointed to pass judgment on complex situations that involved the possibility of different interpretations. The *theoros* passed the judgment, but the judgment itself was conditioned by considerations of order in a concrete historical situation. Theorizing under the circumstances involved not only interpretation but also considerations of public order. See Wlad Godzich, introduction to *Resistance to Theory*, by Paul de Man (Minneapolis: University of Minnesota Press, 1986), xv.

To turn to the other question, whether or not theory means the same thing in the Chinese context as it does in Euro-American contexts, it is necessary to note that while the question of vocabulary across cultural divides is a very vexing question, it needs to be approached with some care in order to avoid the culturalist assumptions built into the question itself. After all, theory has served as a means of communication across cultural boundaries (wherever those may be located), and simple differences in terminology should not lead to automatic assumptions about differences in understanding. The question needs to be raised nevertheless to avoid misunderstanding. The most commonly used Chinese term for theory, *lilun*, which could be translated literally as "discourse on principles," intimates not only the possibility of generalization on principles, but also that generalizations involve interpretations, since discourses on principles offer different portrayals of those principles. The term also carries implications that parallel in remarkable ways what Godzich has to say of theory in its etymology, which may explain why, in most twentieth-century discussions of theory in China, theory often overlaps with "ism" (*zhuyi*). According to Wing-tsit Chan, *li* (principle), used as a verb, means "to establish order." See Wing-tsit Chan, trans. and comp., *A Sourcebook in Chinese Philosophy* (New York: Bobbs-Merrill, 1963),.260 n. 23. Theorizing, therefore, means not only getting at fundamental principles of distinguishing right from wrong, but also that the procedures for doing so involve interpretation with an eye to settling disputes so as to achieve order. But there may also be a significant difference in connotation that involves the question of order. The *theoros* were publically appointed officials charged with interpreting events. *Li*, according to a Chinese etymological dictionary, the *Cihai*, referred in some early Chinese texts (*Guanzi*) to a "prison-official." *Cihai* (Taipei: Zhonghua shu ju), 2: 28. (See also *Hanyu da cidian*, 4: 5686, def. 13, which has citations from Sima Qian and Han Yu to the same effect. I am grateful to Victor Mair for bringing this source to my attention.) If that is indeed the case, the association of theory with a policing function may be much stronger in the one term, *li*, than in the other, theory, which is much more closely associated with the adjudication of difference, although that, too, involves a policing action of sorts. But we need to remember that we are talking about terminology and abstract etymologies, which are not necessarily a guide to understanding twentieth-century usages.

The question of a Chinese or Western theory involves different appreciations, not of the term "theory," but of different representations of reality through abstractions, the part representation plays in the appreciation of reality, and the social and political meanings attached to representation.

2. This question has been raised forcefully in the historiography of China by Paul A. Cohen, *Discovering History in China: American Historical Writing on the Recent Chinese Past* (New York: Columbia University Press, 1984).

3. It is noteworthy that this breakdown of theory into national cultures parallels the breakdown of capitalism into national or continental (such as Asian) capitalisms; in other words, the abandonment (in theory, at least) of universalism with the so-called globalization of capitalism. See, e.g., Charles Hampden-Turner and Alfons Trompenaars, *The Seven Cultures of Capitalism: Value Systems for Creating Wealth in the United States, Japan, Germany, France, Britain, Sweden, and the Netherlands* (New York: Currency/Doubleday, 1993). The counterintuitive distinguishing of universalism from globalism is apparent in many areas of contemporary thought.

4. John Tomlinson, *Cultural Imperialism* (Baltimore: Johns Hopkins University Press, 1991), provides an important discussion of the problems associated with the idea of "cultural imperialism."

5. For a discussion of this problem with reference to the Indian thinker Ashis Nandy, see chap. 5.

6. Jean-François Lyotard, *The Postmodern Condition: A Report on Knowledge*, trans. Geoff Bennington and Brian Massumi (Minneapolis: University of Minnesota Press, 1984).

7. See Raymond Wylie, *The Emergence of Maoism: Mao Tse-tung, Ch'en Po-ta, and the Search for Chinese Theory* (Stanford, Calif.: Stanford University Press, 1980). See also Arif Dirlik, "Mao Zedong and 'Chinese Marxism,'" in *Encyclopedia of Asian Philosophy*, ed. I. Mahalingam and B. Carr (London: Routledge, 1997); and Arif Dirlik, "The Predicament of Marxist Historical Consciousness: Mao Zedong, Antonio Gramsci, and the Reformulation of Marxist Revolutionary Theory," *Modern China* 9, no. 2 (April 1983): 182–211. My remarks on the sinicization of Marxism are drawn from these articles, which discuss at much greater length the theoretical questions presented by sinicization,

8. Cai Yongmei and Xiao Xinhuang (Michael Hsiao), eds., *Shehuixue Zhoongguohua* (The sinicization of sociology) (Taipei: Juliu tushu gongsi, 1985).

9. *Selected Works of Mao Tse-tung*, 4 vols. (Beijing: Foreign Languages Press, 1965–67), 2: 339–84, 380–81, published originally as "Xin minzhu zhuyide zhengzhi yu xin minzhu zhuyide wenhua" (The politics and culture of new democracy), *Zhongguo wenhua* (Chinese culture) 1 (January 1940).

10. Shu Riping, "Shinian lai Mao Zedong zhexue sixiang yanjiu shuping" (An account of research on Mao Zedong's philosophy over the last ten years), *Mao Zedong zhexue sixiang yanjiu* (Research on Mao Zedong's philosophical thought) 5 (1989): 4–10, 6.

11. Stuart S. Schram, *The Political Thought of Mao Tse-tun*, rev. and enl. (New York: Praeger, 1971), 112.

12. For differences among Chinese interpretations, see Shu, "Shinian lai Mao Zedong zhexue sixiang yanjiu shuping," 6. For different interpretations among U.S. analysts, see

"Symposium on Mao and Marx," *Modern China* 2, no. 3 (October 1976), and *Modern China* 3, no. 1 (April 1977).

13. Mao Zedong, "Lun xin jieduan" (On the new stage), speech to the Enlarged Plenary Session of the Sixth Central Committee (12–14 October 1938), in *Mao Zedong ji* (Collected works of Mao Zedong), ed. Takeuchi Minoru, 10 vols. (Hong Kong: Po Wen Book Co., 1976), 6:163–263, 260–61.

14. Wylie, *Emergence of Maoism*, 76–99.

15. See, e.g., the discussions in the collection *Xian jieduande Zhongguo sixiang yundong* (The Chinese thought movement of the present) (Shanghai: Yiban shudian, 1937).

16. A striking example is Roger R. Thompson, ed., *Report from Xunwu* (Stanford, Calif.: Stanford University Press, 1990).

17. One of the first to draw attention to the problem of language was Qu Qiubai. See Paul Pickowicz, *Marxist Literary Thought in China: The Influence of Ch'u Ch'iu-pai* (Berkeley and Los Angeles: University of California Press, 1981). A good discussion of Communist cultural activity may be found in Ellen Judd, "Revolutionary Song and Drama in the Jiangxi Soviet," *Modern China* 9, no. 1 (January 1983): 127–60. Indeed, some Chinese authors, on the basis of Mao's revolutionary practice, carry the origins of sinicization back to the early 1930s.

18. Institute for the Study of Mao Zedong's Philosophy, Sichuan Social Sciences Academy, *Mao Zedong bapian zhuzuo chengyu diangu renwu jianzhu jianjie* (Brief annotations of set phrases, classical allusions, and personalities in eight essays by Mao Zedong) (Chongqing: Chongqing chuban she, 1982).

19. Ai Siqi, "Lun Zhongguode teshuxing" (On China's special characteristics), *Zhongguo wenhua* 1 (January 1940), 31–32.

20. See, e.g., Frederic Wakeman Jr., *History and Will: Philosophical Perspectives of Mao Tse-tung's Thought* (Berkeley and Los Angeles: University of California Press, 1975); Thomas A. Metzger, *Escape from Predicament: Neo-Confucianism and China's Evolving Political Culture* (New York: Columbia University Press, 1977); Benjamin I. Schwartz, "The Reign of Virtue: Some Broad Perspectives on Leader and Party in the Cultural Revolution," *China Quarterly* 35 (1965): 1–17; Joseph Liu, "Mao's 'On Contradiction,'" *Studies in Soviet Thought* 11 (June 1971): 71–89.

21. According to the accounts of this movement, sinicization was already in the air in Taiwan in the late 1970s, but the movement got under way with a conference in 1980 organized by the Institute of Ethnology of the Academia Sinica, "Shehui yu xingwei kexuede Zhongguohua" (The sinicization of social and behavioral sciences). It was followed up by a conference at the Chinese University of Hong Kong in 1983, "Xiandaihua yu Zhongguo wenhua" (Modernization and Chinese culture), which included Chinese scholars from Hong Kong, Taiwan, Singapore, and the People's Republic. While the conference was broader in scope, sinicization apparently became a hot topic of discussion. The concern reached the United States the same year, when at the Western Conference of the Association for Asian Studies in Tempe, Arizona, a roundtable discussion was held on the subject "Sinicization of Sociology: A Collective Portrait of Some American-Trained Chinese Sociologists." The Institute of Ethnology Conference issued a volume, *Shehui ji xingwei kexue yanjiude Zhongguohua* (Sinicization of research in social and behavioral sciences), ed. Yang Guoshu and Wen Chonggyi (Taipei: Zhongyanyuan minzu suo, 1982). American sociologists published their own volume, *Shehui zhuyi Zhongguohua* (hereafter, SHXZGH), that offered Chinese Amer-

ican sociologists' take on the issues involved. Cai Yongmei's introduction to the latter volume gives a personal account of these conferences and publications. For similar concerns about "indigenizing" sociology in Korea, see Park Myoung-Kyu and Chang Kyung-Sup, "Sociology between Western Theory and Korean Reality: Accommodation, Tension, and a Search for Alternatives," *International Sociology* 14, no. 2 (June 1999): 139–56.

22. Bringing a Chinese voice into scholarship has been a concern in recent years in many disciplines, most prominently in history. The concern in the latter case, however, has been almost exclusively with historiographical traditions of high culture, which follow civilizational divides reminiscent of Orientalist mappings of the world. Orientalism may be a misnomer here, or, conversely, may be particularly pertinent, because Chinese historians do the same. See, e.g., a report on a conference on the crisis of history, "Shixue wang nali zou?" (Whither history?), in *Jindai Zhongguo*, 30 April 1989, 1–14, in which the distinguished historian from Hong Kong, Du Weiyun, was the keynote speaker. The speech is devoted exclusively to the accomplishments of historical high culture in China and how its ideals might be reconciled to Western historiography. This question has dominated historiographical discussions in conferences in which I have been a participant. It avoids, needless to say, the changes experienced by Chinese populations everywhere. Sociologists, on the other hand, like anthropologists, draw attention to everyday experience in their dealings with the confrontation between theory and culture—which incidentally may have something to say about the classification of disciplines into nomothetic and ideographic categories. The intrusion of disciplines into the discussion of the relationship between culture and history is also an indication of how much things have changed since the 1930s.

23. See the accounts offered by Lin Nan, "Shehuixue Zhongguohuade xia yibu" (The next step in the sinicization of sociology); and Xiao Xinhuang (Michael Hsiao), "Shehuixue zai Taiwan" (Sociology in Taiwan), in SHXZGH, 29–44 and 271–310, respectively.

24. See the essay by Zhou Yanling, "Shehuixue Zhongguohua yu funu shehuixue" (Sinicization of sociology and the sociology of women), SHXZGH, 105–33, where the author stresses the centrality of women's issues but also qualifies, as do other Third World feminists, the claims of a universalist feminism.

25. Cai Yongmei, introduction to SHXZGH, 9–28, 9–10.

26. Lin Nan, "Shehuixue Zhongguohuade xia yibu," 32. This essay was delivered initially at the Tempe meeting.

27. Lin Nan, "Shehuixue Zhongguohuade xia yibu," 32–33.

28. Xiao, "Shehuixue zai Taiwan," 307.

29. Xiao, "Shehuixue zai Taiwan," 301.

30. Xiao Xinhuang and Li Zhefu, "Youshi sanshi nianlai haixia lianggan shehuixuede fazhan" (Looking at the development of sociology on two sides of the straits in the last thirty years), SHXZGH, 311–28, 315–16.

31. In the course of the 1980s, as attention turned to Taiwanization, *Zhongguohua* was downplayed whereas *bentuhua* became more prominent in the thinking of Taiwan social scientists, with a specific focus on Taiwan. I am grateful to my student, Chuang Ya-chung, for pointing this out to me. Chuang was a graduate student in Taiwan in the late 1980s.

32 Xiao, "LuMei Zhongguo shehuixuezhe tan shehuixue Zhongguohua" (Chinese sociologists in the United States discuss the sinicization of sociology), app., SHXZGH, 329–45, 339.

33. Xiao, "Shehuixue zai Taiwan"; Guo Wenxiong, "Cong shehuixue Zhongguohua

guandian kan Zhongguo shaoshu minzu zhengce yu yanjiu" (Viewing Chinese policy and research on minority nationalities from the standpoint of sinicization), SHXZGH, 151–64; and Zhou Yanling, "Shehuixue Zhongguohua yu funu shehuixue," 122–23.

34. Ma, "Lun shuli yanjiude Zhongguohua" (Sinicization of research in alienation), SHXZGH, 191–212, 206.

35. Ma, "Lun shuli yanjiude Zhongguohua," 209.

36. Guo, "Cong shehuixue Zhongguo guandian kan Zhongguo shaoshu minzu zhengce yu yanjiu," 163.

37. For the appeals of Maoism in the Third World, see Arif Dirlik, Paul Healy, and Nick Knight, eds., *Critical Perspectives on Mao Zedong's Thought* (Atlantic Highlands, N.J.: Humanities Press, 1997).

38. For this interpretation of Mao's Marxism, see the essays in Maurice Meisner, *Marxism, Maoism, and Utopianism* (Madison: University of Wisconsin Press, 1982).

39. J. K. Gibson-Graham, *The End of Capitalism (As We Knew It): A Feminist Critique of Political Economy* (Boston: Blackwell, 1996), 28.

40. L. Althusser, "Contradiction and Overdetermination," in *For Marx* (New York: Vintage Books, 1970): 89–128, esp. 90–94.

41. Jürgen Habermas, *Theory and Practice*, trans. John Vierted (Boston: Beacon Press, 1973), 2, 10–16.

42. Cai Yongmei, introduction to SHXZGH, 14.

43. Ma, "Lun shuli yanjiude Zhongguohua," 208.

5

READING ASHIS NANDY:

THE RETURN OF THE PAST,

OR MODERNITY WITH A VENGEANCE

The discussion in this chapter very likely reads as one big question, rather than an answer to anything. I am aware that Nandy's work has been quite controversial within the immediate Indian context. For someone like myself who is an outsider to Indian intellectual and political life, an attempt to discuss his work seems little different from venturing into a minefield without a reliable mine detector. What makes the risk worth taking is the relevance of what Nandy has to say beyond Indian intellectual borders. I am especially interested here in the triangular relationship between science, history, and developmentalism that informs much of his writing.

Against the grain of Nandy's antihistoricism, I find it important to historicize his work and its impact. In his preface to *The Intimate Enemy*, Nandy writes of the unease with the knowledge-systems underlying theories of progress:

> This awareness has not made everyone give up his theory of progress but it has given confidence to a few to look askance at the old universalism within which the earlier critiques of colonialism were offered. It is now possible for some to combine fundamental social criticism with a defence of non-modern cultures and traditions. It is possible to speak of the plurality of critical traditions and of human rationality. At long last we seem to have recognized that neither is Descartes the last word on reason nor is Marx that on the critical spirit.[1]

The statement may have something to tell us about the conditions of possibility of Nandy's speech: the "confidence" that has been enabled by the discrediting of, or loss of faith in, the "old universalisms." The universalisms that Nandy has in mind are quite evidently Eurocentric universals, including those that informed earlier *radical* critiques of colonialism. This recognition may enable us to evaluate what Nandy has to offer critically—in its crucial insights as well as its limitations. To this end, I would like to place Nandy's thinking within the context of two contradictory intellectual tendencies of our times, which are also products of the retreat of the "old universalisms": a postcolonialism that nourishes off a new universalism under the guise of diasporic globalization, and a contrary tendency to ethnocentrism in the reassertion of alternative civilizational values submerged earlier under the flood of Eurocentric modernity. For all their contradictoriness, these two tendencies both point to a return of the past, not in the negation of modernity, but in its complication; for this contemporary turn to suppressed pasts, while it may be conceived as a reaction to modernity, also represents its triumph.

FROM FRANTZ FANON TO ASHIS NANDY

Nandy's training as a psychologist and the importance of psychology to the way he frames problems of colonialism and modernity immediately recall to mind that other psychologist, Frantz Fanon, whose writings left a deep imprint on an earlier, revolutionary, age, the disappearance of which is one of the fundamental conditions of our own.[2] It is not possible here to engage in a close comparison of two texts such as *The Intimate Enemy* and Fanon's *Black Skin, White Masks*, which offer many interesting parallels.[3] Both texts practice what Nandy calls a "cultural psychology" of colonialism, although it may be revealing that Fanon refers to his undertaking also as "sociodiagnosis."[4] Central to both texts is the colonial subject, the colonized as well as the colonizer, and the psychic damage both suffer as a result of colonialism. Both texts are intended to "decolonize" the colonial subject, although Fanon more often uses the term "disalienation," as he is intensely preoccupied with the alienation of black men and women not only from their own subjectivities but also from, to use a term of Marx's, their "species-being." Central to both analyses are issues of class and sexuality in colonial relations of domination and resistance. Colonialism created a new class of cultural hybrids, the "babus," to use the term from the Indian context, alienated from their own cultures in their feelings of superiority toward their societies and yet despised by the colonialists with whom they strove to identify. It also introduced or exacerbated gender antagonisms. The feminization of the colonized by the colonizer was to find a response on the part of the colonized male in an unhealthy stress on assertions of sexual potency, dichotomizing gender relations in society.

These issues are central to contemporary postcolonial criticism; how they are framed and dealt with goes a long way toward locating not only individual intellectual and political positions but also historical transformations in attitudes toward colonialism and its legacies. Fanon's own legacy has been the subject of debate, occasioned by efforts to appropriate his analyses of the colonial encounter for postcolonialism of a poststructuralist bent.[5] My goal in invoking the parallels between the two texts by Fanon and Nandy is not to assimilate the one to the other but to get at the differences between them, which may be even more significant than what their texts have in common. The thematic parallels between *The Intimate Enemy* and *Black Skin, White Masks* are overshadowed by the different ways in which the two authors handle the themes. These differences are magnified further if we juxtapose two other texts that are not just diagnostic but also point to solutions to the problems created by colonialism: *The Wretched of the Earth* and *Traditions, Tyranny, and Utopias.*[6]

These differences at one level point to the different milieus within which these works were produced. Fanon's Caribbean and Africa are a great distance from Nandy's India in the problems they present. As my intention here is not to engage in an intellectual history of the two thinkers but rather to evaluate how they handle the problems of colonialism and domination, I am more interested in what Nandy's works reveal about the distance of our times from the context within which Fanon's works were produced and received. Even the ways in which we conceive spatial distances have their temporality. An earlier age, which found significant meaning in a term such as "Third World" and in a theory with universal claims such as Marxism, could ignore the distance of India from Africa. That neither "Third World" nor "Marxism" commands such significance any more is a gauge of temporal distance. These distancings may also help us locate Nandy historically with regard both to an earlier problematic of liberation from the colonial and to contemporary postcolonial rephrasings of the problem.[7] If Fanon now sounds like a voice from the past, what he had to say still offers a way to evaluate critically our own voices.

FANON AND NANDY IN POSTCOLONIAL PERSPECTIVES

There is no better place to start in enunciating these differences than an evaluation Nandy has offered of Fanon's answer to the problem of colonialism. What he has to say is worth quoting at some length because of the number of problems it touches upon, as well as his own perception of his differences from Fanon:

> Despite all the indignity and oppression they have faced, many defeated cultures refuse to draw a clear line between the victor and the defeated, the oppressor and the oppressed, the rulers and the ruled. . . . Drawing upon the non-dualist traditions of their religions, myths and folkways, these cultures try to set some vague, half-effective limits on the objectification of living beings and on the violence which flows from it. They try to protect the faith—increasingly lost to the modern world—that the borderlines of evil can never be clearly defined, that there is always a continuity between the aggressor and his victim, and that liberation from oppressive structures

outside has at the same time to mean freedom from an oppressive part of one's own self. . . . The cleansing role Frantz Fanon grants to violence in his vision of a post-colonial society sounds so alien to many Africans and Asians mainly because it is insensitive to this cultural resistance. Fanon admits the internalization of the oppressor. But he calls for an exorcism in which the ghost outside has to be finally confronted in violence, for it carries the burden of the ghost within. The outer violence, Fanon suggests, is the only means of making a painful break with a part of one's own self. If Fanon had more confidence in his culture he would have sensed that his vision ties the victim more deeply to the culture of oppression than any collaboration can. Cultural acceptance of the major technique of oppression in our times, organized violence, cannot but further socialize the victims to the basic values of their oppressors. . . . Perhaps if Fanon had lived longer, he would have come to admit that in his method of exorcism lies a partial answer to two vital questions about the search for liberation in our times, namely, why dictatorships of the proletariat never end and why revolutions always devour their children.[8]

I am concerned here not with the adequacy of this reading of Fanon on the issue of violence but rather with what it has to tell us about Nandy. A careful reading of the last two chapters of Fanon's *Black Skin, White Masks* suggests considerable ambivalence on the issue of violence. This early text, which Gates describes as Fanon's "most overtly psychoanalytic book,"[9] is the preferred text for postcolonial interpretations of Fanon, which seek to find in Fanon an ambivalence similar to that in postcolonial criticism over the relationship of the colonized to the colonizer. On the other hand, an affirmative discussion of violence opens up Fanon's later book, *The Wretched of the Earth*, where Fanon describes the colonial world as "a Manichean world" from which there is no escape except through violence. Not surprisingly, *The Wretched of the Earth* does not easily permit a postcolonial reading of Fanon that would erase the relentless opposition between the colonizer and the colonized.[10] While Nandy cites both of these texts in the footnote to the passage above, it seems that he gives priority to *The Wretched of the Earth* in his evaluation of what Fanon has to say about violence. Unlike in postcolonial interpretations, in other words, he seeks a distance from, not an appropriation of, Fanon.[11] The distancing is not just ideological, it is also temporal, as is implicit in his observation that "if Fanon had lived longer," he would have seen revolutions for what they are, which is clearer to us from *our* vantage point in time.

This double distance—from past revolutionary responses to colonialism and contemporary efforts to erase the revolutionary past by subsuming those responses in new postcolonial narratives—offers one way to place Nandy intellectually and politically. Strangely enough, while Nandy's evaluation of Fanon may differ from that in postcolonial criticism, the premises that inform his evaluation share much with the latter. As far as I am aware, Nandy has only a tenuous relationship to fellow Indian intellectuals who have done much to propagate postcolonial criticism abroad.[12] The Centre for the Study of Developing Societies, of which he has been fellow and director, addresses questions of a nature quite different from those in postcolonial criticism, and draws on a Gandhian legacy to challenge modernity, including a postcolonial modernity.

I will say more on these issues later in this chapter. The differences in Nandy's critique of colonialism from that in postcolonial criticism should not lead us to ignore that the two critiques are contemporaries, that for all their differences they also may share commonalities which distinguish what they have to say about colonialism from past responses to it—and ultimately suggest a broader range to postcolonial criticism than is allowed for in Euro-American conceptions of it informed by diasporic intellectuals. The most obvious commonality may be that both critiques are postrevolutionary, in the sense both of "after" and "anti." This is quite explicit in the case of Nandy. It may also be seen without much effort in postcolonial criticism, which in its repudiation of metanarratives, or fixed identities, also militates against revolutionary possibilities by denying the structural and subjective conditions of revolution. When Nandy writes that "conventional anti-colonialism, too, could be an apologia for the colonization of minds," he might easily be speaking as a "postcolonial critic."[13] The repudiation and the appropriation of Fanon, while quite antithetical in interpretation, nevertheless converge in their denial of revolution as a means to liberation from colonialism.

Second, Nandy is at one with much of postcolonial criticism in his emphasis on colonialism as a cultural or a psychological entity. This, of course, was the case also with Fanon, who was one of the first Third World intellectuals to make a powerful case that liberation from oppressive structures also requires freedom from the self shaped by colonial domination, that decolonization as political act is inseparable from psychological and cultural decolonization. Fanon also argued, as do Nandy and postcolonial critics, that this cultural and psychological colonialism shaped the colonizer as much as the colonized. This is what has enabled the assimilation of his analyses to postcolonial narratives.

On the other hand, the way in which Fanon understood this process of psychological/cultural decolonization distinguishes him from these later interpretations in two significant ways. No reader of *Black Skin, White Masks* can escape the impression of the tragedy of the colonized subject, who has been deprived not only of cultural affinities to the society of origin or the society of the colonizer that she or he mimics, but totally of his or her humanity. Fanon, of course, is speaking not just of colonial oppression but of a racially motivated colonialism that has reduced the black person to a biological minimum. The tragedy of the violence that he proceeds to affirm in *The Wretched of the Earth* follows from this prior tragedy, where the restoration of selfhood may be achieved only by turning that violence against the colonizer. Fanon's works are written in the trope of tragedy.

By contrast, when Nandy refers to "colonialism as a shared culture,"[14] the relationship that he has in mind is a significantly more negotiable one. Much as Homi Bhabha speaks of a "colonial subject" that includes both the colonizer and the colonized, Nandy speaks of "continuity between the oppressor and the oppressed";[15] his, too, is the language of "hybridity" and "interface" against the "dichotomies" of which Fanon speaks. Where the Europeanization of the black intellectual appears in Fanon's work in terms of a zero-sum relationship (the more white, the less black), Nandy's babu is "grudgingly recognized as an interface who processes the West on behalf of his society and reduces it to a digestible bolus. Both his comical and dangerous selves protect his society against the White Sahib."[16] For Nandy, it is in the end the oppressed who have the better deal, as they are able to contain the colonial encounter more successfully than the colonized:

> This is the underside of non-modern India's ethnic universalism. It is a universalism which takes into account the colonial experience, including the immense suffering colonialism brought, and builds out of it a maturer, more contemporary, more self-critical version of Indian traditions. It is a universalism which sees the Westernized India as a subtradition which, in spite of its pathology and its tragi-comic core, is a 'digested' form of another civilization that had once gate-crashed into India. India *has* tried to capture the differentia of the West within its own cultural domain, not merely on the basis of a view of the West as politically intrusive or as culturally inferior, but as a subculture meaningful in itself and important, though not all-important, in the Indian context. This is what I meant when I said that Kipling, when he wanted to be Western, could not be both Western and Indian, whereas the everyday Indian, even when he remains only Indian, is both Indian and Western.[17]

Fanon's attentiveness to questions of political economy is a second distinguishing feature of his approach to the question of colonial domination, which may be deeply psychological but is imbedded in the structures of political economy. Nandy shares with postcolonial criticism a tendency to culturalism, to a displacement of colonialism to the realm of culture. As we shall see below, his emphasis on forms of knowledge in the colonization of the world leads him to rather radical questions about the nature and consequences of modernity, but there are also certain fundamental questions that are raised by the relative absence of attention to questions of political economy in his work. Postcolonialism's avoidance of political economy is rationalized by the repudiation of metanarratives and foundations, which Nandy does not share. It is all the more remarkable, then, that Nandy, no less than postcolonial critics, should give relatively little notice to the importance Fanon assigns to questions of "land and bread."[18] Two out of the six chapters in *The Wretched of the Earth* are devoted to questions of political economy and class in anticolonial struggles for liberation, which in the end shape Fanon's attitude toward revolution not just as a revolution against colonialism but also as an internal class struggle. Nandy in his turn does speak of a relationship between internal and external colonialism, and he shares with Fanon an emphasis on "folkways" (the culture of the masses) as the reservoir of cultural resources that have not been invaded by colonial culture and that are indispensable as such to any struggle for liberation from colonialism. But here too the emphasis is largely on colonialism and liberation as cultural and psychological problems. As Nandy puts it, "the political economy of colonization is of course important, but the crudity and inanity of colonialism are principally expressed in the sphere of psychology and, to the extent the variables used to describe states of mind under colonialism have themselves become politicized since the entry of modern colonialism on the world scene, in the sphere of political psychology."[19] And when he writes of the village in India, presumably the ultimate location for native cultural resources, he is concerned less with the concrete than with the imagined village.[20] In this version of colonialism, the "modern West" itself appears not just as a geographical or a temporal but as a "psychological category."[21] Nandy writes that "colonialism minus a civilizational mission is no colonialism at all."[22] The statement is indicative of his approach to colonialism as well as the distance that separates contemporary critiques of colonialism from those that prevailed just a generation earlier.

Nowhere is Nandy's distance from Fanon more apparent than over the question of history. His reference in the passage above to Fanon's "insensitivity" to resistance to colonialism of native cultures is an interesting understatement that says as much about Nandy as it does about Fanon. As I shall take up Nandy's own ideas of history and culture below, there is little need to elaborate on this question here, except to point out that Fanon and Nandy share some similarities in their repudiation of civilizational or national pasts rewritten to compensate for the lack of "manliness" or civilization indicated by the colonial conquest, which merely deepens colonial hegemony. But beyond this they part ways in very revealing ways. Fanon's is a radical rejection of the past that places the burden for the creation of history and culture on the revolutionary struggle itself.[23] The history thus to be created is a history that is universal: "I am a man, and what I have to recapture is the whole past of the world. . . . Every time a man has contributed to the victory of the dignity of the spirit, every time a man has said no to an attempt to subjugate his fellows, I have felt solidarity with his act. In no way should I derive my basic purpose from the past of peoples of color. In no way should I dedicate myself to the revival of an unjustly unrecognized Negro civilization. I will not make myself the man of any past. I do not want to exalt the past at the expense of my present and my future."[24]

Against this universalist humanism that negates the past in order to ground the future in a revolutionary vision, which may be most striking in a contemporary perspective for its Eurocentric premises, Nandy proposes alternative universalisms embodied in different cultural traditions. His affirmation of different civilizational pasts distinguishes his vision from a revolutionary vision such as Fanon's and also abolishes what affinity he may have to contemporary postcolonialist arguments. Where in the postcolonial argument different pasts return only to lose their authenticities in new, hybrid, rephrasings, Nandy's argument utilizes hybridities produced by the colonial encounter as means to the rediscovery and recovery of authentic pasts. This, in turn, points to a different, contradictory, affinity with contemporary reassertions of alternative civilizational ideals.

NANDY'S WORK IN THE PERSPECTIVE
OF CONTEMPORARY ETHNOCENTRIC REVIVALS

Ours is not only an age of postcolonialist erasure of differences in the name of difference, it is also an age of the reassertion of differences with a vengeance. From Islamic and Hindu reassertions of cultural pasts to the Confucian revival of East Asia to Samuel Huntington's new geopolitics based on civilizations, there is a widespread reassertion of cultural or civilizational authenticities even as authenticity is called into question in Euro-American postmodern or postcolonial circles. Authenticity may be lodged in nations, ethnicities, or civilizations, or it may be lodged in entities as diverse as diasporas and indigenous localisms, but these locations all contribute to the same end: the fragmentation of the world even as slogans of globalization increasingly decorate the roosts of academia, which, ironically, celebrate such fragmentation as a sign of globalization. The fragmentation of politics and culture most importantly calls into question the knowability of the world as knowledge itself is ethnicized, or even biologized.

This may be the "condition of postmodernity" that is most relevant from a global perspective. Or we may describe it as "modernity with a vengeance." Huntington is correct to point out in his celebrated (and notorious) essays that rather than erase "traditions," modernization has strengthened them by empowering the very identities that it endangered.[25] The rapid economic development of East Asian societies during the last two decades has empowered the "Confucian revival" in those societies.[26] Islamic fundamentalists as much as American evangelicals rationalize what they offer in the languages of modernity. Nandy himself writes of his own source of inspiration that "Gandhi, despite being a counter-modernist, re-emerged for the moderns as a major critic of modernity whose defence of traditions carried the intimations of a post-modern consciousness."[27] His own reading of Indian civilization contributes to a contemporary postmodernity by strongly asserting an Indian presence in the contemporary world, but he parts ways quickly with contemporary ethnocentrism by bringing to the idea of Indianness his own postmodern consciousness.

Nandy's challenges to the old universalisms is informed by a conviction that colonialism and modernization, far from erasing India's pasts, have enabled the construction of "a maturer, more contemporary, more self-critical version of Indian traditions."[28] As I have noted several times above, Nandy is quite sensitive to the fact that an anticolonialist rewriting of native pasts may well replicate the premises of colonialism and Orientalism, as he believes was the case with efforts in India to discover masculinity or national consciousness in the past, which rendered "the golden age of Hinduism . . . [into] an ancient version of the modern West."[29] Against such efforts he counterposes what he calls "critical traditionalism," which requires an effort to "take a critical look at Indian traditions, evaluate the nature of the Western impact on them, and update Indian culture without disturbing its authenticity."[30] The statement is one that is likely to grate on postcolonial ears in its affirmation of authenticity. And there is an apparent contradiction between a tradition that is subject to constant revision ("invention"?) and yet manages somehow to retain its authenticity. Nandy's resolution of the problem, I think, distinguishes him from ethnocentrists in India and elsewhere, overcomes the nationalist chauvinism that characterizes much of contemporary nativist revivalism, and opens up critically creative ways of thinking modernity in relation to the past. It is also possible that the same resolution in the end defeats his efforts to salvage the Indian past.

First, the "traditions" that Nandy defends are the traditions of a civilization, which he distinguishes from, and sets against, the nation-state. Nandy is resolutely antinationalist. Like Partha Chatterjee, he sees in the nationalist appropriation of the past a replication of Orientalism, and he perhaps goes beyond Chatterjee in viewing the nation-state's efforts to homogenize national culture as a form of "internal colonialism."[31] As he writes in the preface to his study of Tagore and nationalism, "I hope that young Indians confronting and perhaps resisting the violent emergence of a steam-rolling modern nation-state in their country will discover in this essay a useful construction of the past."[32] A historical survey of Nandy's publications suggests that the concern with nationalism has come to overshadow in recent years the concern with colonialism. Rather than an obstacle to national unity, Nandy's recent writings suggest, communal conflict in India may be a product of "the concept of a 'mainstream national culture' that is fearful of diversities, intolerant of dissent unless it is cast in the language of the mainstream, and panicky about any self-assertion or search for autonomy by ethnic groups."[33] As he (and his collaborators) write in a study of the Ramjanmabhumi Movement,

> South Asia has always been a salad bowl of cultures. For long it has avoided—to the exasperation of modern nationalists and statists of the right and the left—the American-style melting pot model and its individualistic assumptions and anti-communitarian bias. In a salad, the ingredients retain their distinctiveness, but each ingredient transcends its individuality through the presence of others. In a melting pot, primordial identities are supposed to melt. Those that do not are expected to survive as coagulates and are called nationalities or minorities; they are expected to dissolve in the long run. Much of the recent violence in South Asia can be traced to the systematic efforts being made to impose the melting pot model upon time-worn Indian realities.[34]

Second, it should be apparent from these critiques of nationalism that, ironic as it may seem, for Nandy the core values of Indian civilization rest on the repudiation of an authentic Indianness. He writes of a nineteenth-century predecessor, Iswarchandra Vidyasagar:

> He refused to use the imagery of a golden age of the Hindus from which contemporary Hindus had allegedly fallen, he refused to be psychologically tied to the history of non-Hindu rule of India, he resisted reading Hinduism as a 'proper religion' in the Islamic or Western sense, he rejected the ideologies of masculinity and adulthood, and he refused to settle scores with the West by creating a nation of super-Hindus or by defending Hinduism as an all-perfect antidote to Western cultural encroachment. His was an effort to protect not the formal structure of Hinduism but its spirit, as an open, anarchic federation of sub-cultures and textual authorities which allowed new readings and internal criticisms.[35]

This reading of the Indian past pervades Nandy's texts. Nandy's affirmation of an authentic Indian culture resists ethnocentric containment as it is presented throughout in an ironic mode: "Only in recent times have the Hindus begun to describe themselves as Hindus. Thus, the very expression has a built-in contradiction: to use the term Hindu to self-define is to flout the traditional self-definition of the Hindu, and to assert aggressively one's Hinduism is to very nearly deny one's Hinduness."[36] He writes in the closing pages of *The Intimate Enemy*, in terms that almost repudiate his affirmations of an authentic Indian civilization earlier in the book, that

The differentia of Indian culture has often been sought by social analysts, including this writer, in the uniqueness of certain cultural themes or in their configuration. This is not a false trail, but it does lead to some half-truths. One of them is the clear line drawn, on behalf of the Indian, between the past and the present, the native and the exogenous, and the Hindu and the non-Hindu. But, as I have suggested, the West that is aggressive is sometimes inside; the earnest, self-declared native, too, is often an exogenous category, and the Hindi who announces himself so, is not Hindu after all. Probably the uniqueness of Indian culture lies not so much in a unique ideology as in the society's traditional ability to live with cultural ambiguities and to use them to build psychological and even metaphysical defences against cultural invasions. Probably, the culture itself demands that a certain permeability of boundaries be maintained in one's self-image and that the self be not defined too tightly or separated mechanically from the not-self.[37]

An unsympathetic reader could easily dismiss this self-maintained ironic stance as sheer befuddlement. To this reader, Nandy overcomes this befuddlement by carrying his critique to another critical level: to the dehistoricization of Indian civilization, not in the manner of Orientalist dehistoricization, but by taking it outside of history. His inspiration here is Gandhi, whose "specific orientation to myth became a more general orientation to public consciousness. Public consciousness was not seen as a causal product of history but as related to history non-causally through memories and anti-memories. If for the West the present was a special case of an unfolding history, for Gandhi as a representative of traditional India history was a special case of an all-embracing permanent present, waiting to be interpreted and reinterpreted."[38] Nandy attributes to Gandhi an

anti-historical assumption that, because they faithfully contain history, because they are contemporary and, unlike history, are amenable to intervention, myths are the essence of a culture, history being at best superfluous and at worst misleading. Gandhi implicitly assumed that history . . . was one-way traffic, a set of myths about past time . . . built up as independent variables which limit human options and pre-empt human futures. . . . Myths, on the other hand, consciously acknowledged as the core of a culture . . . widen instead of restricting human choice.

Nandy's own conclusion is that "the affirmation of ahistoricity is an affirmation of the dignity and autonomy of non-modern peoples."[39] He writes elsewhere:

The rejection of history to protect self-esteem and ensure survival is often a response to the structure of cognition history presumes. The more scientific a history, the more oppressive it tends to be in the experimental laboratory called the third world. It is scientific history which has allowed the idea of social intervention to be cannibalized by the ideal of social engineering at the peripheries of the world. For the moderns, history has always been the unfolding of a theory of progress, a serialized expression of a telos which, by definition, cannot be shared by communities on the lower rungs of the ladder of history. Even the histories of oppression and the historical theories of liberation postulate stages of growth which, instead of widening the victims' options, reduce them. . . . The ethnocentrism of the anthropologist can be corrected; he is seg-regated from his subject only socially and, some day, his subjects can talk back. The ethnocentrism towards the past mostly goes unchallenged. The dead do not rebel, nor can they speak out. So the subjecthood of the subjects of history is absolute, and the demand for a real or scientific history is the demand for a continuity between sub-jecthood in history and subjection in the present. The corollary to the refusal to accept the primacy of history is the refusal to chain the future to the past. This refusal is a special attitude to human potentialities, an alternative form of utopianism that has survived till now as a language alien to, and subversive of, every theory which in the name of liberation circumscribes and makes predictable the spirit of human rebel-liousness.[40]

Contemporary ethnocentrisms for the most part insist on drawing bound-aries between nations, ethnicities, and civilizations that are so firm that it becomes meaningless to speak of communication across boundaries. National and civilizational characteristics are likewise projected deep into the past so as to render history into an alibi for the divisions of the present. Interestingly, in the case of Nandy, the insistence on civilizational authenticity serves as the means to a new universalism that ends up breaking down the very boundaries with which he starts his argument. Indeed, in his refusal to allow the past to serve as a hindrance to the imagination of the future, he is not very far from Fanon's present-mindedness, which refuses to locate in the past the burden for creating the future. Ironically, for all his refusal to rely on the past, Fanon's writ-ings express a much keener awareness of the burden of the past on the present, of the structures of colonial and precolonial pasts that need to be eliminated so that the future can be created out of the very struggles for liberation. As the statement quoted above indicates, Fanon seems to have envisioned the future thus to be created as a cosmopolitan universalism, where everybody's past would in the end be everybody else's past.

As Dipesh Chakrabarty points out, Nandy has a voluntarist (or "decision-ist," as Chakrabarty puts it) attitude toward the past that, as a product of con-stant invention, allows multiple visions of the future.[41] Nandy, unlike Fanon, is postcolonial—and postmodern—in his readings of the past, no less than in his visions for the future. On the other hand, placing him against contempo-rary ethnocentrisms indicates that he does not easily fall in with those cate-gories either. Against postcolonial and postmodern tendencies to dissolve cul-tural identities into hybridities, or whatever, he insists on authentic and even "primordial" identities, even if those identities are located only in the myths people live by. The insistence is intended to bring into the present the voices of those who have been suppressed in history—national no less than civilizational history. What he and his colleagues wrote of South Asia as a salad bowl may be paradigmatic of the way he envisages the contemporary world: that it consists (or should consist) of ingredients that retain their individuality but that also transcend that individuality through the presence of others. Hence Fanon's cosmopolitan universalism appears in his vision of the future as a dialogue between alternative universalities:

> [T]he search for authenticity of a civilization is always a search for the other face of the civilization, either as a hope or as a warning. The search for a civilization's utopia, too, is part of this larger quest. It needs not merely the ability to interpret and reinterpret one's own traditions, but also the ability to involve the often-recessive aspects of other civilizations as allies in one's struggle for cultural rediscovery, the willingness to become allies to other civilizations trying to discover their other faces, and the skills to give more centrality to these new readings of civilizations and civilizational concerns. This is the only form of a dialogue of cultures which can transcend the flourishing intercultural barters of our times.[42]

MODERNITY, ANTIMODERNITY, NONMODERNITY: HISTORY, SCIENCE, AND DEVELOPMENT

It is difficult (and probably irrelevant) to say whether antimodernism is a source of, or a solution to, the problems thrown up by Nandy's critiques of colonialism, nationalism, and the failure of radical visions of the past. But it is everywhere in his writing. There is nothing new about antimodernism, which may be part and parcel of modernism. On the other hand, the manner in which it is phrased is historical in partaking of the problems of the age. To use the distinction Chatterjee has offered in his study of nationalism, if antimodernism shares the thematic of modernism, its problematic is nevertheless derivative of concrete situations.[43] The globalization of capital since World War II, becoming evident in the 1980s, has resulted in a reconfiguration of the ways in which we think the world, blurring earlier boundaries, including boundaries between the colonizer and the colonized. It has brought forth more sharply than ever the problem of cultural homogenization, especially through the globalization of material habits as embodied in practices of consumption; it makes little sense to speak of cultural imperialism when the culturally colonized willingly embrace their colonization, which casts the whole history of colonialism in a new light. The postcolonial and postsocialist nation-state, in its depredations against its own constituents, appears less as a bulwark against colonialism than as a colonizing agent in its own right. Socialism, in its failures, appears to be not so much an alternative to capitalism as an alternative form of capitalist modernization doomed by its own internal contradictions. Globalization itself internationalizes class exploitation even as it produces a new fragmentation of the globe. In the meantime, the utopian promise of welfare and equality for all recedes ever further into the future, a future that seems less and less attainable as unbridled developmentalism erodes the very material bases of subsistence and survival. In the meantime, our aptly renamed knowledge industries seem to be intent on covering up the global crisis rather than contemplating serious alternatives to the way we plunder the earth and its inhabitants, including its human inhabitants. It is difficult not to be antimodernist in times like these.

And yet it also takes a great deal of courage to be seriously antimodern—not the New Age or the postmodernist variety that nourishes off the very modernity it deplores, but the kind of antimodernism that insists on the indispensable relevance of the nonmodern if we are to be able to think our way out of the problems presented by modernity. One need not agree with everything about such an antimodernism in order to recognize the courage involved in daring to give soft answers to hard questions, that elevates weakness over strength, promotes diversity at the cost of economic nondevelopment, and proclaims that the promise of democracy may lie not with those who spread it around the globe with the force of arms but with those who have never heard the word.

It is not my intention here to render Ashis Nandy into an icon of antimodernism (or nonmodernism, as he might prefer). Other names that I have called upon to similar effect in my own work include his colleague Vandana Shiva, the Amerindian scholar and historian Vine Deloria Jr., and Subcomandante Marcos. Others could be invoked with ease. Many participate these days in the return of the nonmodern.

It is important nevertheless to recognize Nandy as an eloquent voice in the contemporary critique of modernity, a voice that retains a hope in universalism even as it protests against manufactured uniformity. It is a voice that is deeply radical in its willingness to confront what are almost unconsciously accepted faiths of our times. Two of these faiths, those in history and science, are worth noting here.

I have already raised the question of history in Nandy's thinking; suffice it to say here that these days, when Eurocentrism in the writing and conceptualization of history is a major concern within and without Euro-America, Nandy's critique takes us far beyond the limited questions of who is to be included, and how, to confront history and historical thinking as a problem. The argument is deceptively simple, as perhaps a radical critique should be: History, as one mode of thinking about the past, present, and future, has been established in the modern world as the *only* way to think them, consigning all other ways of thinking, along with those who thought in those ways, to the realm of the nonhistorical. The dominance of history "is derived from the links the idea of history has established with the modern nation-state, the secular worldview, the Baconian concept of scientific rationality, nineteenth-century theories of progress, and, in recent decades, development. . . . [O]nce exported to the nonmodern world, historical consciousness has not only tended to absolutize the past in cultures that have lived with open-ended concepts of the past or depended on myths, legends, and epics to define their cultural selves, it has also made the historical worldview complicit with many new forms of violence, exploitation and satanism in our times and helped rigidify civilizational, cultural, and national boundaries."[44] Most available criticisms of history are themselves historical. As in the case of colonial nationalism that assimilates Orientalism in its own self-definition, to be historical in the non-Euro-American world is to rewrite the past under the hegemony of an epistemology that has Eurocentrism built into its very structure.[45] On the other hand, from this same perspective, contemporary efforts in Euro-America to globalize history by writing everyone into it, even in all their differences, appear as little more than an effort to contain genuine difference by rendering all societies historical. Nandy concedes that "at one time not long ago, historical consciousness had to coexist with other modes of experiencing and constructing the past even within the modern world. The conquest of the past through history was still incomplete in the late nineteenth century, as was the conquest of space through the railways. . . . As long as the non-historical modes thrived, history remained viable as a baseline for radical social criticism. That is perhaps why the great dissenters of the nineteenth century were the most aggressively historical."[46] But such is no longer the case, as the historical way has become the only way of knowing the past, when a critical epistemology has turned into a means of dominance. The point presently is not to find alternative histories but *alternatives to history.*[47]

Similarly, where science is concerned, the question Nandy raises is not whether or not science is constructed, and therefore limited in its claims, but rather the more fundamental question that science has become the source of a new authoritarianism. The objectification of the world, which legitimizes claims to scientific truth, is made possible by "the splitting of cognition and affect," which is characteristic of the pathology of "isolation."[48] This pathological condition, associated by some with the psychology of Fascism, is a condition of the modern world as it has been shaped by the domination of the scientific worldview: "[B]y the early fifties it was clear to many that fascism was a typical psychopathology of the modern world, for it merely took to logical conclusions what was central to modernity, namely the ability to partition away human cognition and pursue this cognition unbridled by emotional or moral constraints."[49] The question, however, is not merely that of a pathology in the premises of science but the invasion of the life-world by the scientific worldview, which will allow no competitors in the comprehension of the world:

> Today, in the last decade of the century . . . older, tired and wiser, we can now take courage to affirm that the main civilisational problem is not with irrational, self-contradicting superstitions but with the ways of thinking associated with the modern concept of rationality. . . . According to this world view, the irrationality of rationality in organized normal science is no longer a mere slogan. It is threatening to take over all of human life, including every interstice of culture and every form of individuality. We now have scientific training in modern sports and recreations; our everyday social relations and social activism are more and more guided by pseudosciences like management and social work. Our future is being conceptualized and shaped by the modern witchcraft called the science of economics. In fact, the scientific study of poverty has become more important than poverty itself. If we do not love such a future, scientific child-rearing and scientific psychotherapy are ever ready to certify us as dangerous lunatics. Another set of modern witch-doctors has taken over the responsibility of making even the revolutionaries among us scientific. Even in bed, our sexual performance is now judged according to the objective criteria of some highly scientific, how-to-do-it manuals on sex.[50]

The next step of manufacturing human beings may invalidate many of these objections based on good, old-fashioned humanism, but that is not the point here. Neither is the point the juxtaposition of a scientific to a humanistic worldview. The point is that, similarly to history, science as it has taken over the world has become a negation of its own critical premises:

> [M]odern science was once a movement of dissent. It then pluralized the world of ideas. . . . I am now suggesting that modern science, which began as a creative adjunct to the post-medieval world and as an alternative to modern authoritarianism, has itself acquired many of the psychological features of the latter. In fact, in its ability to legitimize a vivisectional posture toward all living beings and non-living nature, modern science is now moving toward acquiring the absolute narcissism of a new passionless Caligula.[51]

It may be noteworthy that there is an ethical motivation underlying Nandy's criticism of science; to recall the line with which he concludes *The Intimate Enemy*, "knowledge without ethics is not so much bad ethics as inferior knowledge."[52]

The third corner in the triangulation of modernity is development, which is empowered by the faith in science and technology and legitimized by a history informed by its teleology. Science and technology have been crucial to the legit-imation of colonialism as a modernizing force: "When towards the middle of the nineteenth century a proper theory of imperialism began to take shape, the theory used modern technology and its culture as major justifications for colo-nialism and its civilizing mission: Western technology was superior because Western man and Western technological culture were better equipped for tech-nological achievements than their savage counterparts."[53] History, written in terms of various versions of stages of development, was to serve as an alibi to this claim, so that, if I may paraphrase, only those pasts were celebrated that were seen as conducive to modernization and development; and those pasts were rued that were seen as resistant to modernity and development.[54] Devel-opmentalism, or the ideology of development, may be the most enduring lega-cy of colonialism that has outlasted formal colonialism:

> The problem with the idea of development is not its failure. The idea has succeeded beyond the dreams of its early partisans who never imagined that they had hit upon something whose day had come. Developmentalism has succeeded where western colonialism and evangelical Christianity failed. It has established itself as one of the few genuine universals of our time. It has become an intimate part of every surviving civilization and changed the self-definitions of some of the least accessible societies. Development has converted even the seemingly non-proselytizable.[55]

I may add here, in a slight revision of Nandy's sense, that the triumph of developmentalism is testimonial to the ultimate victory of colonialism. Glob-alization in our day has taken over the civilizing mission from modernization, to finish the task that formal colonialism was unable to achieve. The ethno-centrisms that assert themselves against Euro-American hegemony, or even against globalization, are nevertheless colonized to the extent that they legit-imize themselves in terms of development; the appending of the adjective "alternative" to "development" in these cases does not really change the fact that development has become, as Gilbert Rist puts it, a "global faith."[56] Hence the importance to the critique of developmentalism of the nonmodern, the non-scientific, and the nonhistorical—in other words, the indigenous. Indigenous societies around the world that showed no signs of political and economic development toward modernity were shoved out of time, as "peoples without history," to become fair game for physical and cultural extinction. Now, in our awareness of the complicity of history in developmentalism, those societies without history, much more so than the "civilizations" that engaged in *their* various forms of colonialism, occupy a crucial critical place in any considera-tion of alternatives to development—if only as paradigms, for few survive phys-ically or culturally.[57]

CONCLUDING THOUGHTS

How to read Nandy? Some of the ideas that I have pulled out of his work have been subjects of controversy within his Indian context. His discussion of *sati* in terms of a native ideal of womanhood that was perverted by the "masculinization" of Indian society in response to colonialism has drawn the fire of Indian feminists and others.[58] Others have been critical of his advocacy of communitarianism (along with some of his colleagues, including Partha Chatterjee). His defense of faith against secularism has come under criticism. Still others have focused on the "relativism" in his (and his colleagues', most prominently Vandana Shiva's) discussions of science and technology that not only obscure the benefits of science but also elevate knowledge systems that were themselves oppressive. Some, like Aijaz Ahmad, find in Nandy's defense of Indian traditions a cover-up of oppressive native traditions by blaming them on colonialism.[59]

As I wrote at the beginning of this discussion, it is not my intention to get involved in any of these debates. I think I appreciate the concerns of critics who view Nandy's writings from within a society that is torn by communitarian strife, where religious conflict is part of everyday politics, where the practice of sati continues and is condoned. The question for me is whether views such as Nandy's and his associates' should be withheld from public debate for fear of consequences, or whether it is those very circumstances that demand the airing of such views. There is certainly a great deal of irony in the charge of antifeminism against a thinker who bemoans the masculinization of Indian society, or in the suggestion that a rewriting of Indian history to stress the need for pluralism should appear as the condoning of communal violence.

I have stressed above the complexities of Nandy's thinking. These complexities may appear to the unsympathetic as contradictions: Does he really repudiate history when he concedes that history may serve critical perspectives or even calls for "the historicization of history"? Does he really believe that science is merely a tool of authoritarianism, when he concedes that it once served as a source of criticism, and he himself freely draws on the findings of modern psychology to make his case? Is he a relativist when it comes to knowledge, when he states that "cultural relativism . . . is acceptable only to the extent it accepts the universalism of some core values of humankind?"[60] Does he really propose that all the evils in Indian society came with colonialism, when he concedes that this society also had a "dark side"? Is he naive enough to think that the dark side of this civilization had nothing to do with its bright side, when he has a rather integrated view of societies? Does he really oppose secularism, when the pluralism and tolerance he advocates are very much informed by a secular worldview? Is he unaware of the importance of political economy, when the critique of developmentalism is one of his major contributions to contemporary thinking? Finally, is he really unaware of the burden of history, when so much of what he has to say is posthistorical?

Having gone through Nandy's works, and thought through them in the writing of this chapter, I answer all of these questions in the negative. The questions remain, and must remain, open, for Nandy as well as for many others on the contemporary intellectual scene (in India or abroad) who seek radical questions to comprehend the fundamental problems of our times, when earlier answers, and the questions that prompted them, no longer seem sufficient. The failure of earlier radical efforts to confront problems of modernity may have been beneficial to the extent that they now drive the search deeper for those problems. The way we think the world is obviously one of those fundamental problems. As I read Nandy, it seems to me that one thread runs through his work, no matter what question is addressed: to recall what has been suppressed or erased by the teleologies of modernity, so that modernity itself may enrich its cultural repertoire and recover once again the critical impulses that lay at its origins. Everything else is "experimenting with truth."

NOTES

1. Ashis Nandy, *The Intimate Enemy: Loss and Recovery of Self under Colonialism* (Delhi: Oxford University Press, 1993), x.

2. The fact that Fanon was a psychoanalyst does not have any bearing on this discussion.

3. Frantz Fanon, *Black Skin, White Masks*, trans. Charles L. Markmann (London: Macgibbon & Kee, 1968). French original published in 1952. Hereafter, *BSWM*.

4. For "cultural psychology," see Ashis Nandy, *At the Edge of Psychology: Essays in Politics and Culture* (Delhi: Oxford University Press, 1993), vii. For "sociodiagnosis," see *BSWM*, 13.

5. For a critical discussion, see Henry Louis Gates Jr., "Critical Fanonism," *Critical Inquiry* 17 (Spring 1991): 457–70.

6. Frantz Fanon, *The Wretched of the Earth*, trans. Constance Farrington (New York: Penguin Books, 1977), first published in French in 1961; and Ashis Nandy, *Traditions, Tyranny, and Utopias: Essays in the Politics of Awareness* (Delhi: Oxford University Press, 1987).

7. A note is in order here that is of both methodological and political significance. Henry Louis Gates cautions against rendering Fanon into a "type" that deprives him of his historicity, his contradictions, and his own problematic relationship to his audiences and readers (Gates, "Critical Fanonism," 459, 468–69). The point is well taken. Inserting Fanon into the narratives of revolution of his time or postcolonial narratives of a later time no doubt violates his historical specificity. On the other hand, Fanon did address broad questions of revolutionary change beyond specific problems of race and intraracial difference, and the appeals of his texts did not stop at the boundaries provided by the color line.

We should be able, on the basis of textual evidence, to distinguish what he said, how it was received at his time, and how it is received presently in different quarters. Much the same may be said, of course, about Nandy, who focuses on specifically Indian questions and yet also speaks to broader problems of the age. One distinction is important, as the discussion below should reveal: Nandy, as a reader of Fanon, in part responds to Fanon and Fanon's analysis of the problem of liberation.

8. Ashis Nandy, "Towards a Third World Utopia," in *Traditions, Tyranny, and Utopias*, 20–55, 33–34.

9. Gates, "Critical Fanonism," 470 n.

10. See Fanon, *Wretched of the Earth*, 31–40, for the Manichean world. See Gates, "Critical Fanonism," 458–60, for postcolonial readings of Fanon. For a critique that affirms Fanon's manicheanism, see Abdul R. Jan Mohamed, "The Economy of Manichean Allegory: The Function of Racial Difference in Colonialist Literature," *Critical Inquiry* 12 (Autumn 1985): 59–87, 59–60.

11. Likewise, in his preface to *Intimate Enemy*, Nandy writes of Fanon: "Let us not forget that the most violent denunciation of the West produced by Fanon is written in the elegant style of a Jean-Paul Sartre. The West has not merely produced modern colonialism, it informs most interpretations of colonialism." In this case, however, he also bridges his distance from Fanon somewhat by adding that "it colours even this interpretation of interpretation" (xii).

12. The only reference to postcolonial intellectuals that I have been able to locate is one to Dipesh Chakrabarty and Gyan Prakash on history, where Nandy refers admiringly to their questionings of history while also observing that they do not go far enough in their critiques. See Ashis Nandy, "History's Forgotten Doubles," *History and Theory* 34, no. 2 (1995): 44–66, 52–53.

13. Nandy, *Intimate Enemy*, xi. For a further discussion of "postrevolutionary" in the periodization of the contemporary, see Arif Dirlik, "Postcolonial or Postrevolutionary? The Problem of History in Postcolonial Criticism," in *The Postcolonial Aura: Third World Criticism in the Age of Global Capitalism* (Boulder, Colo.: Westview Press, 1997).

14. Nandy, *Intimate Enemy*, 2.

15. Nandy, *Intimate Enemy*, 39.

16. Nandy, *Intimate Enemy*, xv.

17. Nandy, *Intimate Enemy*, 75–76.

18. *Wretched of the Earth*, 34, where Fanon writes that "for a colonized people the most essential value, because the most concrete, is first and foremost the land; the land which will bring them bread and, above all, dignity."

19. Nandy, *Intimate Enemy*, 2.

20. See the remarkable essay—remarkable both for its imaginativeness and for its presentation of the village as a problem in imagination—Ashis Nandy, "The Decline in the Imagination of the Village," *Emergences* 7/8 (1995–1996): 146–54. I should note that my discussion here is based entirely on the place of political economy in Nandy's own texts. The Centre for the Study of Developing Societies is very much concerned with issues of political economy, albeit in a direction quite different from Fanon's Marxist-inspired approach. Nandy's approach, if viewed in terms of a division of labor within the center, would appear differently than I read it here. Still, it suggests problems that I will take up below.

21. Nandy, *Intimate Enemy*, xi.

22. Nandy, *Intimate Enemy*, 11.

23. Fanon, *Wretched of the Earth*, chap. 4; Fanon, *BSWM*, chap. 8.

24. Fanon, *BSWM*, 226.

25. Samuel P. Huntington, "The Clash of Civilizations?" *Foreign Affairs* (Summer 1992): 22–49.

26. Arif Dirlik, "Confucius in the Borderlands: Global Capitalism and the Reinvention of Confucianism," *Boundary 2* 22, no. 3 (Fall 1995): 229–73.

27. Ashis Nandy, *The Illegitimacy of Nationalism: Rabindranath Tagore and the Politics of Self* (Delhi: Oxford University Press, 1994), 2.

28. Nandy, *Intimate Enemy*, 75.

29. Nandy, *Intimate Enemy*, 26.

30. Nandy, *Intimate Enemy*, xvii, for "critical traditionalism"; and 27, for the quotation. I am taking the liberty here of interpreting what Nandy means by "critical traditionalism," since he does not offer a definition in his initial reference.

31. "[T]he rhetoric of progress uses the fact of internal colonialism to subvert the cultures of societies subject to external colonialism and . . . internal colonialism in turn uses the fact of external threat to legitimize and perpetuate itself." Nandy, *Intimate Enemy*, xii. See also Partha Chatterjee, *Nationalist Thought and the Colonial World: A Derivative Discourse?* (Atlantic Highlands, N.J.: Zed Books, 1986).

32. Nandy, *Illegitimacy of Nationalism*.

33. Ashis Nandy et al., *Creating a Nationality: The Ramjanmabhumi Movement and Fear of the Self* (Delhi: Oxford University Press, 1995), 9.

34. Nandy et al., *Creating a Nationality*, vi. See also D. L. Sheth and Ashis Nandy, eds., *The Multiverse of Democracy* (New Delhi: Sage Publications, 1996), where the contributors (mostly critics of modernity from abroad) discuss the ways in which the modern nation-state contributes to the curtailment of diversity and democracy.

35. Nandy, *Intimate Enemy*, 28.

36. Nandy, *Intimate Enemy*, 103.

37. Nandy, *Intimate Enemy*, 107.

38. Nandy, *Intimate Enemy*, 57.

39. Nandy, *Intimate Enemy*, 59.

40. Nandy, "Third World Utopia," 48–49.

41. Dipesh Chakrabarty, "The Modern Indian Intellectual and the Problem of the Past: An Engagement with the Thoughts of Ashis Nandy," *Emergences*.

42. Nandy, "Third World Utopia," 55.

43. Chatterjee, *Nationalist Thought*, chap. 1.

44. Nandy, "History's Forgotten Doubles," 44.

45. This, of course, may be even more of a problem in Marxist than in liberal historiography. For a discussion, see Arif Dirlik, "Marxism and Chinese History: The Globalization of Marxist Historical Discourse and the Problem of Hegemony in Marxism," *Journal of Third World Studies* 4, no. 1 (Spring 1987): 151–64. As this journal is not easily accessible, the essay was also published as "Marxisme et histoire Chinoise: La globalisation du discours historique et la question de l'hégémonie dans la référence marxiste à l'histoire," *Extreme-Orient Extreme-Occident* 9 (August 1987): 91–112.

46. Nandy, "History's Forgotten Doubles," 46.

47. Nandy, "History's Forgotten Doubles," 53. For further discussion of some of these problems, see Vinay Lal, "History and the Possibilities of Emancipation: Some Lessons from India," *Journal of the Indian Council of Philosophical Research* (June 1996): 97–137; and Arif Dirlik, "History without a Center? Reflections on Eurocentrism," in *Historiographical Traditions and Cultural Identities in the Nineteenth and Twentieth Centuries,* ed. E. Fuchs and B. Stuchtey (Washington, D.C.: German Historical Institute, forthcoming).

48. Ashis Nandy, "Modern Science and Authoritarianism: From Objectivity to Objectification," *Bulletin of the Science and Technology Society* 7, no. 1 (1997): 8–12. This essay is an abbreviated version of an earlier discussion included in *Traditions, Tyranny, and Utopias,* 95–126.

49. Nandy, "Modern Science," 9.

50. Nandy, "Modern Science," 10.

51. Nandy, "Modern Science," 11.

52. Nandy, *Intimate Enemy,* 113.

53. Ashis Nandy, "The Traditions of Technology," in *Traditions, Tyranny, and Utopias,* 77–94, 87. The "civilizing mission" of science and technology has been receiving increased attention in recent years. For two prominent examples, see Michael Adas, *Machines as the Measure of Man: Science, Technology, and the Ideologies of Western Dominance* (Ithaca, N.Y.: Cornell University Press, 1990); and Lewis Pyenson, *Civilizing Mission: The Exact Sciences and French Overseas Expansion* (Baltimore: Johns Hopkins University Press, 1993). What distinguishes the work of Nandy and his colleagues at the Centre for the Study of Developing Societies is the critique of modernity that they base on the critique of science and technology, and their search for alternatives.

54. Ashis Nandy, "Development and Violence," working paper, Zentrum fur Europäische Studien, University of Trier, 1995, 2.

55. Nandy, "Development and Violence," 1.

56. Gilbert Rist, *The History of Development: From Western Origins to Global Faith,* trans. Patrick Camiller (London: Zed Books, 1997). It is interesting that with the recent crisis of globalization, the language of colonialism has once again returned to political discourse. Nandy has suggested, drawing on the work of Philip Ariès, that developmentalist history was based on an analogy with a new conception of childhood that emerged in the seventeenth century: the child as an inferior, rather than a smaller, version of the adult (*Intimate Enemy,* 14). It is interesting that as those like Mahathir Mohamed now speak of a new colonialism, his Euro-American counterparts attribute the crisis in Southeast Asia to the "immaturity" of these societies in their lack of experience with capitalism.

57. See chap. 8 for further elaboration.

58. Ashis Nandy, "Sati: A Nineteenth-Century Tale of Women, Violence, and Protest," in *At the Edge of Psychology: Essays in Politics and Culture* (Delhi: Oxford University Press, 1993) 1–31. First published in 1980.

59. For some of these criticisms, see Sumanta Banerjee, "Reviewing a Debate," review of *Secularism and Its Critics,* ed. Rajeev Bhargava, *Economic and Political Weekly,* 11 July 1998, 1826–28; Meera Nanda, "Reclaiming Modern Science for Third World Progressive Social Movements," *Economic and Political Weekly,* 18 April 1998, 915–23; Sarah Joseph, "Politics of Contemporary Indian Communitarianism," *Economic and Political Weekly,* 4

October 1997, 2517–23; and Nivedita Menon, "State/Gender/Community: Citizenship in Contemporary India," *Economic and Political Weekly*, 31 January 1998, 3–10. I am grateful to Vinay Bahl for bringing these critiques to my attention.

60. Nandy, "Towards a Third World Utopia," 54–55.

6

FORMATIONS OF GLOBALITY

AND RADICAL POLITICS

The discussion in this chapter undertakes two tasks. The first is to outline a number of influential representations of globality, mark their distinctions, and point to the ways in which they complement and contradict one another. Second, on the basis of what these representations have to say about the condition of globality, I draw certain conclusions concerning the possibilities for radical politics under contemporary circumstances.

Discussions of geopolitics usually do not concern themselves with radicalism—except perhaps with how to extinguish it. On the other hand, radicals from Marx to Marcos have had to confront geopolitical questions, not only because a grasp of geopolitics is crucial to formulating strategies of revolution, but more fundamentally because radicalism, if it is understood to be something other than an arbitrary commitment to radical politics for its own sake, needs to grapple with the social and political circumstances of which it is itself a product in order to account for the necessity, form, and direction of radical change. The discussion here is not geopolitical in the strict sense of the term, as it has little to say on questions of power and strategy. Rather, it is most concerned with the reconfiguration in recent years of global relations, why these changes have rendered irrelevant earlier forms of radicalism, associated mostly with socialism, and why the largely invisible radical activities of the present take the forms that they have taken.

My point of departure is globalization, which over the last decade has replaced modernization as a paradigm of change—and a social imaginary. The discourse of globalization claims to break with the earlier modernization discourse in important ways, most notably in abandoning a Eurocentric teleology of change, which in many ways has been compelled by real economic, political, and cultural challenges to Eurocentrism. It is rendered plausible by the appearance of new centers of economic and political power, assertions of cultural diversity in the midst of apparent cultural commonality, intensifying motions of people that scramble boundaries, and the emergence of new global institutional forms to deal with problems that transcend nations and regions. All of this suggests that institutional arrangements informed by a Eurocentric modernization process are no longer sufficient to grasp and to deal with the world's problems. Globalization has an obvious appeal to a political left that has been committed all along to internationalism, equality, and closer ties between peoples. That the most visible reactions to globalization emanate from the political right reinforces the image of globalization as a move toward left or, at the very least, liberal left, aspirations.

The euphoria over globalization, however, has served to disguise the very real social and economic inequalities that are not merely leftovers from the past but are also products of the new developments. There is some question as to whether globalization represents the end or the fulfillment of a Eurocentric modernization. Globalization as a discourse would seem to be increasingly pervasive, but it is propagated most enthusiastically from the older centers of power, most notably the United States, fueling suspicion of the hegemonic aspirations that inform it. Economic and political power may be more decentered than earlier, but globalization is incomprehensible without reference to the global victory of capitalism, and pressures toward the globalization of "markets and democracy" are at the core of globalization, as they once were of modernization. Cultural conflicts are played out even more evidently than before on an ideological and institutional terrain that is a product of Eurocentric modernization. Finally, unlike in an earlier period of socialism and Third World alternatives, challenges to Eurocentrism come mostly from those who have been empowered by their very success in making capitalist modernity their own, whose challenges are voiced in the language of that modernity, and whose vision of alternatives is inescapably refracted through the lens of their incorporation into a capitalist world economy. Globalization, for all the new kinds of conflicts to which it has given rise, may well represent the universalization of developmentalism in its capitalist guise (as its socialist counterpart is no longer an issue).

It is not clear, in other words, whether globalization is the final chapter in the history of capitalist modernity as globalized by European power or the beginning of something else that is yet to appear with any kind of concreteness. What is clear, however, is that globalization discourse is a response both to changing configurations in global relations—new unities as well as new fractures—and to the need for a new epistemology to grasp those changes. But globalization is also ideological, as it seeks to reshape the world in accordance with a new global imaginary that serves some interests better than others. A triumphalist account of globalization, as appealing to cosmopolitan liberals or leftists as it is to transnational capital, celebrates the imminent unification of the world, overlooking the fact that the problems that persist are not just leftovers from the past but products of the very process of globalization with the developmentalist assumptions built into its ideology. That other than Euro-

Americans now participate in the process does not make it any the less ideological or devastating in its consequences but merely points to changes in the global configuration of classes. In this sense, the preoccupation in globalization discourse with the problem of Eurocentrism is a distraction from confronting new forms of power.[1] The emancipatory promise of globalization is just that: a promise that is perpetually deferred to the future, while globalization itself creates new forms of economic and political exploitation and marginalization. Some problems thrown up by globalization, most importantly environmental ones, are conceded by its very engineers. Others are represented merely as legacies of the past that will be eliminated as globalization fulfills its promise. Ideologues of globalization may promise plenty for all, but as a number of studies have revealed, the actual forecast of what globalization promises is much more pessimistic: the marginalization of the majority of the world's population, including many in the core societies. Economic marginalization also implies political marginalization, as, in the midst of spreading democracy, the most important decisions concerning human life are progressively removed from the reach of electorates. The world may be reconfigured, but the reconfiguration takes place under the regime of capitalism that continues to reproduce under new circumstances, and in new forms, the inequalities built into its structuring of the world.[2]

This is what makes a radical critique as relevant today as it has ever been, and perhaps more so. Such a critique, if it is to be meaningful, must be informed by a recognition of changed circumstances rather than a nostalgic attachment to its historical legacy. It is important, therefore, to begin with a few words about what may or may not be new about globalization as a contemporary phenomenon.

GLOBALIZATION: OLD AND NEW

There is a paradox in arguments for globalization. Its proponents represent it at once as a novel phenomenon of the contemporary world *and* as a process that has characterized the human condition since its origins. The latter on occasion takes trivial forms that are not easily distinguishable from earlier diffusionist arguments. It is hardly big news that human beings have been on the move since their origins somewhere in East Africa more than two million years ago. Nor is it a major breakthrough in views of the past that there have been all along interactions among societies, some of them quite consequential. That we should analyze the histories of societies in terms of these relationships rather than in their isolation is an important epistemological argument, but that too has been around for quite some time, perhaps going back to Herodotus and

Sima Qian but most conspicuously to Enlightenment views of history. What may be novel about the present, at least in the United States, is the projection of a contemporary consciousness of globality onto the entire past, thereby erasing important historical differences between different forms and dimensions of globality not only in material interactions among societies but also, perhaps more important, in the consciousness of globality. It also erases critical consciousness of its own conditions of emergence.

The confounding of these differences also obviates the need to account for the relationship of contemporary globalization and its material/mental consequences to its historical precedents, including its immediate historical precedents. Is it possible that consciousness of globalization ebbs and flows in response to historical circumstances, but that the ebbs and flows carry different meanings at different times and for different peoples occupying different locations in global arrangements of power? If so, what is the relationship between power and ideologies of globalization? On the other hand, if there is a secular trend to globalization, where in the past do we locate it?

The preferred answer to the last question is the origins of capitalism, because it is with the emergence of capitalism that it is possible to detect a continuing trend toward the globalization, not only of economic activity, but also of politics and culture. This does not mean, as I will suggest below, that the "ebbs and flows" either of globalization or of consciousness of it therefore disappeared, but aside from culminating in the eighteenth century in the mapping of the world as we know it today, capitalism not only provided a sustained motive force for globalization but also served as the vehicle for the unification of the world under a new European hegemony. If the origins of capitalism lay in its prehistory in earlier modes of production, that fact neither negates the unprecedented historical role capitalism was to play in unifying the world nor renders the whole of human history, rather than the structures of capitalism, as the historical context for contemporary globalization. What Karl Marx and Friedrich Engels wrote in the middle of the nineteenth century might have seemed fantastic in their day, but it is an eerily apt description of ours:

> The discovery of America, the rounding of the Cape, opened up fresh ground for the rising bourgeoisie. The East-Indian and Chinese markets, the colonisation of America, trade with the colonies, and increase in the means of exchange and in commodities generally, gave to commerce, to navigation, to industry, an impulse never before known. . . . Modern industry has established the world market, for which the discovery of America paved the way. . . . The bourgeoisie, historically, has played a most revolutionary part. . . . The bourgeoisie cannot exist without constantly revolutionising the instruments of production, and thereby the relations of production, and with them the whole relations of society. . . . The need of a constantly expanding market for its products chases the bourgeoisie over the whole surface of the globe. It must

nestle everywhere, settle everywhere, establish connexions everywhere. The bourgeoisie has through its exploitation of the world given a cosmopolitan character to production and consumption in every country. . . . All old-established national industries have been destroyed or are daily being destroyed. They are dislodged by new industries, whose introduction becomes a life and death question for all civilised nations, by industries that no longer work up indigenous raw material, but raw material drawn from the remotest zones; industries whose products are consumed, not only at home, but in every quarter of the globe. In place of the old wants, satisfied by the productions of the country, we find new wants, requiring for their satisfaction the products of distant lands and climes. In place of the old local and national seclusion and self-sufficiency, we have intercourse in every direction, universal inter-dependence of nations. And as in material, so also in intellectual production. The intellectual creations of individual nations become common property. National one- sidedness and narrow-mindedness become more and more impossible, and from the numerous national and local literatures there arises a world-literature. . . . The bourgeoisie, by the rapid improvement of all instruments of production, by the immensely facilitated means of communication, draws all, even the most barbarian, nations into civilisation. The cheap prices of its commodities are the heavy artillery with which it batters down all Chinese walls, with which it forces the barbarians' intensely obstinate hatred of foreigners to capitulate. It compels all nations, on pain of extinction, to adopt the bourgeois mode of production; it compels them to introduce what it calls civilisation into their midst, *i.e.,* to become bourgeois themselves. In a word, it creates a world after its own image.[3]

The language of the last few sentences may betray a Eurocentric bias and is certainly offensive from a contemporary perspective—though even there the irony the authors introduce ("what it calls civilisation") should not be overlooked. And the very last sentence is problematic in its assumption of a single bourgeois "self-image," which is blind to the possibility of the emergence of a multiplicity of self-images and interests as the bourgeoisie became more cosmopolitan in content, paving the way for the many internal contradictions that would mark the subsequent history of capitalism. It is hard to disagree otherwise with what the passage has to say concerning both material and cultural globalization. As Giovanni Arrighi has argued recently, capital has been globalizing all along, even before there was a structured and structuring entity that could be recognized as a "capitalist world-system."[4] Arrighi in turn draws on the work of Fernand Braudel, which in its analysis of the emergence of a European world-system recognizes the existence of a multiplicity of regional world-systems, with their own interactions, insertion into which enabled the bourgeoisies of Europe first to construct a European world-system and subsequently to create the economic and political institutions that enabled them to draw all these other world-systems within the orbit of Europe to create a world-system that was global in scope.[5]

While the capitalist world-system as it emerged in the fifteenth to the seventeenth centuries may provide the historical-structural context for contemporary globalization, however, it is necessary to comprehend the particular features of the latter to account for the history of capitalism itself and for what I referred to above as "ebbs and flows" both in its processes and in the consciousness of globalization. Globalization may be viewed as an irrevocable process, at least from the time when Marx and Engels penned the *Communist Manifesto*. And consciousness of globality would proceed apace, not just among Euro-Americans, who through imperialism and colonialism imposed it upon increasingly broader constituencies in the world. But the very process of globalization created its own parochialism, including the parochialism of the European bourgeoisie, as Marx and Engels noted in their ironic reference to what the bourgeoisie calls "civilization." If globalization was to become an ever inescapable phenomenon, it was through colonialism, nationalism, and socialism, which were at once products of globalization and efforts to shape it in some ways, or even to restrain it, as in the case of nationalism and socialism. The immediate predecessor for contemporary conceptualizations of globalization is modernization discourse, grounded in what the (by then predominantly U.S.) bourgeoisie called "civilization" and the alternative to it provided by socialist modernization. While locked in deadly opposition, these two alternatives ironically shared a common commitment to developmentalism, and each sought to draw into its orbit the nations of the postcolonial world, themselves anxious to develop so as to overcome the legacies of colonialism and enhance national autonomy and power. The "three worlds" of modernization discourse, moreover, all conceived of modernization in terms of national units, which disguised the fundamental ways in which both the "three worlds" idea and the idea of the nation were premised on prior assumptions and processes of globalization.[6]

The immediate context for contemporary forms and consciousnesses of globality is the breakdown of this mapping of the world, first with the transformations that rendered increasingly questionable the idea of the Third World, and subsequently with the abandonment and/or fall of the socialist alternative. Already in the late 1960s and early 1970s important alternatives had emerged that questioned the nation-based, culturalist assumptions of modernization discourse. As a new global situation emerged in the 1980s with transformations within capitalism, most importantly the decentering of economic power with the appearance of competitors to U.S. hegemony, the analysis of capitalism itself assumed greater complexity. Finally, as the post–Cold War promise of a "new world order" in the early 1990s has given way to evidence of new kinds of disorder, drawing upon sources of identity that are as old as, if not older than, modernity, still other analyses of globality have become an urgent necessity.

Contemporary analyses of globality may be divided roughly between those that stress changes in the political economy of capitalism and those that are primarily culturalist in orientation. Most important among the former, in my view, is world-system analysis, which has its origins in the radical response of the 1960s to modernization discourse; analyses emerging in the 1980s that are based on a "new international division of labor"; and, most recently, the important contribution of Manuel Castells in his idea of a "network society." Culturalist approaches may be viewed best through the left-liberal proponents of globalization who eschew, or are explicitly critical of, political economy approaches, and the more conservative culturalism of Samuel Huntington, who perceives in culture not a unifying but a divisive force in a renewed fracturing of the world.

THE POLITICAL ECONOMY OF GLOBALIZATION

The term "world-system" became current in the early 1970s, primarily in connection with Immanuel Wallerstein's studies of the origins of capitalism. It is necessary, however, to place Wallerstein's own work within the context of the 1970s in order to appreciate its impact. World-system analysis was received with enthusiasm above all because of its challenge to modernization discourse, which had dominated the social sciences in the United States and Europe since the end of World War II. It is not surprising that it found the greatest favor among young radical scholars who had come of scholarly age in the 1960s and who were for the most part students of the Third World. Equally influential (intellectually if not institutionally) were the works of Samir Amin, Andre Gunder Frank, and the Latin American "dependency" theorists who proposed alternatives to modernization discourse that had much in common with the work of Wallerstein in their theoretical assumptions and political conclusions. In all cases, the new approaches to the study of development were informed by the radical movements of the 1960s against imperialism. Wallerstein's work was distinguished by his efforts to go beyond contemporary problems of development to offer a systematic account of the rise of capitalism from its origins in Europe to its globalization in the twentieth century.[7]

For the last two decades, world-system analysis has offered the foremost alternative to modernization discourse in the explanation of problems of development and underdevelopment. Modernization discourse, as it took shape in the years after World War II, was basically culturalist in the explanations it offered to problems of development, something that was evident in the initial phrasing of the problem of development in terms of "modernity" and "tradition." Modern societies were those societies (in Europe and North America, soon to be joined by Japan) that had somehow liberated themselves from the hold of the past to create rational modes of thought and rational institutions; traditional societies were those that remained wedded to the past both culturally and institutionally and were unable, therefore, to break into modernity. In this distinction, backward and traditional were nearly synonymous while development was associated very closely with progress toward the norms embodied by Euro-American societies. Before the 1980s, modernization proponents rarely spoke of "modernity" with reference to capitalism but, rather, represented Euro-American modernity as the norm of progress that all societies must follow in order to escape their backwardness. Modernization discourse was Weberian in inspiration in its emphasis on the normative power of values associated with Euro-American modernity; what was missing from it was Max Weber's recognition of the fundamental significance of material conditions (necessary but not sufficient) as well as Weber's critique of "rationalization." Modernization discourse took the norms of Euro-American modernity as positive values that guaranteed ceaseless human progress. We should note, finally, that modernization discourse, because of its emphasis on cultural values, represented the problem of modernization as a problem internal to societies, a function of their own internal institutional and value structures, without reference to relationships between societies. Hence the impact of Europe and the United States on "traditional" societies appeared as a progressive force, and any impediments to progress derived from the historical inertia of the "backward" societies themselves. It is ironic that for all its emphasis on the burden of the past, modernization discourse was quite unhistorical in ignoring vast differences among "traditional" societies, as well as the shaping of *their* modernities by Euro-American capitalism. Similarly, revolutions, understood primarily as Communist revolutions, appeared in modernization discourse as some form of inertial resistance to progress that must disappear as modern rationality overtook revolutionary societies.

By the late 1960s, even some modernization theorists, most notably S. N. Eisenstadt and Samuel Huntington, had come to be critical of the teleological assumptions of modernization discourse. But their own efforts to deal with these problems, rather than question the premises of modernization as progress, primarily addressed the question of how to bring under control the disorder created by modernity to salvage the whole process of modernization. Huntington's recognition that revolutions were products not of historical inertia but of the very process of modernization, for instance, was a significant revision of the politics of modernization. His concern, however, was less with what revolutions had to say about modernity than with ways to control their emergence, which was to lead to an affirmation of authoritarian regimes—modernization minus democracy, in other words. What he has had to say about globalization in recent years, which I will discuss below, is in many ways continuous with this earlier position, now shifted to the terrain of civilizations.[8]

The main challenge to modernization discourse was to come from world-system analysis, which, informed by a neo-Marxist understanding of capitalism from Third World perspectives, questioned basic assumptions of modernization. To recapitulate briefly what I take to be the fundamental propositions of world-system analysis that also enunciate its differences from modernization discourse, world-system analysis takes capitalism as the central datum of modernity and seeks to understand the structuring of the modern world by capitalism as a mode of production. In this, it is clearly Marxist in inspiration. Also, world-system analysis differs from orthodox Stalinist Marxism in its insistence that capitalism may not be understood in terms of the internal development of individual nations but must be understood in terms of spatial relationships that transcend nations and give form to them—hence the term "world-system," which refers not to the whole world (except in its ultimate fulfillment) but to spaces that are more or less self-contained in terms of commodity production and exchange. As a world-system adherent has written, "rather than taking states as self-evident units of analysis that are then related to each other through trade, investment flows, and labor exchanges, world-system scholars view these units as being constituted and continually reconstituted by the relations between and among them."[9]

It follows that world-system analysis introduces space into the analysis of development as a central datum; the relations between different societies are not merely relations in time (say, between advanced and backward, developed and underdeveloped) but also simultaneous relations in space. One consequence of this emphasis on space, to which I will return below, is to question the teleology of modernization: that all societies must move in a single temporality of which Europe and North America are the most advanced instances. In the analysis of spatial relations, world-system analysis takes as the most crucial relationship that between "core" and "periphery," which refer respectively to the centers of capital marked by economic and social complexity, relatively autonomous in their economic structure, and the areas that are economically, socially, politically, and culturally dependent on the cores. A third term, "semi-periphery," is used to refer to those areas that do not clearly belong in either one or the other. These premises imply that world-system analysis focuses, not on independent and autonomous economic, social, and political units, but on relationships between such units and how the units themselves are constituted by such relationships. Core-periphery relations are not the premises but the consequences of capitalist development; development and underdevelopment do not describe states that are independent of one another, but are consequences of capitalist relationships. "Underdeveloped" societies are not underdeveloped according to some abstract measure but are underdeveloped by the relations between core and periphery (in Gunder Frank's memorable words, "the development of underdevelopment"), just as the developed owe much of their development to the underdevelopment of others. From this perspective, there are no "modern" and "traditional" societies. All societies that are part of the capitalist world-system are "modern" societies. The difference is that some belong in the capitalist core, others in the capitalist periphery. It is impossible to argue, therefore, that all societies may progress once they have broken with the past; peripheral societies are condemned to underdevelopment by their very peripheral status. This also suggests that within the capitalist world-system it is impossible for all societies to advance, since the core-periphery relationship is essential to the structure of capitalism. What may happen, however, is that these relationships may be reconstituted so that cores and peripheries may shift spatially. It is necessary, finally, to note an implication of world-system analysis for socialism. So long as the capitalist mode of production and exchange is the structuring principle of the world-system, socialism is possible only on condition of "delinking" (the term is Samir Amin's, and the inspiration Maoist), since incorporation into the capitalist world-system by definition precludes the possibility of economic organization directed to the satisfaction of local needs rather than the demands of capital. This, I may note, was a central issue of Chinese Marxism in the 1920s, inspired by Lenin's and Trotsky's analyses of imperialism.

As I noted above, Fernand Braudel, whose own work was an inspiration for world-system analysis, was to carry world-system analysis further back in time to explain the emergence of a Europe-dominated world. According to Braudel, at the beginning of the modern world, there were a number of world-systems, of which the European was only one, and a peripheral one at that. Others were East and Southeast Asia, with China at the core; South Asia, with India at the core; the Ottoman Empire; the Russian Empire; Central African kingdoms; and the Indian empires of the Americas. The history of the modern world is, then, the emergence of capitalism in Europe as Europeans progressively inserted themselves as intermediaries between these more or less self-contained world-systems and managed in the end to incorporate them into a capitalist world-system emanating from Europe. This is the process through which, by the twentieth century, a global world economy was to come into existence, ultimately with the United States at its core.

I am not concerned here with the merits and the demerits of world-system analysis, which has been criticized from a number of perspectives. These criticisms have not been successful in undermining its explanatory power.[10] World-system analysis presupposed globalization before that term acquired popularity and retains its importance as one representation of global formations. Already by the 1980s, however, changes within capitalism, the emergence of other centers of economic power, particularly in East Asia, and the increasingly visible turn to capitalism in socialist societies were to bring globalization to the forefront of consciousness and necessitate new analyses that were to produce different representations of globality.

Following my earlier usage, I will describe this new phase of capitalism as global capitalism,[11] although others have described it variously as "the regime of flexible production," "the regime of flexible accumulation," and "disorganized capitalism." Fundamental to the structure of the new global capitalism is what F. Frobel and others have described as "a new international division of labor";[12] in other words, the transnationalization of production where, through subcontracting, the process of production (even of a single commodity) is globalized. While world-system analysts have rightly indicated that "commodity chains" (or "integrated production processes") are as old as the history of capitalism, it is undeniable that new technologies have expanded the spatial extension of production, as well as its speed, to an unprecedented degree in what David Harvey has described as "time-space compression."[13] Nor is it possible to deny the political, social, and cultural consequences of the new practices. Beginning with East Asia, the new practices have brought into the processes of production Third World locations, scrambling earlier mappings of the world. As production cuts across national boundaries, it also calls into question economic sovereignty as a definition of national integrity. Socially, the new technologies have endowed capital and production with unprecedented mobility, so that the location of production seems to be in a constant state of flux, seeking maximum advantage for capital against labor as well as the avoidance of social and political interference in the activities of capital (hence, "flexible production"). Combined with new media practices, its cultural consequences have been equally drastic; as the new capitalism cuts across political boundaries, so it also does across cultural ones. Its globalization is accompanied by a localization, as capital moves from location to location.

For purposes of the discussion here, the situation that emerged in the 1980s, or became apparent then, may be summarized as, first, the decentering of capitalism, with the emergence of new centers that were themselves the products of globalization of capital but that in turn contributed to the reality and consciousness of a new globality. East Asia is the most conspicuous but may not be the only one. World-system analysts, among others, point to East Asia as a possible new core in the unfolding of the world-system. The recent crisis in East and Southeast Asia may be only temporary, the product of a transition. On the other hand, it has also revealed fundamental structural weaknesses in the new "miracle" economies that have been there all along but that remained unacknowledged so long as the economies seemed to be flourishing. It is also possible that we are witnessing the reconfiguration of global relations that is implicit in the description of the new economic configuration as "a high-tech Hanseatic League"—a network of "global cities" (in Saskia Sassen's term), in other words, that together form the core of the global economy.[14] Other observers, such as Kenichi Ohmae, perceive it more as a network of "regional economies," many Silicon Valleys linked together by the "information high-way."[15] Central to a core thus envisaged are transnational corporations, which have taken over from national markets as the loci of economic activity, not just providing a passive medium for the transmission of capital, production, and commodities, but also determining the nature of the transmission and its direction. The interesting thing about a core thus envisaged is that it may be a core without a periphery, because what used to be peripheries increasingly may be marginal to the operations of the core. Hope of survival, not to speak of power, seems to be contingent under the circumstances on the possibility of joining the core. I may note here, if only in passing, that the globalization of capitalism was a crucial reason for the fall of socialist states that insisted on creating their own alternative spaces, for they faced the alternative of joining in, which for the most part they have, or being marginalized.

Second, the transnationalization of production is the source at once of unprecedented unity globally and unprecedented fragmentation that is systemic (hence "disorganized capitalism"). The homogenization of the globe economically, socially, and culturally is such that Marx's comments above, premature for his time, finally seem to be on the point of vindication. At the same time, there is a parallel process of fragmentation at work—globally, in the absence of a center to capitalism; and locally, in the fragmentation of the production process into supra- or subnational regions and localities. As supranational regional organizations manifest this fragmentation at the global level, localities within the same nation competing to place themselves in the pathways of capital represent it at the basic local level. Nations themselves, it can be argued, represented attempts historically to contain fragmentation; but under attack from the outside (transnational organizations) and the inside (subnational economic regions and localities), it is not quite clear how this new fragmentation is to be contained. A global level of governance, which the new economic configuration urgently demands, further restricts the ability of nation-states to answer to their constituencies. At the same time, fragmentation of state power encourages the resurfacing of dormant conflicts contained earlier by the nation-state.

A final important consequence of the transnationalization of capital may be that for the first time in the history of capitalism, the capitalist mode of production appears as an authentically global abstraction, divorced from its historically specific origins in Europe. In other words, the narrative of capitalism is no longer a narrative of the history of Europe, so that for the first time non-

European capitalist societies, the very products of European capitalist globalization, make their own claims on the history and culture of capitalist modernity. Apparent cultural homogenization accompanying globalization produces its own cultural fragmentations.

The simultaneous globalization and fragmentation that has characterized the world since the 1980s is visible in many other phenomena, from movements of populations to the emergence of new transnational institutions, challenges to Eurocentrism in the very language that was created by a Eurocentric capitalism, the resurgence of ethnic and religious fundamentalisms in the midst of homogenization of everyday cultural habits, and so forth. And at some point, I would hesitate to assign causative priority to some phenomena over others as, all of a sudden, both the products of capitalist modernity and cultural habits long suppressed by capitalism and the nation-state find themselves on the same stage, engaging in cooperation as well as deadly conflict. Challenges to the hegemonies of the past are very much the order of the day, but the challenges themselves would seem to be limited in their horizon by their inability to think beyond their past legacies or present circumstances.

If I may repeat what I suggested at the beginning, globalization as it emerged in the 1980s and gained strength in the 1990s represents significant departures from the immediate past but also contains as some of its vital elements longstanding characteristics of the dynamics of capitalism. World-systems analysts are wrong to the extent that they view contemporary globalization as just another cycle in the history of capital waiting for the appearance of a new core before it once again achieves a structural order.[16] But they are also quite right to point out that claims to globalization as a new departure simply ignore all that the present shares with the history of capitalism. In its final fulfillment, capitalist modernity both points in new directions and reproduces all the contradictions that have marked its history.

Analyses of global capitalism share much in their logic with world-system analysis, but the conclusions to which they point depart in significant ways from world-system analysis, most importantly in global configurations of power. Most significant is the status of the nation-state. While it recast modernization discourse in a new frame by pointing to spatialities beyond the nation, world-system analysis nevertheless continued to take the nation as the unit of analysis when it came to questions of development and emancipation, as with the concept of delinking, in which the national unit separated itself from the world-system to seek alternatives. Contemporary analyses of globalization (as, indeed, the fate of socialist societies that attempted such delinking) would suggest that this is no longer a viable option. None but the most naive would suggest that the nation-state is already a thing of the past or that it no longer may have a part to play in countering the effects of globalization, but it is also the case that any reconceptualization of the nation-state must account for both the supranational and the subnational forces that have once again acquired crucial significance in determining the shape of the nation.

Such is also the case with core-periphery relationships, which are central to world-system analysis. Such relationships do indeed persist, but it is increasingly difficult to assign them to neatly delineated spatialities of "Third Worlds" or nations. As the core has assumed fluidity, so has the periphery. It is possible now to find First Worlds in Third World locations, and Third Worlds within the First. Even more so than in the case of the nation-state, this scrambling of cores and peripheries requires new kinds of analyses of problems of development, as well as of political power.

It is necessary nevertheless to exercise some caution not to mystify power by equating the scrambling of power with its disappearance. The "disorganizing" of capital does not imply that there are no longer centers to power. The recent crisis in East and Southeast Asia and the measures adopted for its resolution are revealing of the power of the capitalist core in shaping global policy. Transnational corporations are not as homeless as they appear on the surface, as their power in some measure depends on state action; it is no accident that the most powerful corporations are those that identify with core states in the world-system. To speak of Third Worlds in the First is not to incorporate them into a condition of "Third World–ness" that is the same everywhere. Even the emergence of a transnational capitalist class or the need for core states to share power with others is no indication that relations of dependency have therefore been eliminated. Globalization points to the need for accommodating new realities of power. On the other hand, it is also quite evidently more of a concern in the ideologies of core states, particularly the United States, that represent an effort to recomprehend the world in its totality. Such a vision of totality is not available equally to all who participate in global practices. Neither are all participants in those practices equally concerned to contain global chaos, though they may all feel its effects in one way or another.

One possible way of bringing some analytical coherence to the conflicting phenomena of global capitalism has been offered by Manuel Castells in his recent work.[17] Castells's metaphor of networks in the description of contemporary capitalism is derived from the central importance he assigns to information technologies, which then serve as a paradigm for the reconfiguration of global relations. The metaphor of "network" offers ways for envisaging the new global capitalism in both its unities and its disunities, in its pervasiveness as well as in the huge gaps that are systemic products of the global economy. The metaphor of network shifts attention from surfaces to "highways" that link nodes in the global economy. A network has no boundaries of any permanence but may expand or contract at a moment's notice and shift in its internal configurations as its nodes move from one location to another. Marginality to the global economy may mean being outside of the network, as well as in the many surfaces within that are in its many gaps. Marginality does not imply being untouched by the networks, as the inductive effects of network flows affect even those that are not direct participants in its many flows. Finally, the network metaphor offers new ways of accounting for power. It is possible to state that the most powerful nodes in the global economy—for example, Sassen's global cities—may be those locations where nodes of economic, political, and cultural power coincide. The network militates against neat spatialities, but it also allows for their inclusion in considerations of power; while any location may be included in the network, the most powerful, and controlling, nodes are still located in national spaces of commanding global presence.

While some of these conclusions may be beyond what Castells intended, they are consistent, I think, with what he has to say about "the architecture" and "the geometry" of global power. In his words, "there is a basic architecture, inherited from history, that frames the development of the global economy."[18] As he explains further:

> The architecture of the global economy features an asymmetrically interdependent world, organized around three major economic regions and increasingly polarized along an axis of opposition between productive, information-rich, affluent areas, and impoverished areas, economically devalued and socially excluded. Between the three dominant regions, Europe, North America, and the Asian Pacific, the latter appears to be the most dynamic yet the most vulnerable because of its dependence upon the openness of the markets of the other regions. However, the intertwining of economic processes between the three regions makes them practically inseparable in their fate. Around each region an economic hinterland has been created, with some countries being gradually incorporated into the global economy.[19]

"Within this visible architecture," however, "there are dynamic processes of competition and change that infuse a variable geometry into the global system of economic processes." As Castells explains this "variable geometry":

> What I call the newest international division of labor is constructed around four different positions in the informational/ global economy: the producers of high value, based on informational labor; the producers of high volume, based on lower-cost labor; the producers of raw materials, based on natural endowments; and the redundant producers, reduced to devalued labor. . . . The critical matter is that these different positions do not coincide with countries. *They are organized in networks and flows, using the technological infrastructure of the informational economy.* They feature geographic concentrations in some areas of the planet, so that the global economy is not geographically undifferentiated. . . . Yet the newest international division of labor does not take place between countries but between economic agents placed in

the four positions I have indicated along a global structure of networks and flows. . . . [A]ll countries are penetrated by the four positions. . . . Even marginalized economies have a small segment of their directional functions connected to a high-value producers network. . . . And certainly, the most powerful economies have marginal segments of their population placed in a position of devalued labor. . . . Because the position in the international division of labor does not depend, fundamentally, on the characteristics of the country but on the characteristics of its labor . . . and of its insertion into the global economy, changes may occur, and indeed do, in a short span. . . . The newest international division of labor is organized on the basis of labor and technology, but is enacted and modified by governments and entrepreneurs. The relentlessly variable geometry that results from such processes of innovation and competition struggles with the historically produced architecture of the world economic order, inducing the creative chaos that characterizes the new economy.[20]

The power of Castells's analysis lies in its ability to bring together contemporary changes with the legacies of the past, observable concentrations of power with ultimate powerlessness to control the uncertainties of the global economy, globalization with regionalization and the continued relevance of the nation-state, and the persistence of earlier mappings of the globe with its reconfigurations. The world-system all along may have been not so much a stable "system" as a process of systematizations and desystematizations. This may be the condition of the contemporary global economy, with the processes speeded up to a point where order becomes indistinguishable from chaos. The very fulfillment of capitalist modernization issues not in the fulfillment of the promise of modernization discourse but in its final dissolution.

THE CULTURES OF GLOBALIZATION

One by-product of globalization discourse is the return of culture. Not that culture ever disappeared from discussions of development, but it was driven to the background for a brief while in the preoccupation with political economy, and with the social, that accompanied the repudiation of modernization discourse with its culturalist assumptions. Contemporary preoccupation with culture has more than one source. The emergence of East Asian economies from the late 1970s on gave rise once again to questions of whether or not culture had anything to do with development. The scrambling of boundaries with globalization, but especially the increasingly visible motions of populations, not only gave rise to questions of identity but also empowered the reassertion of suppressed identities; the reemergence of sub- and supranational ethnicity is one of the outstanding phenomena that have accompanied globalization. The stress on culture is also propagated not only by the immense power commanded by culture industries (including the media) but also, perhaps even more fundamentally, by the importance of information, a basically cultural force, in production and consumption.

In the perspective of political economy, culturalist approaches to globalization appear not just as expressions of this new situation but also as efforts to bring some order to the untidiness of everyday life. I will look briefly here at two versions of contemporary culturalist paradigms of globality: the one representative of left-liberal approaches that perceive in contemporary cultural formations an unprecedented globalization (as distinct from homogenization) in the human experience of the world; the other representative of, for lack of a better term, a "geopolitical realism" that postulates culture as the defining feature of the new fracturing of the globe by past legacies. I describe both approaches as "culturalist" because they give priority to culture above all other elements; if anything, the left-liberal alternative is more hostile to political economy than the "realist" one.

Anthony Giddens has written that "the 'world' in which we now live is in some profound respects . . . quite distinct from that inhabited by human beings in previous periods of history. It is in many ways a single world, having a unitary framework of experience (for instance in respect of basic axes of time and space), yet at the same time one which creates new forms of fragmentation and dispersal."[21] For Giddens, the media play a "central role" in this world, as it is through them that "the influence of distant happenings on proximate events, and on intimacies of the self, becomes more and more commonplace."[22] Nevertheless, the media do not homogenize the world but only provide a "unitary framework." He writes:

> The globalisation of social activity which modernity has served to bring about is in some ways a process of the development of genuinely world-wide ties—such as those involved in the global nation-state system or the international division of labour. However, in a general way, the concept of globalisation is best understood as expressing fundamental aspects of time-space distanciation. Globalisation concerns the intersection of presence and absence, the interlacing of social events and social relations 'at distance' with local contextualities. We should grasp the global spread of modernity in terms of an ongoing relation between distanciation and the chronic mutability of local circumstances and local engagements. . . . [G]lobalisation has to be understood as a dialectical phenomenon, in which events at one pole of a distanciated relation often produce divergent or even contrary occurrences at another. . . . *The dialectic of the local and global* is . . . basic.[23]

The juxtaposition of the global and the local is common to most writing on globalization in the left-liberal disposition and represents one of its most important contributions to the debate on globalization, pointing to new kinds of fragmentation that have accompanied globalization. While the local may on occasion refer to the national, more often than not it points to levels below and within the nation, where the global meets concrete contexts of everyday existence. Similarly, the global in this usage needs to be distinguished from the "international," as it transcends and provides the context for relationships between nations and even regions. The global also shapes the local, we might add, as the local, while by no means just a passive recipient of the global, is most important nevertheless for pointing to the different ways in which the global works over localized configurations. The refusal to entertain the possibility that the local, having been worked over by the global, may in turn shape the global is one of the problems with these analyses.

Giddens's suggestion of a break between the present and the past is shared by most expositions of the left-liberal position on globalization. Roland Robertson, whose enthusiasm for globalization is matched by his extremist culturalism, insists on the necessity of distinguishing globalization even from the forces and the processes of which it is the product:

> I argue that systematic comprehension of the macrostructuration of world order is essential to the viability of any form of contemporary theory and that such comprehension must involve *analytical separation of the factors which have facilitated the shift towards a single world—e.g., the spread of capitalism, western imperialism and the development of a global media system—from the general and global agency-structure (and/or culture) theme.* While the empirical relationship between the two sets of issues is of great importance (and, of course, complex), conflation of them leads us into all sorts of difficulties and inhibits our ability to come to terms with *the basic and shifting terms* of the contemporary world order.[24]

In the extreme nature of its presentist culturalism, Robertson's statement reveals both the virtues and the serious shortcomings of globalization in left-liberal analyses. The assertion of the autonomy of a culture of globality underlines the importance of viewing culture not as a by-product of material conditions but as a constituent of globality. While Robertson has refrained from clarifying his own idea of culture,[25] he is nevertheless correct in pointing out the power of "global culture" as a social imaginary that shapes the behavior even of those who are in no evident position to gain from globalization. This culture, however vague, is also not a functional product of capitalism alone but is nourished by many sources, including the very idea of globality; it makes some sense, therefore, to view it separately from the functioning of global capitalism, even if global capitalism continues to empower it. Given the power of globalization in reshaping conceptualizations of the world, finally, the effort to grasp the "macrostructuration" of the world independently of its origins has some epistemological value in uncovering how a present situation of globality may differ from its historical antecedents.

These virtues, however, seem to me to be achieved at the cost of an intellectual and political mystification of globalization. Forte observes that "Robertson's approach is 'cultural' in a purely ideational or symbolic sense," resting the evidence of globality on the diffusion of global awareness—or awareness of globality.[26] While left-liberal advocates of globalization, including Robertson, concede that globalization has a long history that is coeval with the history of capitalist modernity, there seems to be a reluctance to investigate the implications of the connection between contemporary globality and its context in capitalist modernity, seemingly out of an anxiety about falling back upon functionalist explanations, but also because of a possibility that too much preoccupation with globality's relationship to capitalist modernity might reveal globalization as "modernity writ large"[27] and the culturalist approach to globalization as a contemporary variant of the culturalism that marked modernization discourse, minus its Eurocentrism. Failure to do so, however, also obviates the need to inquire into the immediate context of globalization discourse within a contemporary global capitalism where the mere repudiation of Eurocentrism does not in and of itself signify an escape from it, as capitalism even in its globalization carries upon it the stamp of its origins and modern development. This becomes even more evident if we consider that globalization is not of equal concern to all populations globally but is propagated most enthusiastically from the earlier centers of global power, which continue to shape global economic and political futures.[28] Challenges to Eurocentrism within this context emanate not from populations at large, which may feel the effects of globalization without being players in it, but from global elites empowered by their participation in a global capitalist economy and that may well represent, therefore, the deployment of culture in intraelite struggles within a context of shared economic interests. Exemplary in this regard may be the "socialist" government of the People's Republic of China, which in its dealings with the United States (or with Taiwan) consistently insists that negotiations focus on economic issues, leaving aside thorny questions of culture and politics—which does not prevent culture and politics from becoming issues of contention nevertheless.

The failure of cultural globalists to address issues of power mystifies questions of the spatial and social limits of globalization. The elevation of globality to a transcendental status, on the other hand, renders globalization into a mystical force that compels all who live under its regime to follow its dictates at any cost, raising the question of the complicity of this representation of globality with the globalization discourse of transnational capital, the core states of global power, and an emergent transnational capitalist class (in Leslie Sklair's term). It is ironic that globalists such as Roland Robertson spend considerable time attacking political economy analyses of capital, such as world-system analysis, while they have little to say about the relationship of globalization as ideology to contemporary structures of power. The compelling power with which globalization is endowed is seen to some extent even in the works of analysts such as Giddens who are more cognizant of such a relationship.

Interestingly, the most important intellectual challenge to globalization in recent years has come not from the left but from a political scientist who long has been associated with conservative causes. Samuel Huntington's critique of globalization is in many ways consistent with his earlier criticism of modernization discourse; as he contended earlier that modernization bred not democracy but disorder, he now argues that globalization breeds not global unity but division and disorder. If there is a major difference from his earlier analysis, it is in the hardening of the boundaries of the units of his analysis. Huntington believes that nation-states remain important, and will remain important for the foreseeable future, but shifts attention from nations to "cultural entities" called civilizations. In the article where he first outlined his position, he wrote that "the interactions among peoples of different civilizations enhance the civilization-consciousness of people that, in turn, invigorates differences and animosities stretching or thought to stretch back deep in history."[29] The conflicts he perceives between civilizations are products of globalization, which creates not unity—or the erasure of history—but new fractures along historical/cultural legacies. His own understanding of these fractures is exemplary of the ethnicization of learning that has accompanied globalization. Huntington's point of departure is the premise that in the post–Cold War world, "the most pervasive, important and dangerous conflicts will not be between social classes, rich and poor, or other economically defined groups, but between peoples belonging to different cultural entities."[30] He conceives cultural entities at the broadest level in terms of civilizations, which are "culture[s] writ large."[31] Huntington perceives a regrouping of the world's peoples around civilizations that in their origins predate modernity. There are seven or eight of these civilizations, of which the most important in his analysis are the Western, the Eastern Orthodox (or Slavic), Islamic, and Sinic (Chinese). Language and religion are in his analysis the most crucial defining elements of civilizations, although he views culture most broadly as "the overall way of life of a people."[32] Ways of life long assumed to be things of the past are on the resurgence, ironically, as a consequence of modernization, which, on the one hand, has enhanced the economic, military, and political power of non-Western societies and, on the other hand, has created alienation and identity crisis: an expression at once, in other words, of alienation and empowerment.[33] Rather than lead to Westernization, modernization, and the increased contact among peoples that has accompanied it, has intensified the human propensity to hate outsiders.[34]

The problem that Huntington sets out to address is how to secure world order when the Western-dominated world of modernity is being challenged by non-Western civilizations that have made a comeback, thanks to modernity, and assert the universality of *their* real or imagined civilizational legacies against the Western. Under the circumstances, "the concept of a universal civilization helps justify Western cultural dominance of other societies and the need for those societies to ape Western practices and institutions."[35] This is impossible and unsustainable because the West itself represents a unique civilization with values that are not easily adaptable to the norms of other civilizations.[36] Worse, it is arrogant and dangerous; "Western intervention in the affairs of other civilizations [not least efforts to export human rights and democracy] is probably the single source of most instability and potential conflict in a multicivilizational world."[37] The best that the West can do is to retreat behind its own boundaries, mind its own affairs, and leave "the primary responsibility for containing and resolving regional conflicts . . . [to] the leading states of the civilizations dominant in those regions."[38] The formation of fortress "West" in Huntington's analysis, includes control of immigration to the "West" in order to preserve its own unique heritage.

Huntington's civilizational units may seem quaint, if not outrageous, at a time when the "constructedness" of culture has become a matter of faith among Euro-American, especially American, intellectual circles, among which intellectuals from other "civilizations" are prominently visible. Methodologically his discussion of current and impending conflicts between civilizations draws on scattered examples, held together by "commonsense" homilies about human propensities of one kind or another. For all its insistence on the power of the past, the argument is deeply ahistorical. Huntington recognizes the constructedness of cultures and differences internal to civilizations, as well as the permeability of boundaries that divide them from one another. And yet these qualifications do not find their way into the argument, which is sustained by an assumption that the values characteristic of civilizations persist against the transformative pressures of time and space. The analysis is marred seriously by his inability to draw clear physical boundaries around "civilizations," which are intermixed in most locations. Having committed himself to "civilizations" as the units of conflict in the contemporary world, he cannot do much better in the end than concede that "the relations between civilizations are complicated, often ambivalent, and they do change. . . . Conflicts also obviously occur within civilizations, particularly Islam. . . . The relatively simple bipolarity of the Cold War is giving way to the much more complex relationships of a multipolar, multicivilizational world."[39] The analysis is also oblivious to the globalization of capitalism and the common interests as well as new kinds of divisions it is in the process of creating; he makes little, for instance, of his own quite accurate observation that "the ability of Asian regimes to resist Western human rights pressures was reinforced by several factors. American and European businesses were desperately anxious to expand their trade with and their investment in these rapidly growing countries and subjected their governments to intense pressure not to disrupt economic relations with them."[40] Perhaps most important, for all its cultural relativism, Huntington's analysis, as with his earlier work on modernization, is intended to secure global order in accordance with a conceptualization of the world that is rooted in the history of Euro-American modernity—minus values such as democracy and human rights that legitimized that modernity.

It would be a mistake, nevertheless, to dismiss Huntington's analysis as a mere reassertion of Eurocentrism or American power, or as an ethnocentrism that borders on racism. This is not just because the author is well connected to influence decision making in U.S. circles of power.[41] His analysis has been received with great interest outside of the United States. The "remaking of world order" that he advocates not only refers freely to U.S. imperialism but also suggests that the United States should share world power with regional hegemons, in the form of "core states" of civilizations. The appeal of such an arrangement, say, to the leaders of "Sinic civilization," should be obvious.[42] Above all, however, I would like to suggest that Huntington's analysis is appealing because it is exemplary of a growing ethnicization/racialization not only in world politics but also of the ways in which it is conceptualized; it therefore speaks to a real situation, as he claims. Huntington himself recognizes that cultures are internally divided, or constructed, which may not matter, because constructed or not, faith in their reality leads to the kinds of results that Huntington describes. Faith in all Chinese being Confucian is no less a faith because it may be a construction of the contemporary world. Huntington himself may be engaged in just such a construction with regard to "Western civilization"; the ideological nature of his analysis does not detract from its power to persuade the faithful.[43]

From a critical perspective, what needs to be pointed out are the resistances that are also outstanding phenomena of the contemporary world, about which Huntington has little to say. Not everyone in the world is equally engaged in the remanufacturing of civilizations, although everyone may feel its effects one way or another. In Huntington's analysis, as in culturalist arguments for globalization in general, there is little accounting for the relationship between culture and power, as if globalization or civilizational resurgence were products of invisible processes. The reification of culture in either alternative, mutually contradictory though they are, also disguises the conflicts over life and culture that are imbedded not at the off-ground levels of globality or civilizations but in everyday struggles for survival and democracy.

PLACE-BASED IMAGINATION

Alternative readings of globalization offer insights into different aspects of globality that are complementary but in their contradictory conclusions also reveal the complexity of global formations. Political economy analyses point to the context of contemporary globalization both within the history of capitalist modernity and in terms of recent changes in the configurations of capital. World-system analysis that in the post–World War II period challenged modernization discourse to adopt a global perspective still retains its power to reveal structural inequalities built into the capitalist system. On the other hand, these structural inequalities are obscured to some extent both by the decentralization of capital and by an intensified fluidity in its operations that "disorganize" the system on an ongoing basis. The virtue of the network analysis offered by Manuel Castells is to reconcile these two aspects of contemporary global formations.

Political economy analyses are not as innocent of questions of culture and agency as culturalist critics maintain, but they do display a bias toward structures and the impersonal workings of capital.[44] It is arguable even that political economy analyses have done a better job of formulating explanations that integrate culture and politics than those culturalist analyses that consciously set themselves against political economy. On the other hand, employed wisely, cultural globalism has done invaluable service in pointing out the part played by culture and agency in the dynamics of globalization. What I have described above as left-liberal culturalism has reinforced the revelations of political economy analyses in underlining the localization of cultures in the very process of, and as a consequence of, globalization. Huntington's culturalism, for all its reductionism, points to the new fracturing of the globe at both the macro- and the microlevels by a recuperation of historical legacies in response to pressures of globalization.

These analyses are nevertheless lacking in their inattention to still another way of constructing globality: what has been termed "globalization from below" by more than one analyst with reference to the proliferation of place-based movements that cut across the customary East/West, North/South, "civilizational" and national divides. Castells recognizes their importance but relegates them to a secondary role in favor of ecological and gender-based movements. The recognition is also implicit in left-liberal identification of the local in the global, which stops short, however, of recognizing the global in the local. Place-based movements are not new, but they have acquired a new significance under the conditions of globalization, which, on the one hand, completes modernity's "invasion of the life-world" and, on the other hand, generates "places" as locations for new kinds of politics.[45] The politics of place of necessity differs from location to location in its concerns and constitution; what renders it global is its appearance globally in response to "the unitary framework of experience" of which Giddens speaks. The challenge to radical politics is how to translate reactive politics of place that are limited to resistance to the ravages and uncertainties of globalization into proactive politics that point to alternative futures. This raises the question of how to coordinate diverse politics of place into a coordinated movement—without abolishing diversity.

To speak of place-based politics as a possible and necessary option requires an "unthinking" of radical politics, much as Wallerstein has spoken of "unthinking social science." The various analyses of globalization discussed above all share one thing: that earlier forms of radical politics have become largely irrelevant under contemporary circumstances. Capitalism is too decentered to permit any realistic option of systemic change, such as was envisaged earlier in socialism. Socialism, at any rate, was concretely manifested only in nation-states; both past experience with socialism and the increasingly problematic nature of the nation-state rule out as a radical option nation-based movements that may delink from the world-system and point the way to alternative futures. Labor, women's, and ecological movements, while quite important, also suffer from the fragmenting dynamics of uneven development as well as the ethnicization of politics of which Huntington speaks. They may be quite crucial, nevertheless, to providing the necessary links between places, which require new kinds of transnational vision and organizational flexibility.

It is possible to argue presently that even such radical movements may have a hope of success only if they challenge the hegemony of globalization and seek ways to ground themselves without giving up their international or global commitments. The nation-state, too, has not yet exhausted all its utility or possibilities, as it may have a protective role to play against the "creative chaos" of globalization. What seems clear is that while globalization requires a response that is also national and global, it is necessary most fundamentally to challenge its premise that an off-ground existence is the fate of humankind, which calls for renewed attention to places—not places as they have been inherited from the past, with their own inequalities and oppressions, but places as they have been worked over by modernity, which in their reaffirmation of everyday life seek also to counter past legacies. Instead of urging places to go global in order to survive, which undermines both economic and political democracy, the crucial task at the present time may be to create those democratic spaces in which to secure livelihood and to reaffirm the priorities of everyday existence against the visions of future welfare.[46] Places thus conceived are not the givens of history but projects to be realized. If such projects seem utopian, they are no more so than a globalization with its indefinitely deferred promises. The difference between the two projects lies not in degrees of utopianism but in their relationship to power.

Unfortunately, a left caught up in visions of globalization, rather than challenge its premises, celebrates its promises of cosmopolitanism or ethnic multiculturalism and contributes to the very hegemony that it would undermine. Wedded to modernity, left-liberals in our day seem to have hitched their aspirations to the bandwagon of globalization, in which they wishfully perceive not a fulfillment of a program of modernization but a way to overcome some of its less desirable legacies. It is arguable to the contrary that globalization has finally exposed as an illusion the hope (as much Marxist as it is bourgeois) that the answer to the problems of modernity is more modernization. While globalization compromises some of the more valuable promises of modernity, it places beyond the control of everyday life (and even of states and capital) modernity's most destructive consequences. Its celebration by radicals in postmodernism (the contemporary counterpart to modernism) reinforces the ideology of capital in persuading us that we are all condemned to following the dictates of globalization that do not emanate from a single source but represent the cumulative effects of bits and pieces of human progress. Some progress, that in its march continues to negate the very ideas of human welfare and democracy that justify it!

Recognition of the fundamental contradictoriness of globalization might enable an antimodernism that may be essential to asking hard questions about capitalist modernity and formulating alternatives to it. Presently, the most visible protests against globalization, especially in the United States, would seem to bear an unmistakably right-wing character. That they are right-wing is no reason for dismissing them, for they still represent the anxieties and fears of real people who find themselves at the mercy of globalization. At the same time, these protests offer little more than a commitment to preserving accustomed privileges and are highly limited, therefore, in their ability to address past legacies of inequality and injustice; indeed, they exacerbate these legacies by finding scapegoats for their woes among even less privileged groups.

If the right seems to be addressing problems of globalization more effectively at present, it may be because the left, with its cosmopolitan developmentalist biases, has been all too ready to concede places to the political right. The right may also be better at it because the right is more willing to affirm particularity against theoretical generalization. While it may be possible to theorize places, the politics of place is ultimately based on diversity and difference, because each place is marked not only by a particular location but also by a particular legacy. If there is a challenge in that to "unthinking" theory, it is the challenge of everyday political and economic democracy that yet remains to be realized, not just in Chiapas or the Three Gorges of the Yangtze River, but also in Cleveland, Ohio, and Durham, North Carolina.

NOTES

This chapter originally appeared as "Formations of Globality and Radical Politics," *Review of Education/Pedagogy/Cultural Studies* 21, no. 2 (1999): 300–338. The author gratefully acknowledges the permission of this publication to reprint the article here.

1. Indeed, without an account of the relationship between Eurocentrism and the enormous power of capitalism that enabled Euro-American expansion, the criticism of Eurocentrism may perpetuate Eurocentric assumptions in new guises. See chap. 3. To repeat what I have remarked elsewhere, without capitalism, Eurocentrism might have remained just another parochial ethnocentrism.

2. Among the works that are notable for what they reveal about globalization are Hans Peter-Martin and Harald Schumann, *The Global Trap: Globalization and the Assault on Democracy and Prosperity*, trans. Patrick Camiller (London: Zed Books, 1997); Richard J. Barnet and John Cavanagh, *Global Dreams: Imperial Corporations and the New World Order* (New York: Simon & Schuster, 1994); and William Greider, *One World, Ready or Not: The Manic Logic of Global Capitalism* (New York: Simon & Schuster, 1997). Martin and Schumann, citing globalizationists, point out that globalization is expected to produce a "20:80" society sustained by "tittytainment"; that is, a society where only 20 percent of the world's population will benefit from globalization, while the rest will be kept occupied by entertainment. The "20:80" figure was originally forecast by the European Union. See Ricardo Petrella, "World City-States of the Future," *NPQ (New Perspectives Quarterly)* (Fall 1991): 59–64.

3. Karl Marx and Frederick Engels, *Manifesto of the Communist Party* (1888; reprint, Peking: Foreign Languages Press, 1968), 31–36.

4. Giovanni Arrighi, *The Long Twentieth Century: Money, Power, and the Origins of Our Time* (London: Verso, 1994).

5. Fernand Braudel, *The Perspective of the World*, vol. 3 of *Civilization and Capitalism, Fifteenth to Eighteenth Century*, trans. Sian Reynolds (New York: Harper & Row, 1986). Braudel himself drew upon Immanuel Wallerstein's world-system analysis, adding a recognition of other world-systems that predated the emergence of capitalism. He also restricted the definition of capital, identifying it with large enterprises devoted to accumulation. In his case, as in the case of Arrighi, the emphasis is on the role of finance in globalization. Financial expansion required an alliance between the territorial state and a globalizing capital but also created contradictions between the two because of their conflicting orientations to territorial grounding. The argument is highly plausible, but it is questionable in ignoring both production and issues of culture, especially for the period after the eighteenth century. Accumulation is the goal (and the defining feature) of capital, but production may be essential to comprehending both sources of national power and the foreshortening of the cycles of financial accumulation and dispersion that is important in Arrighi's analysis. On the other hand, it is also important to explain why the creation of the nation-state accompanied mechanisms of accumulation at one stage of globalization while its dissolution or the qualification of its powers would seem to be a feature of contemporary globalization. Such questions require greater attention, I think, to the relationship between accumulation, production, and national markets. It is also important to recognize that national cultures, once they had come

into existence, have also played autonomous roles in influencing, if not shaping, the actions of both states and capital.

6. For a more detailed discussion, see Arif Dirlik, "Three Worlds or One, or Many? The Reconfiguration of Global Relations under Contemporary Capitalism," in *The Postcolonial Aura: Third World Criticism in the Age of Global Capitalism* (Boulder, Colo.: Westview Press, 1997): 146–62; first published in *Nature, Society, and Thought* 7, no. 1 (1994): 19–42.

7. Wallerstein himself points to "the discovery of the contemporary reality of the Third World" as an important moment in the formulation of world-system analysis, which he refuses to describe as "theory." See Immanuel Wallerstein, "The Rise and Future Demise of World-System Analysis," *Review* 21, no. 1 (1998): 103–12, 104.

8. Samuel P. Huntington, *Political Order in Changing Societies* (New Haven: Yale University Press, 1972). First published in 1968, by 1972 the book was into its sixth printing. It was seminal in its disassociation of democracy from markets in the modernization process.

9. Ravi Arvand Palat, *Pacific Asia and the Future of the World-System* (Westport, Conn.: Greenwood, 1993), 6.

10. For a brief but informative recapitulation of debates over the world-system, see Giovanni Arrighi, "Capitalism and the Modern World-System: Rethinking the Nondebates of the 1970s," *Review*, 21, no. 1 (1998): 113–29.

11. Arif Dirlik, *After the Revolution: Waking to Global Capitalism* (Hanover, N.H.: Wesleyan University Press/University Press of New England, 1994).

12. F. Frobel, J. Heinrichs, and O. Kreye, *The New International Division of Labor* (Cambridge: Cambridge University Press, 1980).

13. David Harvey, *The Condition of Post-Modernity* (Cambridge, Mass.: Blackwell, 1989).

14. Saskia Sassen, *The Global City: New York, London, Tokyo* (Princeton, N.J.: Princeton University Press, 1991).

15. Kenichi Ohmae, *The End of the Nation State; The Rise of Regional Economies: How Capital, Corporations, Consumers, and Communication Are Shaping Global Markets* (New York: Free Press, 1995).

16. There is also the possibility of complete dissolution, with no hint of what might come next. See Immanuel Wallerstein, "The Global Possibilities, 1990–2025," in *The Age of Transition: Trajectory of the World-System, 1945–2025*, ed. Terence K. Hopkins and Immanuel Wallerstein (London: Zed Books, 1996), 226–43.

17. Manuel Castells, *The Rise of the Network Society*, vol.1 of *The Information Age: Economy, Society and Culture* (Malden, Mass.: Blackwell, 1997).

18. Castells, *Network Society*, 146.

19. Castells, *Network Society*, 145–46.

20. Castells, *Network Society*, 146–47 (emphasis in original).

21. Anthony Giddens, *Modernity and Self-Identity: Self and Society in the Late Modern Age* (Stanford, Calif.: Stanford University Press, 1991), 4–5.

22. Giddens, *Modernity and Self-Identity*, 4.

23. Giddens, *Modernity and Self-Identity*, 21–22 (emphasis in original).

24. Roland Robertson, "Mapping the Global Condition: Globalization as the Central Concept," in *Global Culture: Nationalism, Globalization, and Modernity*, ed. Mike Featherstone (London: Sage Publications, 1994), 15–29, 23. Emphasis in the longer section is mine.

25. Maximilian C. Forte, "Globalization and World-Systems Analysis: Toward New Paradigms of Geo-Historical Social Anthropology (A Research Review)," *Review* 21, no. 1 (1998): 29–99, 80.

26. Forte, "Globalization and World-Systems Analysis," 79.

27. Mike Featherstone, "Localism, Globalism, and Cultural Identity," in *Global/Local: Cultural Production and the Transnational Imaginary,* ed. Rob Wilson and Wimal Dissanayke (Durham, N.C.: Duke University Press, 1996), 46–77, 46.

28. Noteworthy in this regard is the enthusiasm for globalization of "rational choice" political scientists, who, in their very claims to the scientificity of their undertaking, are products of a Eurocentric scientism. A globalized culture, to the extent that it erases cultural particularities, is quite obviously convenient for an approach to politics that assumes the possibility of universal methodologies. While cultural globalists such as Giddens recognize local permutations of globalization, globalists such as Robertson may have something in common with "rational choice" analysts; the specifically stated goal of dehistoricizing globalization in the quotation cited above is to evolve a "contemporary theory" without telling the reader whose theory it is to be.

29. Samuel P. Huntington, "The Clash of Civilizations?" *Foreign Affairs* (Summer 1993): 22-49, 26.

30. Samuel P. Huntington, *The Clash of Civilizations and the Remaking of World Order* (New York: Simon & Schuster, 1996), 28.

31. Huntington, *Clash of Civilizations,* 41.

32. Huntington, *Clash of Civilizations.*

33. Huntington, *Clash of Civilizations,* 76–77.

34. Huntington, *Clash of Civilizations,* 130.

35. Huntington, *Clash of Civilizations,* 66.

36. Samuel P. Huntington, "The West Unique, Not Universal," *Foreign Affairs* (November/December 1996): 28–46. See also Huntington, *Clash of Civilizations,* chap. 3.

37. Huntington, *Clash of Civilizations,* 312.

38. Huntington, "West Unique, Not Universal," 42.

39. Huntington, *Clash of Civilizations,* 245.

40. Huntington, *Clash of Civilizations,* 194.

41. Shortly after Huntington's first discussion was published, a conference of nongovernmental organizations in Washington, D.C., entitled "Managing Chaos," featured him as a keynote speaker. The others, according to the program, were Henry Kissinger and Ted Koppel. See also his policy recommendations (*Clash of Civilizations,* 312) that are intended to shore up "Western" power, which, contrary to his arguments, include Western "intervention" in the affairs of others to rebuild world order.

42. It is also worth remembering that Huntington's earlier arguments on order were quite popular in the People's Republic of China in the late 1980s in the guise of a "new authoritarianism."

43. It may be revealing that in the concluding part of his book, Huntington states that "culture . . . follows power" (*Clash of Civilizations,* 310). The statement seems somewhat surprising in light of what he has to say about the lasting power of civilizational values, but not if we take into account his underlying motivation to reassert Euro-American power.

44. World-system analysis does not stand or fall with core-periphery structures; nor does a recognition of the fundamentalness even of technology require obliviousness to questions

of culture, agency, and identity. See Wallerstein, "Global Possibilities, 1990–2025," for an example of the former; and Manuel Castells, *The Power of Identity*, vol. 2 of *The Information Age: Economy, Society, and Culture* (Malden, Mass.: Blackwell, 1997), as an instance of the latter.

45. For a more thorough discussion, see Arif Dirlik, "Place-Based Imagination: Globalism and the Politics of Place," *Review* 22, no. 2 (1999):151–87. See also a related symposium on the question of place, Arif Dirlik, "Globalism and the Politics of Place, *Development* 41, no. 2 (June 1998): 7–13. The term "invasion of the life-world," is Jürgen Habermas's.

46. This, too, is a demand that has acquired audibility globally with globalization. References to works devoted to the subject are many; some of them may be found in the bibliography of Dirlik, "Place-Based Imagination." See also Michael H. Shuman, *Going Local: Creating Self-Reliant Communities in a Global Age* (New York: Free Press, 1998), for a recent and thoughtfully argued example.

7

BRINGING HISTORY BACK IN: OF DIASPORAS,

HYBRIDITIES, PLACES, AND HISTORIES

At a conference in Singapore in December 1997, a U.S. anthropologist gave a presentation on the Chinese diaspora or, as she preferred it, Chinese transnationality. When she was finished, a well-known Singapore sociologist stood up to object to her conceptualization, declaiming that he was a Singaporean, not a diasporic or transnational and adding for good measure that American scholars were always imposing identities of that kind on other people. He was joined by a distinguished historian of Chinese Overseas, who added that rather than impose diasporic identity on all Chinese Overseas, it would be much more productive to think of them in terms of recent migrants, not yet settled in their places of arrival, and classes who were in a position to exploit or benefit from transnationality. For both scholars, the issue was not one of Singapore nationalism, or an "essentialized" Singapore identity (Singapore prides itself in many ways on being a multicultural society), but a place-based identity against a transnational or diasporic one.[1]

Discussions of diasporas or diasporic identities in much of contemporary cultural criticism focus on the problematic of national identity or the necessity of accommodating migrant cultures. The concept of diaspora or diasporic identity serves well when it comes to deconstructing claims to national cultural homogeneity. It is also important in expanding the horizon of cultural difference and challenging cultural hegemony at a time when the accommodation of cultural difference may be more urgent than ever in the face of the proliferating transnational motions of people. It may be because of the urgency of these issues that relatively less attention has been paid to problems presented by notions of diaspora and diasporic identity, especially the quite serious possibility that they may reproduce the very homogenizations and dichotomies that they are intended to overcome. I will take up these problems in this chapter, with some attention to the question of hybridity, which has acquired considerable prominence with the emergence of a diasporic consciousness. As my goal is to stimulate questions on various aspects of diasporas, I present my thoughts as a series of reflections, without too much effort to achieve a tight coherence of argument. If diasporas are my point of departure, I rest my reflections on places and place consciousness, which I offer as a counterpoint to globalism and diasporas. While on occasion I may refer to other groups, my concern here is mainly with Chinese populations in motion, and it is those populations that I draw on for purposes of illustration.

The reconceptualization of Chinese Overseas in terms of diaspora or transnationality responds to a real situation: the reconfiguration of migrant societies and their political and cultural orientations. But diaspora and transnationality as concepts are also discursive or, perhaps more appropriately, imaginary; not only do they have normative implications, but they also articulate—in a very Foucauldian sense—relations of power within populations so depicted, as well as in their relationship to societies of origin and arrival.[2] Diaspora discourse has an undeniable appeal in the critical possibilities it offers against assumptions of national cultural homogeneity, which historically has resulted in the denial of full cultural (and political) citizenship to those who resisted assimilation into the dominant conceptualizations of national culture, were refused entry into it, or whose cultural complexity could not be contained easily within a single conception of national culture. Taking their cue from Paul Gilroy's concept of "double consciousness" with reference to the African diaspora, Ong and Nonini write of Chinese in diaspora that "they face many directions at once—toward China, other Asian countries, and the West—with multiple perspectives on modernities, perspectives often gained at great cost through their passage via itineraries marked by sojourning, absence, nostalgia, and at times exile and loss."[3]

This critical appeal, however, also disguises the possibility that diasporic notions of culture, if employed without due regard to the social and political complexities of so-called diasporic populations, may issue in reifications of their own, opening the way to new forms of cultural domination, manipulation, and commodification. To quote Ong and Nonini once again, "there is nothing intrinsically liberating about diasporic cultures."[4] In pursuit of their interests, diasporic Chinese elites have collaborated with despotic political regimes, pursued exploitative practices of their own, and utilized the notion of "Chineseness" as a cover for their own class interests. The danger of reification is implicit in a contemporary culturalism that easily loses sight of the distinction between recognizing autonomy to culture as a realm of analysis and the rendering of culture into a self-sufficient explanation for all aspects of life, therefore rendering culture once again into an off-ground phenomenon available to exploitation for a multiplicity of purposes. Moreover, since much of the discussion of culture and cultural identity is mediated by the new discipline of "cultural studies," there has been a tendency to carry questions and findings concerning one group of people to all groups similarly placed, in effect erasing considerable differences in the experiences of different populations through the universalization of the language of cultural studies. In either case, the erasure is the erasure of the social relations that configure difference within and between groups and, with them, of historicity.

Ambiguities in the discourses on diasporas and related discourses of hybridity warrant some caution concerning projects of overcoming "binarisms." While there is little question about the desirability of such projects where they seek to overcome debilitating (and worse) divisions between ethnicities, genders, et cetera, it is also important to note that they may also serve as ideological covers for proliferating divisions in the contemporary world, especially the new forms of class divisions that accompany the unprecedented concentrations of wealth within nations and globally. It is important, in any case, not to take such projects at face value, but to distinguish progressive efforts to overcome divisions from their manipulation in the service of new forms of power.

◆

The problems presented by diaspora discourse may be illustrated through the recent case of John Huang, the Chinese American fund-raiser for the Democratic National Committee. When Huang was charged with corruption on the grounds that he raised funds from foreign sources, the Democratic National Committee proceeded immediately to canvass all contributors with Chinese names to ascertain whether or not they were foreigners, turning a run-of-the-mill case of political corruption into a racial issue. The committee's action reactivated the long-standing assumption that anyone with a Chinese name might in all probability be foreign, reaffirming implicitly that a Chinese name was the marker of racial foreignness. What followed may not have been entirely novel but seemed quite logical nevertheless in terms of contemporary diasporic "networks" (perhaps more appropriately in this case, "webs"). John Huang's connections to the Riady family in Indonesia, which surfaced quickly not only underlined the probable foreignness of Chinese contributors but also suggested further connections between Chinese Americans and other Chinese Overseas that seemed to be confirmed by revelations that several other Chinese American fund-raisers or contributors had ties to Chinese in South and Southeast Asia. As these overseas Chinese had business connections in the People's Republic of China, before long a petty corruption case was to turn into a case of possible conspiracy that extended from Beijing, through Chinese Overseas, to Chinese Americans.[5]

This linking of Chinese Americans to diasporic Chinese and the government in Beijing has provoked charges of racism among Asian Americans and their many sympathizers. Racism is there, to be sure. But is this racism simply an extension of the historical racism against Asian Americans, or does it represent something new? If it is something new, is it possible that at least some Asian Americans have been complicit in producing a new kind of racist discourse? The question is fraught with difficulties, chief among them shifting responsibility to the victim, but it must be raised nevertheless. My goal in raising the question is not to erase racism but to underline the unprecedented depth to which race and ethnicity have become principles of politics, not just in the United States but globally. If the Democratic National Committee used Chinese names as markers of racial foreignness, is it possible that the government in China, or some Chinese transnational looking for recruits, might do the same? Immigration and Naturalization Service agents at the U.S.-Mexican border, upon finding out the Turkish origins of my name, have stopped me for a special search. On account of the same name, I have been approached by Turkish "grassroots" organizations mobilizing against condemnations of Turkey for its activities against the Kurds or its refusal to acknowledge the Armenian massacres. The name does bring a burden, but the burden is the ethnicization and racialization of politics that is open to all for exploitation.

The new consciousness of diaspora and diasporic identity cutting across national boundaries is at least one significant factor in this racialization of politics in its current phase. The linking of John Huang, Chinese Overseas, and the Beijing government, I would like to suggest here, has been facilitated by the new discourse on the Chinese diaspora, which, in reifying Chineseness, has created fertile ground for nourishing a new racism. The idea of diaspora is responsible in the first place for abolishing the difference between Chinese Americans and Chinese elsewhere (including in China). In response to a legacy of discrimination against Chinese Americans, which made them hesitant even to acknowledge their ties to China and other Chinese, some Chinese Americans and their sympathizers have been all too anxious to reaffirm such ties, in turn suppressing the cultural differences arising from the different historical trajectories of different Chinese populations scattered around the world. The antiassimilationist mood (expressed most fervently in liberal "multiculturalism") itself has contributed in no small measure to such cultural reification by a metonymic reduction of the culture of the Other to "representative" ethnographic elements or texts divorced from all social and historical context, which may then serve purposes of self-representation by the diasporic population or self-congratulatory consumption in the carnivals of the society at large. While in much of contemporary diaspora discourse the preferred term for representing difference is "culture," the question of culture, to quote Gilroy, is "almost biologized by its proximity to 'race.'"[6] *Because* of the fact that the very phenomenon of diaspora has produced a multiplicity of Chinese cultures, the affirmation of "Chineseness" may be sustained only by recourse to a common origin, or descent, that persists in spite of widely different historical trajectories, resulting in the elevation of ethnicity and race over all the other factors—often divisive—that have gone into the shaping of Chinese populations and their cultures. Diasporic identity in its reification does not overcome the racial prejudices of earlier assumptions of national cultural homogeneity but in many ways follows a similar logic, now at the level not of nations but of off-ground "transnations." The "children of the Yellow Emperor" may be all the more of a racial category for having abandoned its ties to the political category of the nation.

Let me add a note of clarification here. In taking a critical stance toward the notion of diaspora, I am not suggesting that Chinese Americans should therefore renounce ties to China or other Chinese Overseas. The question is how these ties are conceived and articulated, and whether or not they erase very significant historical differences among the Chinese populations in different locations around the globe. I will illustrate again by reference to the John Huang case. A very important part was played in publicizing the case by Professor Ling-chi Wang of the University of California at Berkeley, who alerted and informed many of us about the case by gathering and electronically disseminating information on the case. Over the past year, Professor Wang's communications have ranged widely from the John Huang case to the election of Chinese officials around the country, from defense of the People's Republic of China against various allegations to reportage on anti-Chinese activity in Southeast Asia. Now a discursive field that covers all these elements appears at first sight to differ little from what I have been calling diaspora discourse, motivated as it is by bringing together information on Chinese regardless of place. What disrupts this field, however, is its unwavering focus on concrete problems of its immediate environment. Professor Wang was quick from the beginning to distance Asian Americans from "foreign money," drawing a national boundary between Chinese here and Chinese donors of campaign funds from Southeast Asia.[7] The communications throughout have stressed issues of class and community, distinguishing community interests of Chinese Americans from the activities of transnationally oriented diasporic Chinese with economic and political interests of their own. And this electronic discourse has remained focused throughout on the issue of campaign finance reform in the United States, as campaign corruption rather than the color of money has been defined as the basic problem. In other words, the discourse, while ranging transnationally, has been quite grounded in its immediate environment. This, I think, is what distinguishes it from the diaspora discourse in the way I understand that term here.

I will return to this issue of "groundedness" later in this chapter. First, I will take a brief look at two products of this diasporic discourse in the realm of culture that are on the surface quite antithetical but that may also reinforce one another in surprising ways: the reification of Chineseness by erasure of the boundaries among different Chinese populations, and the contrary move to break down such reification through the notion of hybridity.

◆

In its failure to specify its own location vis-à-vis the hegemonic, self-serving, and often financially lucrative reification of Chineseness in the political economy of transnationalism, critical diaspora discourse itself has fallen prey to the manipulation and commodification made possible by cultural reification and contributes to the foregrounding of ethnicity and race in contemporary political and cultural thinking. There has been a tendency in recent scholarship, publishing, and arts and literature, for instance, to abolish the difference between Asians and Asian Americans. In scholarship, contrary to an earlier refusal of Asian studies specialists to have anything to do with Asian American studies, there have been calls recently to integrate Asian American studies into Asian studies, which partly reflects the increased prominence of trans-Pacific population flows but also suggests the increasingly lucrative promise of reorienting Asian American studies in that direction. Publishers' catalogues, especially those devoted to "multiculturalism" and ethnic relations, freely blend Asian with Asian American themes, and it is not rare to see these days a catalogue in which *Woman Warrior* is placed right next to *The Dream of the Red Chamber*. A film series on "Asian American film" at the University of North Carolina mysteriously includes many more films from Asia than from Asian America, either because of the imaginary China of its China specialist organizer, or to increase the appeal of the series. The reason may not matter much, however, as the ideological effect is the same.

Moreover, and more fundamentally, within the context of flourishing Pacific economies (at least until very recently), some Asian Americans—most notably Chinese Americans—have been assigned the role of "bridges" to Asia, which role they have assumed readily for its lucrative promises. The metaphor of bridge as a depiction of Asian Americans is not quite novel. In a recent dissertation that analyzes with sensitivity Asian Americans' relationship to the Chicago School of Sociology, Henry Yu argues that in their association with the Chicago sociologists, second-generation Asian Americans internalized an image of themselves as bridges between American society and societies of origin in Asia, advantageously placed to serve as cultural interpreters.[8] The advantage, however, came at a high price. The condition for successful service as bridges between cultures was marginality; it was their status as "marginal men" who existed between two societies without belonging fully to either that enabled the status of cultural interpreter. As one such "marginal man," Kazuo Kawai, wrote:

My decision to be an interpreter has improved my relations with both races. I am happy because I don't try to be a poor imitation of an American. I am happy because I don't vainly try to be a poor imitation of a genuine Japanese. I am simply what I am. I don't try to imitate either, so I am never disappointed when I find myself excluded from either side.[9]

Kawai, of course, was not qualified to be a cultural interpreter in any serious sense of the term. He was Japanese by birth but American by culture, and his claims to access to Japanese culture were forced on him by alienation from American society, which excluded him, necessitating an imaginary affinity with his parents' society of origin. The notion that someone who did not belong to either society was for that very reason qualified to serve as cultural interpreter between the two glossed over fundamental problems of cultural orientation, which seems to have escaped both Kawai and his Chicago School mentors. Be that as it may, what is important here is that the metaphor of bridge between two societies was ultimately a product of alienation from a society that refused to recognize him as anything but a foreigner.

While alienation may not be the case in any obvious way presently, the metaphor of bridge nevertheless continues to invoke the foreignness of Asian Americans. Much more so than in the case of those like Kawai, a diasporic identification may be a matter of choice rather than necessity. Contemporary bridges, moreover, are most prominently economic brokers rather than cultural interpreters. Nevertheless, there is a racialization at work when diasporic populations, regardless of their widely different cultural trajectories internally, are expected to bridge the gap between places of arrival and places of origin by virtue of presumed cultural legacies that are more imagined than real. Thus Ronnie C. Chan, the chairman of the Hang Lung Development Group, a Hong Kong real estate company, urges Chinese Americans in Hawaii to become "bi-cultural" so as to serve as bridges between Chinese and U.S. business, telling them that, "We all need our cultural roots, but put them away for a while and become truly bi-cultural." Roots in this case take precedence over history, so that Chan urges Chinese Americans not to learn to be Chinese again but to learn to be Americans![10]

The economic emergence of Chinese populations across the Pacific may be the single most important factor in the cultural rehomogenization of Chineseness. The most significant by-product of this economic emergence may be the recent Confucian revival, which attributes the economic success of Chinese (in some versions also of Japanese and Koreans), without regard to time or place, to the persistence of "Confucian values." Those values were viewed earlier as obstacles to capitalism, but they have been rendered now into the source of everything from economic development to the production of "model minorities." As

I have discussed this problem extensively elsewhere, I will simply note here that this so-called Confucian revival reproduces within a context of transnationality the most egregious prejudices of Orientalism.[11] It is also a transnational product itself, for its emergence in the late 1970s and early 1980s involved, at least by way of intertextual collusion, experts on Chinese philosophy, U.S. futurologists, and authoritarian regimes in East and Southeast Asia. According to its more enthusiastic proponents, Confucian values of thrift, diligence, educational achievement, family loyalty, discipline, harmony, obedience to authority—a list that reads like a dream list of the ideal worker or employee—have been responsible for the unquestioning commitment of Chinese (and East Asian) populations to capitalist development. In the more socially based versions of the argument, Confucian values owe their persistence to the central importance throughout Chinese societies of kinship and pseudo-kinship ties, themselves products of the social diffusion of Confucian values: the networks of *guanxi* that distinguish the socially oriented capitalism of the Chinese from individualistic and conflict-ridden "Western" capitalism. As with the Confucian argument, there is little sense of time and place in these social arguments, as if social relations and networks were not subject to change and fluctuation. The net result is a portrayal, where, networked through *guanxi* and driven by Confucianism, Chinese around the world are rendered into a "tribe," in the words of the Pacific visionary Joel Kotkin, committed to a relentless search for wealth. These same networks, needless to say, also make Chinese into ideal bridges with Asia.

Some of this argumentation, where it is promoted by Chinese scholars or leaders, no doubt draws upon a newfound sense of economic power and presence to reassert a Chinese identity against the century-old cultural hegemony of Eurocentrism that utilizes earlier Orientalist representations to turn them against claims of Euro-American superiority. Nevertheless, they have been attached most prominently to questions of economic success, with a consequent commodification not only of the so-called Confucian values but also of Chinese. To quote from a recent piece by the same Joel Kotkin, "With their cultural, linguistic, and family ties to China, Chinese-American entrepreneurs like [Henry Y.] Hwang are proving to be America's secret weapon in recapturing a predominant economic role in the world's most populous nation."[12] Even putting aside the problematic question of "cultural and linguistic ties to China" on the part of many Chinese Americans, it may not be very far from Kotkin's portrayal of Chinese Americans as American economic moles in China to William Safire's depiction of John Huang as a Chinese political mole in Washington, D.C.

The attitudes that lie at the root of these recent tendencies are not the less productive of racism for being produced by, or sympathetic to, Chinese and other Asian populations. They are also quite unstable, in that the sympathy itself may be subject to significant fluctuation, on occasion even turning into its opposite. This has happened to some extent with the recent so-called economic meltdown in Asia, with which "Asian values," among them Confucianism, once again lost their luster. It turns out now that "Asian values" have been responsible for creating a corrupt "crony capitalism" that inevitably led to economic breakdown.

Chinese populations are no less divided by class, gender, ethnic, and place differences than other populations. Not the least among those differences are differences of place and history. Reification of diaspora erases, or at the least blurs, such differences. As Appadurai has written of "ethnoscapes":

> the central paradox of ethnic politics in today's world is that primordia (whether of language or skin color or neighborhood or kinship) have become globalized. That is, sentiments whose greatest force is their ability to ignite intimacy into a political sentiment and turn locality into a staging ground for identity, have become spread over vast and irregular spaces as groups move, yet stay linked to one another through sophisticated media capabilities. This is not to deny that such primordia are often the product of invented traditions or retrospective affiliations, but to emphasize that because of the disjunctive and unstable interaction of commerce, media, national policies and consumer fantasies, ethnicity, once a genie contained in the bottle of some sort of locality (however large), has now become a global force.[13]

While the globalization of ethnicity is no doubt bound up with abstract forces that contribute to global restructurations, it is important nevertheless to draw attention to agencies engaged actively in inventing traditions and producing retrospective affiliations. If differences of history and place are erased by the shifting of attention to a general category of diaspora (which I take to be equivalent to Appadurai's "ethnoscapes"), it is necessary to raise the question of whom such erasure serves. There is no reason to suppose that the government in Beijing (or, for that matter, Taiwan) is any more reluctant than the government in Washington or U.S. transnational corporations to use diasporic Chinese for its own purposes. On the other hand, both from a political and an economic perspective, some diasporic Chinese are obviously of greater use than others and in turn benefit from the erasure of differences among Chinese, which enable them to speak for all Chinese.[14] Reconceptualization of Chinese populations in terms of diasporas, in other words, serves economic and political class interests (it is not accidental that the Chinese American John Huang was connected with the Riady family, which made him useful in a number of ways).

♦

The concept of hybridity is intended to destabilize cultural identities of all kinds, and at least on the surface, it provides a clear alternative to the reification of identity described above. Popularized through the works of influential theorists such as Stuart Hall, Paul Gilroy, Homi Bhabha, and Edward Soja, among others, hybridity is an important keyword of contemporary cultural studies. Judging by the pervasiveness of the term in discussions of identity, hybridity also has come to define the self-identification of intellectuals around the world, in effect becoming a social force of sorts. In the field of Asian American studies, Lisa Lowe, through an influential article, has been a prominent proponent.[15] Hybridity, too, has a lineage in its application to Asian Americans, which may not be very surprising given its kinship with marginality. While some Asian Americans may have found a resource for hope in their marginality or hybridity, others viewed it as an undesirable condition to be overcome. Rose Hum Lee, another product of the Chicago School, observed in a discussion of the "marginal man" that "when the 'cultural gaps' are closed . . . the cultural hybrid no longer poses a problem to himself and others. This is brought about by the processes of acculturation and assimilation."[16]

The contemporary idea of hybridity is in a basic way quite the opposite of what Rose Hum Lee had in mind. Hybridity (along with associated terms such as "in-betweenness" and "third space") is intended to challenge the homogenization and essentialization of cultural identity, most important in the present context, ethnic, national. and racial identity. (It has also been influential in discussions of gender and class identity, especially the former.) Its goal is to undermine the assumption that boundaries may be drawn around nationality, ethnicity, and race on the grounds of cultural homogeneity. What marks it as diasporic is that the argument is directed not only against the society of arrival, where the dominant culture demands assimilation of the migrant for full political and cultural citizenship, but also against the society of origin, which likewise denies political and cultural citizenship to the migrant on the grounds that emigration is inevitably accompanied by distancing and degeneration from the culture of origin. Thus placed at the margins of two societies, the migrant is denied cultural identity and autonomy. Hybridity in contemporary culture is in a fundamental sense a rebellion of those who are culturally dispossessed, or who feel culturally dispossessed, who not only assert hybridity as an autonomous source of identity but go further to challenge the cultural claims of the centers of power.

There is no doubt much that is radical in the challenge. And it is not difficult to see why the notion of hybridity should be appealing at a time of proliferation of the culturally dispossessed. Hybridity is appealing for a different, more intellectual, reason. Its breakdown not just of political and cultural entities but also of the categories of social and cultural analysis releases the imagination to conceive the world in new ways. This has been most persuasively argued recently by Edward Soja, who locates "third space" not just in between societies but between society and imagination, where the imaginary may claim as much reality as the real of conventional social science.[17]

Why then should hybridity also be a deeply problematic concept, especially in its social and political implications, and how could it reinforce the reification of identity when its intention is exactly the opposite? It is problematic, I think, because in its vagueness it is available for appropriation for diverse causes, including highly reactionary and exploitative ones. It reinforces the reification of identity not only because the metaphor of hybridity invokes the possibility of uncontaminated identities but also because such identities are essential to the discourse on hybridity as its dialogical Other. The discourse of hybridity is a response to racial, ethnic, and national divisions, but it is sustained in turn by foregrounding race, ethnicity, and nation in problems of culture and politics.

Apparently transparent, hybridity is in actuality quite an elusive concept that does not illuminate but rather renders invisible the situations to which it is applied—not by concealing them, but by blurring distinctions among widely different situations. Pnina Werbner has observed as a "paradox" of the fascination with hybridity that it "is celebrated as powerfully interruptive and yet theorized as commonplace and pervasive."[18] If hybridity is indeed pervasive, it is in and of itself meaningless—if everything is hybrid, then there is no need for a special category of hybrid—and can derive meaning only from the concrete historical and structural locations that produce it. While some theorists of hybridity such as Paul Gilroy, Stuart Hall, and Gayatri Spivak have been attentive to distinguishing hybridities historically and structurally, others such as Homi Bhabha and Edward Soja have rendered hybridity (and its associated concepts of third space and in-betweenness) into abstractions with no identifiable locations. It is my impression that in recent years the use of the concept has unfolded in the latter direction, as hybridity has been universalized in its application, to be rendered into a "universal standardization," as Feroza Jussawalla puts it, gaining in abstraction but progressively deprived of meaning.[19] The off-grounding of hybridity no doubt derives additional force from the postmodern but especially postcolonial suspicion of history and structures; the demand to historicize hybridity appears from this perspective to imprison the concept within the very categorical prejudices it is intended to overcome.

This may indeed be the case. After all, theorists such as Bhabha and Soja do not intend hybridity or third space in a physical descriptive sense but rather to disrupt the hegemony of social and historical categories and to overcome binary modes of thinking. On the other hand, there is an elision in almost all discussion of hybridity between hybridity as a strategically disruptive idea, operating at the level of epistemology, and hybridity as an articulation of an actual human condition. And it is this elision that may account for the elusiveness and opaqueness of the term. Thus Katharyne Mitchell is quite correct, I think, to inquire of Bhabha's boundary-crossings, "what are the actual physical spaces in which these boundaries are crossed and erased?" or to point out with regard to Soja's liberating claims for third space that "this space is able to accomplish all these marvelous things, precisely because it does not exist."[20] As I noted above, hybridity no longer appears as an intellectual or psychological stratagem but seems to be pervasive in certain quarters, mostly among intellectuals, as a self-definition, which makes it into a social and ideological force. What is not clear is whether the hybrid is "everyman" (what Werbner observes to be the commonplaceness of hybridity), or "nowhereman" (the stranger, as Bauman puts it, who disrupts the existing order of things).[21] The confounding of the two has led to a situation where the promotion of hybridity, out of political correctness or universal standardization, has taken the form of an intellectual and ethical imperative that will brook no alternative, as when Iain Chambers states, "We are drawn beyond ideas of nation, nationalism and national cultures, into a post-colonial set of realities, and a mode of critical thinking that is forced to rewrite the very grammar and language of modern thought in directing attention beyond the patriarchal boundaries of Eurocentric concerns and its presumptive 'universalism.'"[22] Hybridity is no longer disruptive or just descriptive, but prescriptive; if you are not hybrid, you are a Eurocentric patriarch!

Hybridity, abstracted from its social-historical moorings for critical purposes, but then returned to society as an abstraction, most importantly blurs, in the name of difference, significant distinctions between different differences. Hybridity reduces all complexity to a "statement of mixture,"[23] as if the specific character of what is being mixed (from class to gender to ethnicity and race) did not matter—partly stemming from its originary assumptions that all "binarisms" are equally undesirable, regardless of context. It also reads into all mixtures a state of hybridity, disregarding the possibility that mixtures and hybridization may produce new identities. As Jussawalla puts it, "despite mixing and merging, like a martini in a cocktail shaker, the [South Asian] writers do not become hybrids or 'mongrels,' and we do not need a median point along the 'scale' or 'cline' of authenticity to alienation indicating 'hybridity.'"[24] Indeed, hybridity in its abstraction serves not to illuminate but to disguise social inequality and exploitation by reducing to a state of hybridity all who may be considered "marginal," covering up the fact that there is a great deal of difference between different marginalities: between, say, a well-placed social elite hybridized and marginalized ethnically and members of the same ethnicity further incapacitated by their class and gender locations. We have had a good illustration of this only recently, in the flare-up of anti-Chinese violence in Indonesia, which the ordinary Chinese have to deal with as best as they can, while the wealthy Chinese plan refuges in western Australia, in the same spaces occupied by Indonesian generals![25] Given such inequality, the claims to undifferentiated marginality and hybridity on the part of the elite confounds the culturally dispossessed with the culturally privileged, who travel with ease across cultural spaces. The result is the appropriation by the elite of the margins, making hybridity available as a tool in intraelite competition but further erasing the concerns of the truly marginal. As Friedman puts it,

> hybrids and hybridisation theorists are products of a group that self-identifies and/or identifies the world in such terms, not as a result of ethnographic understanding, but as an act of self-definition—indeed, of self-essentialising—which becomes definition for others via the forces of socialisation inherent in the structures of power that such groups occupy: intellectuals close to the media; the media intelligentsia itself; in a certain sense, all those who can afford a cosmopolitan identity.[26]

The "unmooring" (in Mitchell's term) of hybridity from concrete social-historical referents also invites by the back door the very cultural essentializations that it has been intended to overcome, which is the second problem with hybridity. While it may be possible to speak of the hybridization of hybridity, as I will suggest below, most writing on hybridity ignores this possibility, perhaps because the acknowledgment of hybridity as a perennial condition would weaken considerably, or even render irrelevant, the claims made for hybridity, which is the paradox posed by Werbner. As a result, the discourse of hybridity is sustained by a tacit premise, reinforced by its claims to offer a radical alternative, of the purity of hybridity's constituent moments. "Hybridity," Friedman states, "is founded on the metaphor of purity."[27] Referring specifically to Bhabha's use of hybridity, Nira Yuval-Davis writes that "it may interpolate essentialism through the back door—that the old 'multiculturalist' essentialist and homogenising constructions of collectivities are attributed to the homogeneous collectivities from which the 'hybrids' have emerged, thus replacing the mythical image of a society as a 'melting-pot' with the mythical image of society as a 'mixed salad.'"[28] Hybridity taken out of history also dehistoricizes the identities that constitute hybridity, which, if it does not necessarily rest on an assumption of purity, nevertheless leaves unquestioned what these identities might be.

The biological associations of the term contribute further to this underlining of an assumption, if not of purity, then at least of clearly identifiable entities that go into the making of hybridity. In fact the biological notion of hybridity, on the basis of clearly definable identities, even renders hybridity quantifiable; this is quite visible in the human realm in the prolific racial categories employed in nineteenth-century Latin America, still alive in the United States in "the blood quantum" used to define the authenticity of Amerindians.[29]

While such quantification would be difficult to transfer to the realm of culture, it does point to serious questions that are elided in discussions of hybridity, chief among them degrees of hybridity: are all hybrids equally hybrid? There are other questions as well. Robert Young has documented the centrality historically of biological assumptions in the conceptualization of hybridity, which persist in contemporary usages of hybridity if only as traces and as inescapable reminders of the biological associations of the term, as with the author who remarked to Jussawalla that "hybridity smacks of biological blending of plants."[30] While it is not my intention in the slightest to ascribe a racial intention to those who speak of cultural hybridity, it is nevertheless unavoidable that the use of a biological term as a metaphor for culture and society is pregnant with the possibility of confounding cultural, social, and political with racial entities—especially where the term is divorced from its historical and structural referents. Such is the case, I suggested above, with the reified concept of diaspora, where discussions of culture slip easily into identification by descent.

While hybridity could easily refer to in-betweens other than national, ethnic, or racial ones, such as the in-betweens of class and gender, it is remarkable that most discussions of hybridity revolve around the former categories. The mutual articulation of categories of gender, class, and race have been present all along as a basic concern in recent discussions of hybridity;[31] it is remarkable nevertheless that questions of race and ethnicity—often conflated—overshadow all others. This may or may not be a consequence of the logic of hybridity as biological concept. I am inclined to think, however, that the discourse on hybridity, while it may refuse to engage the limitations of its historical and social context, is itself subject to the forces of that context. Within a social and historical context where identity claims are very much alive, and proliferating, the condition of hybridity itself is quite unstable. The benign reading of hybridity perceives in such instability the possibility of opening up to the world. That may well be the case. But it is staked too much on a libertarian faith in the autonomy of the hybrid self, which can negotiate its identity at will in a marketplace of equals, as it were. There is another possibility as well: oscillation between the identities out of which hybridity is constructed and fragmentation into one or another of those identities in response to the pressures of everyday life. How else to explain the simultaneous breakdown and proliferation of identities in the contemporary world? There are also the personal stakes involved. It is worth pondering Jussawalla's observation, which may be familiar from the everyday circumstances of cultural encounters even within academia, "that true hybridity cannot be achieved because those who would most speak for hybridity most want to retain their essentialisms—the natives, the insiders of cultural studies, those who feel they best represent the post-modern condition and can speak for it."[32] Hybridity may be like interdisciplinarity in academia, which everyone lauds but no one really wants, unless it can be shaped according to their disciplinary orientations. It is difficult to avoid the impression that more often than not, the motivation underlying the promotion of hybridity is to center the marginal and render visible cultural identities that have been rendered invisible by coercive or hegemonic suppression. The quite apparent predicament here is how to achieve this quite significant and worthwhile goal without slippage into the reification of the marginalized, as in the case of the diasporic identity I discussed above; to achieve genuine dialogue, rather than merely assert one "essentialism" against another, especially under circumstances of unequal power.

With so much uncertainty over the content of the concept, it is not surprising that the political implications of hybridity in action should be equally indeterminate or that hybridity should lend itself to a variety of politics, ranging from the radical to the reactionary. Hybridity in and of itself is not a marker of any kind of politics but a deconstructive strategy that may be utilized for different political ends. To a bell hooks, Stuart Hall, Homi Bhabha, or Edward Soja hybridity may be a significant means to create new kinds of radical political alliances by opening up and articulating to one another categories of race, class, and gender. To a John Huang, or to the Hong Kong investors in Vancouver of whom Mitchell writes, hybridity is a means to creating alliances (bridges) between different states or between national and diasporic capital, the consequence if not the intention of which is to erase those radical alliances. As Mitchell writes,

> The overuse of abstract metaphors, particularly within frameworks which foreground psychoanalytic approaches, often leads to thorny problems of fetishization. As concepts such as hybridity become disarticulated from the historically shaped political and economic relations in which identities and narratives of nation unfold, they take on a life and trajectory of their own making. Second and third readings, borrowings, interventions, elaborations-all can contribute to conceptualizations that are not only removed from the social relations of everyday life, but which also, because of this very abstraction, become ripe for appropriation. The disingenuous move of the 'third space' is to occupy a position 'beyond' space and time, and beyond the situated practices of place and the lived experience of history. The space thus satisfyingly transcends the kind of essentializing locations that characterize a certain branch of work in historical materialism and feminism. But without context, this 'in-between' space risks becoming a mobile reactionary space, rather than a traveling site of resistance.[33]

Abstraction is one problem, as in its very divorce from its own social and historical locations, hybridity conceals and contains the differential relationship to power of different hybrids, making the concept available for appropriation by those whose goals are not to promote alternatives to the present but to gain entry into existing spaces of power, further consolidating its domination. What Peter McLaren and Henry Giroux write of postmodern and postcolonial preoccupation with language also applies, I think, to hybridity as discursive liberation:

> As essential as these theoretical forays have been, they often abuse their own insights by focusing on identity at the expense of power. Language in these texts becomes a discursive marker for registering and affirming difference but in doing so often fails to address how they are related within broader networks of domination and exploitation. In part, this may be due to the ahistorical quality of this work. Lacking a historical context, they fail to engage the political projects that characterized older versions of critical pedagogy and end up failing to locate their own politics and its value for larger social, political, and pedagogical struggles.[34]

To engage those political projects, it is necessary, I think, to overcome the anxiety that seems to legitimize an unquestioning commitment to hybridity. anxiety over what Werbner describes as "the bogey word of the human sciences": essentialism.[35] Essentialism is surely one of the most inflated words of contemporary cultural studies. It seems that any admission of identity, including the identity that may be necessary to any articulate form of collective political action, is open to charges of essentialism, so that it is often unclear whether the objection is to essentialism per se or to the politics, in which case essentialism serves as a straw target to discredit the politics.[36] In its extremist logic, such suspicion of essentialism may be resolved only at the level of a libertarian individualism, if even that, since the run-of-the-mill libertarianism also essentializes the subject. Notions of hybridity informed by such extremism rule out any kind of serious radical politics, which requires at least some assumption of commonality, what Gayatri Spivak has described by way of compromise as "strategic essentialism." As bell hooks has written:

> One exciting dimension to cultural studies is the critique of essentialist notions of difference. Yet this critique should not become a means to dismiss differences or an excuse for ignoring the authority of experience. It is often evoked in a manner which suggests that all the ways black people think of ourselves as "different" from whites are really essentialist, and therefore without concrete grounding. This way of thinking threatens the very foundations that make resistance to domination possible.[37]

While an antiessentialist hybridity at its extreme undercuts the possibility of "resistance to domination," no less important is its failure to come to terms with the world as it is, so as to confront its very real challenges. As a commitment to hybridity takes hold of intellectuals, the world at large presently is experiencing a proliferation of identity claims, often in the most obscurantist essentialist guise. It will not do to dismiss this historical phenomenon as an aberration, as some kind of a deviation from normalcy as stipulated by the principles of hybridity, which not only reifies hybridity contrary to its claims to open-endedness but also shows how much the contemporary discourse of intellectuals may be in need of a reality check. What needs urgent confrontation is whether or not hybridity and essentialism generate one another.

I will conclude this discussion of hybridity by returning to the paradox posed by Werbner: if hybridity is indeed a condition of everyday life, what is radical about it? One possible answer has been suggested by Robert Young in his invocation of Bakhtin's idea of hybridity in the novel.[38] According to Young, Bakhtin's idea of hybridity was itself hybrid. Bakhtin referred to two kinds of hybridity, unconscious "organic hybridity" and "intentional hybridity." As Bakhtin put it:

> Unintentional, unconscious hybridization is one of the most important modes in the historical life and evolution of all languages. We may even say that language and languages change historically primarily by hybridization, by means of a mixing of various 'languages' co-existing within the boundaries of a single dialect, a single national language language, a single branch, a single group of different branches, in the historical as well as paleontological past of languages.[39]

On the other hand,

> The image of a language conceived as an intentional hybrid is first of all a *conscious hybrid* (as distinct from a historical, organic, obscure language hybrid); an intentional hybrid is precisely the perception of of one language by another language, its illumination by another linguistic consciousness. . . . What is more, an intentional and conscious hybrid is not a mixture of two *impersonal* language consciousnesses (the correlates of two languages) but rather a mixture of two *individualized* language consciousnesses (the correlates of two specific utterances, not merely two languages) and two individual language-intentions as well. . . . In other words, the novelistic hybrid is not only double-voiced and double-accented . . . but is also double-languaged; for in it there are not only . . . two individual consciousnesses, two voices, two accents, as there are two socio-linguistic consciousnesses, two epochs, that, true, are not here unconsciously mixed (as in organic hybrid) but that come together and fight it out on the territory of the utterance.[40]

Bakhtin, Young observes, "is more concerned with a hybridity that has been politicized and made contestatory," rather than hybridity that "remains mute and opaque," for the former is by far the more radical in its consequences.[41] He continues, "Bakhtin's doubled form of hybridity therefore offers a particularly significant model for cultural interaction: an organic hybridity, which will tend towards fusion, in conflict with intentional hybridity, which enables a contestatory activity, a politicized setting of cultural differences against each other dialogically."[42]

If I may revise the vocabulary slightly, it seems to me that "organic hybridity" refers to what we might otherwise call historicity; that language, or in our case, cultural identity, in its historical progress is subject to transformation in the course of daily encounters with different consciousnesses, so that it becomes impossible to speak of a pure, self-enclosed consciousness traveling through time and space untouched by its many encounters. The transformations are, moreover, unarticulated but concrete and specific. Intentional hybridity, on the other hand, is self-conscious and contestatory, bringing out into the open the encounters that remain unarticulated in organic hybridity and confronting them as structural contradictions. It is radical because this very revelation of everyday encounters as contradictions may bring to the surface the relations of inequality and hegemony in everyday life, demanding some kind of resolution.

While this opposition may help explain why hybridity may be both pervasive and radical, it raises other questions. If hybridity is a condition of history, why does it remain silent most of the time, while finding a voice at other times? The question is easier posed than answered, but it seems to me that the articulation as structural opposition of what is lived ordinarily as a condition of life suggests at the least that some kind of sense of empowerment is necessary to even risk the articulation. This may be as much the case with the assertion of cultural hybridity as with class, gender, and ethnic structurations of everyday life.

The thornier, and more immediate, question is whether or not, having found expression in the recognition of structural contradictions, it is possible to resolve those contradictions to return cultural identity to its historicity. The question is crucial, I think. In his reading of Bakhtin, Young tends to overemphasize the conflictual nature of intentional hybridity. While endless contestation and conflict may have a place in the novel or in academia (which I also doubt), it is hardly a desirable condition of everyday life, which requires some coherence and unity. Intentional hybridity is important to Bakhtin in challenging the hegemony of a single voice, but equally important, I think, is Bakhtin's stress on the illumination of one consciousness by another, which binds together the contestants in their very contest, in a "unity of opposites"—reminiscent readily of the dialectical notion of "contradiction," which in many ways is preferable to the term hybridity itself because it allows for the same open-endedness as hybridity while remaining attentive to questions of historicity and concreteness. While intentional hybridity interpreted as conflict may be radical for revealing the inequalities and hegemonies imbedded in everyday life, it also fragments, not just collectivities, but "the dialogical self" itself.

I borrow the latter term from Hubert Hermans and Harry Kempen, who apply Bakhtin's ideas to the study of individual psychology. The authors caution against the confounding of "multiplicity of characters," implicit in the idea of the dialogical self, with the pathological state of "multiple personality." The difference lies in the ability of the multiplicity of characters to engage in a dialogue, rather than speak sequentially, one at a time, unaware of the existence of other characters, as in the case of multiple personality.[43] The goal of the dialogue is to synthesize the self, "to create a field in which the different characters form a community."[44] This mental community, moreover, resonates with the social context of the individual:

> The inside and the outside world function as highly open Systems that have intense transactional relationships. The self, as a highly contextual phenomenon, is bound to cultural and institutional constraints. Dominance relations are not only present in the outside world but, by the intensive transactions between the two, organize also the inside world. . . . [T]he possible array of imaginal positions becomes not only organized but also restricted by the process of institutionalization. . . . [S]ome positions are strongly developed, whereas others are suppressed or even disassociated.[45]

The synthesizing activity takes place in a definite social context, which has a strong presence in the nature of the synthesis achieved. The inquiry into the hybrid or the dialogical self returns us to the social context of the self, without reducing it to the former but underlining nevertheless the crucial importance of concrete circumstances in the shaping of subjectivity. One implication is that even intentional hybridity as a form of subjectivity is subject to organization, a return to the historicity of organic hybridity.

Returning from the self to the collectivity, we may well inquire where this synthesis, this rehistoricization of hybridity, may be achieved most effectively without abandoning the self-consciousness necessary to the nonhegemonic cultural identity, and how. Other questions follow inevitably, most crucial among them, what kind of histories could accommodate the new consciousness, and what kind of social transformation and political projects might produce such histories?

♦

Diasporas do not provide an answer. While the diasporic imaginary is obviously capable of disrupting a world conceived in terms of nations as homogeneous entities, or even transgressing against the borders of nation-states, diasporas themselves may serve as sources of new identities in only the most off-ground, reified sense. Diasporic consciousness has no history; indeed, its claims may be sustained only in negation of history and historicity. This consciousness, whether in its homogenizing or its hybrid forms, may serve the purpose of cultural projects of various kinds; it is much more difficult to imagine what progressive political projects it might produce—unless it is qualified with a consciousness of place.

Criticism of diasporic consciousness need not imply an urge to return to the nation with its colonial, homogenizing, and assimilationist ideology. While recent critiques of the nation have introduced new insights, they often fail to address the question of who stands to benefit most from the erasure of national boundaries. Whatever its colonizing tendencies may be, the nation is still capable, properly controlled from below, of offering protection to those within its boundaries.[46] It is not very surprising, therefore, that those Chinese Americans devoted to social issues and community building should be suspicious of the claims of diasporas or the questioning of national boundaries. In this case, too, place consciousness is a fundamental issue, for it leads to a different conception of the nation, bottom-up rather than top-down.[47]

To raise the question of place is to raise the issue of difference on a whole range of fronts, including those of class, gender, and ethnicity. It is also to raise the question of history in identity. Identity is no less an identity for being historical (is there any other kind?). Contrary to a hegemonic cultural reification or a whimpering preoccupation with the location of "home," which seems to have acquired popularity as an alternative expression of diasporic consciousness, what is important is to enable people to feel at home where they live.[48] This does not require that people abandon their legacies, only that they recognize the historicity of their cultural identities and that those identities are subject to change in the course of historical encounters. In the words of the Indian writer Farrukh Dhondy, "what makes people is not their genes, is not their nostalgia, it's their interactions of daily existence."[49]

The historicity of identity is by no means transparent, since history itself makes sense in terms of its social locations. One of the prominent phenomena of our times is the fragmentation of history into a number of seemingly irreconcilable spaces, most importantly ethnic spaces. The proliferation of histories that have no apparent connections to one another, or that consciously repudiate such connections, has led to the substitution for history of heritage, as David Lowenthal puts it, or more pessimistically, a condition of "schizophrenic nominalism," in Fredric Jameson's words, that has deprived history of all temporal and spatial meaning.[50]

Such negative evaluations stem at least partially from the breakdown of a Eurocentric temporality that provided coherence, but only at the cost of repressing histories other than its own. The breakdown of history may be viewed, from a less pessimistic perspective, as the assault on a hegemonic history of the previously repressed, who have now returned to visibility to demand a presence for themselves. The challenge is how to create new unities out of this fragmentation, which may be a precondition for achieving a more democratic unity to transcend an earlier illusion of unity that could be sustained only through a hegemonic history. A further, and crucial, question is where to locate this new history or histories. The effort no doubt has to proceed at more than one location; but one location that is indispensable, I think, is place.

Diasporas are dispersals from some remembered homeland, from some concrete place, which after the fact is conceived in terms of the nation (at least over the last century), although concrete places of origin retain their visibility even in their incorporation into the language of the nation or of diaspora. The dispersed also land in concrete places in the host society, which, too, is captured in national terms, even if the very fact of diaspora disturbs efforts to define nation and national culture. Ling-chi Wang tells us that one Chinese metaphor for the diasporic condition is "growing roots where landed" (*luodi shenggen*).[51] While a prejudice for the nation makes it possible to speak of "national soil" and demands assimilation to some "national culture," rootedness as a metaphor points inevitably to concrete places that belie easy assumptions of the homogeneity of national soil or culture. Kathleen Neil Conzen writes of German immigrants to the United States that "as change occurred, it could proceed without the kinds of qualitative shifts implied by the familiar notions of acculturation and assimilation. Culture was more strongly localized—naturalized in the literal botanical sense of the term—than it was ethnicized, and the structures of everyday life, rather than being assimilated to those of some broader element within American society, responded to the transforming pressures of modern life on a parallel trajectory of their own."[52] The statement points to both the concrete place-basedness and the historicity of diasporic identity. James Clifford uses the metaphor of "routes" to capture the spatiotemporality of cultural identity; I will describe it simply as "historical trajectory through places."[53] Encounters in places traversed involve both forgetting and new acquisitions. The past is not erased, therefore, but rewritten. Similarly, the new acquisitions do not imply disappearance into the new environment but rather the proliferation of future possibilities.

What attention to place suggests is the historicity of identity. The "assimilation theory" to which Conzen objects presupposed dehistoricized and placeless notions of culture; assimilation implied motion from one to the other.[54] One could not be both Chinese and American but had to move from being Chinese (whatever that might mean) to being American (whatever that might mean); hence failure to become "fully American" could produce such notions as "dual personality," which precluded being American, as well as suggesting that such an identity represented the degeneration of the components out of which it was formed. The very formulation of the problem precluded what from our vantage point would seem to be an obvious answer: that it is possible to be Chinese without being like other Chinese, and it is possible to be an American without being like other Americans. In either case the history traversed makes a crucial difference in the formation of new identities that unite and divide in new ways.

Ironically, contemporary critiques of assimilation theory, to the extent that they ignore place and history, end up with similar assumptions. Multiculturalism may evaluate hybridity differently than an earlier monoculturalism permitted, but it nevertheless retains similar culturalist assumptions (some notion of Chineseness conjoined to some notion of Americanness to produce a hybrid product). And since culturalism still runs against the evidence of difference, it is still potentially productive of the reification of ethnicity and, ultimately, race. If diasporic reification erases the many historical legacies of the past, hybridity disallows the future. Without a clear account of how different "hybridities" may be productive of new cultures, hybridity in the abstract points merely to an existence between cultures frozen in time.

On the other hand, place consciousness is quite visible in Asian American literary texts. The inhabitants of these texts move through ethnic spaces out of choice or necessity, but the ethnic spaces are themselves located in places with a variety of cohabitants. The classic example may be Carlos Bulosan's *America Is in the Heart*, which literally traces the author's motions from place to place, starting in Philippine places, and then up and down the U.S. West Coast. Place-consciousness is most readily evident in contemporary Asian American literature in the literature of Hawaii—of writers such as Milton Murayama, Gary Pak, and Wing Tek Lum—whose forays into the histories of different ethnic groups share in common a language that marks them as irreducibly Hawaiian. Another example, especially interesting because of the deep contrast between the author's literary output and his more formal discussions, is that of Frank Chin. Chin's literary works are quite attentive to places and to the historicity of Chinese American identities. On the other hand, when the author turns to formal discussions of identity, his representations of Chinese identity match the most egregious reifications of an earlier Orientalism. This itself may be revealing of a gap between depictions of concrete everyday life and an imagined ethnicity constructed very much in the course of daily life but lifted out of it to be represented as an identity that transcends history. The contrast raises interesting questions concerning the ways in which transnationalization and diasporic consciousness may affect a place-based understanding of ethnicity.

◆

The insistence on places against diasporic reification has consequences that are not only analytical in an abstract sense. It draws attention, in the first place, to another, place-based, kind of politics. One of the dangerous consequences of undue attention to diasporas is to distance the so-called diasporic populations from their immediate environments, to render them into foreigners in the context of everyday life. Given the pervasiveness of conflicts in American society that pitch different diasporic populations against one another, rather than retreat behind reified identities that further promote mutual suspicion and racial division, it is necessary to engage others in political projects to create political alliances where differences may be bridged and common social and cultural bonds formed to enable different populations to learn to live with one another.[55] A Chinese living in Los Angeles has more of a stake in identifying with his/her African or Hispanic American neighbors than with some distant cousin in Hong Kong (without implying that the two kinds of relationships need to be understood in zero-sum terms). Following the logic of the argument above, I suggest that place-based politics offers the most effective means to achieving such ends. Place-based politics does not presuppose communities that shut out the world but refocuses attention on building society from the bottom up.

Radical (perhaps unrealistically radical)[56] as a place-based politics may seem, it is unlikely to fulfill its radical promise unless it also challenges the hegemony of the global imaginary that utopianizes transnationalism. My use of places is somewhat different from discussions of the "local" in some postcolonial literature, which tends to view places in isolation from the larger structures that inform them and the categorical allegiances (such as class or gender) that enter into their constitution. The reassertion of place that I am suggesting could hardly be accomplished, therefore, without challenging those larger structures and working over such categorical allegiances. Without reference to structures, the notion of historicity itself readily disintegrates into a jumble of empirical phenomena with no meaning outside themselves. To speak of places presently is to set them against the new global or transnational imaginaries, with their fetishism of a dehistoricized developmentalism and placeless spaces.

Liberal multiculturalism seeks to make room for different cultures, but with a hegemonic containment of difference within the structures of capitalism assumed to offer a common destiny for all, which perpetuates fundamental hegemonies under the new requirements of broadened cultural tolerance. Culturalism without history may serve to divide (as it does), but it may also serve to consolidate hegemony. It may not be too surprising that we witness exactly such a hegemonic unity at the level of transnationalized ruling classes, whose claims to cultural difference are negotiated with the assumption of common interests, while the same culturalism is often manifested in deadly conflicts among the population at large. The return to history from culture is important precisely because it may serve as a reminder of how people at the level of places are not just divided by different cultural legacies but are also united by common histories and interests without which those differences themselves may be incomprehensible. What needs to be resolved at this level are different memories: not just histories remembered differently but also histories remembered jointly.

History is important for another reason than the possibilities it offers for resolution of past and present differences. Released from a hegemonic containment within contemporary structures of power, the recognition of different pasts inevitably invites the possibility of envisioning the future differently. The historicization of cultures—the recognition of different historical trajectories—may have a crucial role to play in opening up a dialogue over different futures. Political projects that account for the different historical possibilities offered by their constituents may fulfill their radical promise if they may, on the basis of those possibilities, imagine alternative futures as well.

The other consequence is also political, but within the context of academic politics, for there is a pedagogic dimension to realizing such political goals. It is rather unfortunate that recent ideological formations, backed by the power of foundations, have encouraged the capturing of ethnicities in "diasporic" American or cultural studies. In the case of studies of Asian Americans in particular, the most favored choices these days would seem to be to recognize Asian American studies as a field of its own, to break it down into various national components (Chinese, Japanese, Filipino, et cetera), or to absorb it into American or Asian studies. Each choice is informed by political premises and goals. Asian American studies as a field is under attack from the inside for its homogenizing implications, as well as its domination by some groups over others. Breaking it down, however, does not offer any readily acceptable solution, as it merely replaces continental homogeneity by national homogeneities; why should there be a Chinese American rather than, say, Fuzhounese American studies? And why stop at Fuzhou?

On the other hand, absorbing Asian American studies into either Asian or American studies would seem to achieve little more than bringing it as a field under the hegemony of the study of societies of origin or arrival. On the surface, American studies would seem to be an appropriate home for Asian American studies, as Asian American history is grounded in U.S. history, which continues to be the concrete location for Asian American experience. On the other hand, it is also clear that Asian American history extends beyond the boundaries of U.S. history, and, by virtue of that, has special requirements—chief among them language—that are not likely to be accommodated with ease within the context of American studies as presently organized. These needs have prompted some scholars to advocate some kind of a merger between Asian and Asian American studies. After all, Asian studies would benefit from greater awareness of Asian American populations, which might complicate their notions of Asia with beneficial results. On the other hand, closer integration with Asian studies would bring into Asian American studies a closer grasp of societies of origin, as well as a disciplinary training in languages, which may be necessary for more sophisticated scholarship, as is indicated by the growing number of Asian American scholars who have extended the boundaries of Asian American studies. I am thinking here of scholars such as Yuji Ichioka, Him Mark Lai, Marlon Hom, Sau-ling Wong, and Scott Wong, to name a few, who have produced works that have enriched the field by using non-English language sources.

Dialogue between the different fields is not only desirable, therefore, but is necessary. Mergers are a different matter. The reasoning underlying these proposed mergers is full of pitfalls, especially when viewed from the perspective of politics. Absorption of Asian American into American studies prima facie would perpetuate the hegemonies that do not disappear but are in fact consolidated under the guise of multiculturalism. The case with Asian studies is even more problematic, as the justification for it is fundamentally diasporic, with all the implications of that term that I have discussed above. One of the most important characteristics of Asian American studies, as of all the ethnic studies projects that were born of the political ferment of the 1960s, was its insistence on ties to community projects. This was a reason that Asian studies scholars for long disassociated themselves from Asian American scholarship, for such explicit ties to political projects made the field suspect in terms of scholarship (which, of course, did not apply to scholars of Asia with ties to other kinds of political projects, respectable because of their ties to power). The new interest of scholars of Asia in Asian American studies may be attributed to something as mundane as the lucrative promise of a field in demand all of a sudden as the result of the explosion in the numbers of students of Asian origins. I suspect, however, that what makes the association tolerable is the respectability Asian American studies has acquired as it is transnationalized, or diasporized, achieving respectability at the cost of alienation from its radical political projects. It may be noteworthy here that a panel in the recent annual meeting of the Association for Asian Studies ("Crossing Boundaries: Bridging Asian American Studies and Asian Studies") "bridges" the gap not by addressing Asian American issues but by including in the panel Evelyn Hu-De Hart, the only participant recognizable as a serious scholar of Asian America (to be distinguished from being Asian American). Judging by the titles of the papers listed, the panel reveals little recognition of the integrity and coherence of Asian American studies as a field with its own problems and paradigms, not to speak of the intellectual and political implications of those paradigms.[57] The danger (and the quite real possibility) here is the disappearance into some vague diasporic field of problems specific to Asian America.

If education has anything to do with politics—and it does have everything to do with it—the wiser course to follow in overcoming ethnic divisions would be to reinforce programs in ethnic studies, which initially had as one of its fundamental goals the bridging of ethnic divisions and the pursuit of common projects (based in communities) to that end. Ethnic studies since its inception has been viewed with suspicion by the political and educational establishments and has suffered from internal divisions as well. Whether or not these legacies can be overcome is a big question, imbedded as they are in the structures of U.S. society and academic institutions. The irony is that while ethnic studies might help ideologically in overcoming ethnic divisions, it is not likely to receive much support unless interethnic political cooperation has sufficient force to render it credible in the first place. The ideology of globalization, of which diasporic ideology is one constituent, further threatens to undermine its promise (and existence). Here, too, place-based politics may have something to offer in countering the ideologies of the age.

NOTES

This chapter originally appeared as "Bringing History Back In: Of Diasporas, Hybridities, Places, and Histories," *Review of Education/Pedagogy/Cultural Studies* 21, no. 2 (1999): 95–131. The author gratefully acknowledges the permission of this publication to reprint the article here.

1. While the issue of place against transnationality is quite central, in this case the criticism was not entirely fair. The anthropologist in question, Nina Glick-Schiller, is among the earliest critics of transnational cultural homogenization and its manipulation by business and political interests. See, e.g., Nina Schiller, Linda Basch, and Christina Szanton-Blanc, "Transnationalism: A New Analytic Framework for Understanding Migration," *Annals of the New York Academy of Sciences* 645 (1992): 1–24. The colleagues in Singapore were Chua Beng-huat and Wang Gung-wu. A colleague in Hong Kong, Siu-woo Cheung, responded in similar fashion, this time to a talk by Greg Lee on Chinese hybridity. Cheung informs me that he feels "silenced" by a concept such as hybridity, which erases his differences from other Chinese, not just elsewhere but also in Hong Kong.

2. This double aspect of the concept is investigated in several of the essays, especially the editors' introduction and epilogue in *Ungrounded Empires: The Cultural Politics of Modern Chinese Nationalism,* ed. Aihwa Ong and Donald Nonini (New York: Routledge, 1997).

3. "Chinese Transnationalism as an Alternative Modernity," in *Ungrounded Empires,* Ong and Nonini, 3–33, 12. For Gilroy, see Paul Gilroy, *The Black Atlantic: Modernity and Double Consciousness* (Cambridge: Harvard University Press, 1993).

4. Ong and Nonini, "Toward a Cultural Politics of Diaspora and Transnationalism," in *Ungrounded Empires,* 323–32, 325.

5. There is a great deal of material on the John Huang case, although no studies as yet. For a blatant example of the unscrupulous linking of John Huang with the Riadys and the

People's Republic of China, see William Safire, "Listening to Hearings," *New York Times*, 13 July 1997.

6. Paul Gilroy, "'The Whisper Wakes, the Shudder Plays': Race, Nation and Ethnic Absolutism," in *Contemporary Postcolonial Theory: A Reader*, ed. Padmini Mongia (London: Arnold, 1996), 248–74, 263.

7. Ling-chi Wang, "Foreign Money Is No Friend of Ours," *Asian Week*, 8 November 1997, 7.

8. Henry Yu, "Thinking about Orientals: Modernity, Social Science, and Asians in Twentieth-Century America" (Ph.D. diss., Princeton University, 1995). See 162–89.

9. Quoted in Yu, "Thinking about Orientals," 184.

10. "Entrepreneur Applauds U.S. Money Move," *Hawaii Tribune-Herald*, 18 June 1998, 1, 10.

11. Arif Dirlik, "Global Capitalism and the Reinvention of Confucianism," *Boundary 2* 22, no. 3 (November 1995): 229–73.

12. Joel Kotkin, "The New Yankee Traders," *INC*, March 1996, 25.

13. Arjun Appadurai, "Disjuncture and Difference in the Global Economy," *Public Culture* 2, no. 2 (Spring 1990): 124, 15.

14. For an important discussion, see Peter Kwong, *Forbidden Workers: Illegal Chinese Immigrants and American Labor* (New York: New Press, 1997), esp. chap. 5, "Manufacturing Ethnicity."

15. Lisa Lowe, "Heterogeneity, Hybridity, Multiplicity: Marking Asian American Differences," *Diaspora* 1, no. 1 (Spring 1991): 24–44.

16. Quoted in Yu, "Thinking about Orientals," 229. For another study that also stresses the debilitating consequences of hybridity, see William Carlson Smith, *Americans in Process: A Study of Our Citizens of Oriental Ancestry* (1937; reprint, New York: Arno Press and the New York Times, 1970).

17. Edward W. Soja, *Third space: Journeys to Los Angeles and Other Real and Imagined Places* (Cambridge, Mass.: Blackwell, 1996).

18. Pnina Werbner, "Introduction: The Dialectics of Cultural Hybridity," in *Debating Cultural Hybridity: Multi-Cultural Identities and the Politics of Anti-Racism*, ed. Pnina Werbner and Tariq Modood (London: Zed Books, 1997), 126, 1.

19. Feroza Jussawalla, "South Asian Diaspora Writers in Britain: 'Home' versus 'Hybridity,'" in *Ideas of Home: Literature of Asian Migration*, ed. Geoffrey Kaine (East Lansing: Michigan State University Press, 1997), 17–37, 20, 21. Lawrence Grossberg says there has been an increasing tendency in cultural studies to identify it with problems of identity, which may well have something to do with the abstraction and universalization of hybridity. See Grossberg, "Identity and Cultural Studies: Is That All There Is?" *Questions of Cultural Identity*, ed. Stuart Hall and Paul Du Gay (London: Sage Publications, 1997), 87–107, 87.

20. Katharyne Mitchell, "Different Diasporas and the Hype of Hybridity," *Environment and Planning: Society and Space* 15 (1997) 533–53, 537, 534 n.

21. Zygmunt Bauman, "The Making and Unmaking of Strangers," in *Debating Cultural Hybridity*, Werbner and Modood, 46–57.

22. Iain Chambers, *Migrancy, Culture, and Identity* (London: Routledge, 1994), 77; quoted in Jonathan Friedman, "Global Crises, the Struggle for Cultural Identity, and Intellectual

Porkbarrelling: Cosmopolitans versus Locals, Ethnics, and Nationals in an Era of Global De-Hegemonisation," in *The Dialectics of Hybridity*, ed. Pnina Werbner (Cambridge: Zed Books, 1997), 70–89, 77.

23. Friedman, "Global Crises," 87.

24. Jussawalla, "South Asian Diaspora Writers," 26.

25. For a discussion of class differences, see Leo Suryadinata, "Anti-Chinese Riots in Indonesia: Perennial Problem but Major Disaster Unlikely," *Straits Times* (Singapore), 25 February 1998. For the Indonesian Chinese elite's plans, see "Elite Making Contingency Plans to Flee to Australia," *South China Morning Post*, 28 February 1998. It might be worth remembering that some members of this same elite were implicated in the John Huang case.

26. Friedman, "Global Crises," 81.

27. Friedman, "Global Crises," 82–83.

28. Nira Yuval-Davis, "Ethnicity, Gender Relations, and Multiculturalism," in *Debating Cultural Hybridity*, Werbner and Modood, 193–208, 202.

29. See Robert J. C. Young, *Colonial Desire: Hybridity in Theory, Culture, and Race* (London: Routledge, 1995), 176, for a tabulation of degrees of "mongrelity" in Peru. See also Anthony P. Maingot, "Race, Color, and Class in the Caribbean," in *Americas: New Interpretive Essays*, ed. Alfred Stepan (New York: Oxford University Press, 1992), 220–47, 229, for similar categorizations in Santo Domingo. For "blood quantum," see Mariana Jaimes Guerrero, "The 'Patriarchal Nationalism' of Transnational Colonialism as Imperialist Strands of Genocide/Ethnocide/Ecocide" (paper presented at Asian Pacific Identities Conference, Duke University, March 1995).

30. Young, *Colonial Desire*; Jussawalla, "South Asian Diaspora Writers," 34.

31. Theorists of abstract hybridity such as Bhabha and Soja nevertheless refer to the quite grounded work of bell hooks, who seeks such articulation from a black feminist perspective. See the essays in bell hooks, *Yearning: Race, Gender, and Cultural Politics* (Boston: South End Press, 1990).

32. Jussawalla, "South Asian Diaspora Writers," 35.

33. Mitchell, "Different Diasporas," 534.

34. Peter McLaren and Henry A. Giroux, "Writing from the Margins: Geographies of Identity, Pedagogy, and Power," in *Revolutionary Multiculturalism: Pedagogies of Dissent for the New Millennium*, by Peter McLaren (Boulder, Colo.: Westview Press, 1997), 16–41, 17.

35. Pnina Werbner, "Essentialising Essentialism, Essentialising Silence: Ambivalence and Multiplicity in the Constructions of Racism and Ethnicity," in *Debating Cultural Hybridity*, Werbner and Modood, 226–54, 226.

36. I have in mind here the essentialism that Lisa Lowe discovers in the early Asian American movement of the late 1960s and the 1970s. There is little in the texts of that movement to suggest that Asian American radicals assumed any kind of ethnic or social (class and gender) homogeneity for the groups encompassed under the term. If there was erasure of gender differences to begin with, that was challenged very quickly. On the other hand, the movement did have political goals that have become less desirable to new generations of Asian Americans. See Lowe, "Heterogeneity, Hybridity, Multiplicity."

37. bell hooks, "Culture to Culture: Ethnography and Cultural Studies as Critical Intervention," in *Yearning*, 123–33, 130. See also Stuart Hall, "Cultural Identity and Diaspora," in *Contemporary Postcolonial Theory: A Reader*, ed. Padmini Mongia (London: Arnold Publishers, 1996), 110–21, for the importance of history and place in identity. Hall distin-

guishes the "hegemonising" form of ethnicity from a hybrid one, which is subject to change but does not therefore deny the importance of ethnic identity. ("Difference, therefore, persists in and alongside continuity" [114].) For a similar reaffirmation, this time contrasting ethnicity to race, see Werbner, "Essentialising Essentialism."

38. Young, *Colonial Desire*, 20–22.

39. M. M. Bakhtin, *The Dialogic Imagination*, ed. Michael Holquist, trans. Caryl Emerson and Michael Holquist (Austin: University of Texas Press, 1981), 358–59. Quoted in Young, *Colonial Desire*, 21.

40. Bakhtin, *Dialogic Imagination*, 359–60.

41. Young, *Colonial Desire*, 21.

42. Young, *Colonial Desire*, 22.

43. Hubert J. M. Hermans and Harry J. G. Kempen, *The Dialogical Self: Meaning as Movement* (San Diego: Academic Press, 1993), 89.

44. Hermans and Kempen, *Dialogical Self*, 93.

45. Hermans and Kempen, *Dialogical Self*, 78.

46. For a defense of the nation from what may seem to be a surprising source, see Subcomandante Marcos, "Why We Are Fighting: The Fourth World War Has Begun," *Le Monde Diplomatique* (August–September 1997).

47. For a parallel argument, see Partha Chatterjee, "Beyond the Nation? Or Within?" *Economic and Political Weekly*, 4–11 January 1997, 30–34.

48. I am referring here to the title of a conference held in early November 1997 at New York University, "Where Is Home?" (previously the title of an exhibition on the Chinese in the United States). The preoccupation has its roots in a particularly narcissistic and manipulative offshoot of cultural studies. The "yearning" for home need not be a consequence of such narcissism. Jussawalla defends her case for "home" in response to the oppressive refusal of the society of arrival to recognize genuine political and cultural citizenship of the ethnically, racially, and culturally different, even after generations of residence in the new "home," which indeed has been the experience of many. On the other hand, I find implausible her alternative that "the answer is to assimilate and yet to keep our distinctness, our senses of nationality" (Jussawalla, "South Asian Diaspora Writers," 36).

49. Quoted in Jussawalla, "South Asian Diaspora Writers," 32.

50. David Lowenthal, *Possessed by the Past: The Heritage Crusade and the Spoils of History* (New York: Free Press, 1995); and Fredric Jameson, *Postmodernism, or the Cultural Logic of Late Capitalism* (Durham, N.C.: Duke University Press, 1991). Jameson's pessimism is related to a yearning for an earlier class politics of socialism. He describes the contemporary fragmentation of history with the same vocabulary that he uses to describe the new social movements: as having emerged from the "rubbles" of an earlier unified and coherent history and politics. This yearning does not allow him to see the progressive potential of the new "rubble."

51. Ling-chi Wang, "Roots and Changing Identity of the Chinese in the United States," *Daedalus* (Spring 1991): 181–206, 199–200.

52. Kathleen Neils Conzen, "Making Their Own America: Assimilation Theory and the German Peasant Pioneer," German Historical Institute, Washington, D.C., Annual Lecture Series, no. 3 (New York: Berg Publishers, 1990), 9.

53. See the collection of Clifford's essays, James Clifford, *Routes: Travel and Translation in the Late Twentieth Century* (Cambridge: Harvard University Press, 1997). I may note here

an aspect of the contemporary dissatisfaction with history for supposedly ignoring questions of space out of a preoccupation with questions of time. While this may be a legitimate criticism for certain kinds of histories, such criticism itself seems to be more concerned with nineteenth-century historicism and conceptions of history than with the actual practice of historians. To this historian at any rate, the concept of historicity as a concrete concept is inseparable from location in time *and* space—within a *social* context (to complete Soja's "trialectics"!).

54. Henry Yu argues that the Chicago sociologists dehistoricized the experiences of their "oriental" subjects by rendering into static universal categories what were stages in their life histories. See the discussion in Yu, "Thinking about Orientals," 185–88.

55. The divisive effects of diasporic discourse as I approach it here is similar to the divisive effects of the idea of a "model minority."

56. The difficulties are obvious, but then we do not seem to have too many choices. For a sensitive discussion of the difficulties involved in what she calls "transversal politics" (a term coined by Italian feminists), see Yuval-Davis, "Ethnicity, Gender Relations, and Multiculturalism." I have discussed the problems and the possibilities at greater length in "Place-Based Imagination: Globalism and the Politics of Place," *Review* 22, no. 2 (1999): 151–87.

57. A concomitant roundtable discussion subtitled "Where Do Asia and Asian America Meet?" may have been more promising, with the participation of Gail Nomura and Scott Wong.

8

THE PAST AS LEGACY AND PROJECT:

POSTCOLONIAL CRITICISM IN THE PERSPECTIVE

OF INDIGENOUS HISTORICISM

> Men make their own history, but they do not make it just as they please; they
> do not make it under circumstances chosen by themselves, but under cir-
> cumstances directly encountered, given and transmitted from the past. The
> tradition of all the dead generations weighs like a nightmare on the brain of
> the living.
>
> —Karl Marx, *The 18th Brumaire of Louis Bonaparte*

After nearly a century and a half, Marx's statement still provides a most cogent
affirmation of historicity against both a libertarian obliviousness to the burden
of the past and a determinist denial of the possibility of human agency. But I
begin with this statement for still another reason. While Marx's own work lies
at the origins of so much of present-day theorizing about society and history,
against our theory-crazed times, when once again the logic of abstraction seems
to take precedence over the evidence of the world, the statement is comfort-
ingly commonsensical.

Issues of historicity and common sense are both pertinent to the problem
I take up in this discussion. The problem is derivative of a paradox in contemporary cultural criticism and politics. In academic circles engrossed with
postmodernity/postcoloniality as conditions of the present, it is almost a matter of faith these days that nations are "imagined," traditions are "invented,"
subjectivities are slippery (if they exist at all), and cultural identities are myths.
Claims to the contrary are labeled "essentialisms" and dismissed as perpetua-
tions of hegemonic constructions of the world. The denial of authenticity to
cultural claims beyond localized constructions is accompanied by the denial to
the past of any authority to authenticate the present. In the words of one
"postcolonial critic," criticism, if it is to be thoroughly antihegemonic, needs
to learn from the experiences of "those who have suffered the sentence of history—subjugation, domination, diaspora, displacement." Recognition of
these experiences

forces us . . . to engage with culture as an uneven, incomplete production of meaning and value, often composed of incommensurable demands and practices, produced in the act of social survival. . . . It becomes crucial to distinguish between the
semblance and similitude of the symbols across diverse cultural experiences . . . and
the social specificity of each of these productions of meaning as they circulate as signs
within specific contextual locations and social systems of value. The transnational
dimension of cultural transformation—migration, diaspora, displacement, reloca-
tion—makes the process of cultural translation a complex form of signification. The
natural(ized), unifying discourse of 'nation', 'peoples' or authentic 'folk' tradition,
those embedded myths of culture's particularity, cannot be readily referenced. The
great, though unsettling, advantage of this position is that it makes you increasingly
aware of the construction of culture and the invention of tradition.[1]

As if by some devilish design to mock the postcolonial argument, cultural
politics in our day exhibits an abundance of such claims to cultural authenticity that, rather than disappear, would seem to be proliferating in proportion to
the globalization of postmodernity—with deadly consequences for millions.
Cultural nationalism, ethnicism, indigenism have emerged as markers of cultural politics globally; over the last decade ethnicity has moved to the center of
politics, overshadowing earlier concerns with class and gender. Claims to cultural authenticity, moreover, have been accompanied by efforts to discover or
restore authentic pasts as foundations for contemporary identity, most urgently among those who have suffered "the sentence of history."

The most basic problem presented by this paradoxical situation is the disjuncture between cultural criticism and cultural politics. Even as cultural criticism renders the past into a plaything at the hands of the present, the burden of
the past haunts contemporary politics in a reassertion of cultural identities. Post-
modern/postcolonial criticism would seem to have little to say on this situation,
except to insist even more uncompromisingly on its own validity. Where the
postmodern/postcolonial intellectuals themselves are concerned, the repudiation
of essentialized identities and authentic pasts seems to culminate in a libertarianism that asserts the possibility of constructing identities and histories almost at
will in those "in-between" spaces that are immune to the burden of the past (and
the present, in its repudiation of "foundational" structures). Ironically, however,
postmodern/postcolonial critics are unwilling to recognize a similar liberty for
those who seek to invoke the past in the assertion of cultural identities, labeling
all such attempts as misguided (or ideological) essentialisms that ignore the constructedness of the past. That groups that have "suffered the sentence of history"
are internally divided and differentiated is not a particularly novel insight; what
seems to be new about the current historical situation is the erasure, in the name
of difference, of differences among such groups in their efforts to cope with the

sentence of history, especially those efforts that contradict the new ideology of postmodernism/postcolonialism. In-betweenness, universalized as a human condition and extended over the past, is thus naturalized in the process and becomes a new kind of determinism from which there is no escape. At the same time, the label of essentialism, extended across the board without regard to its sources and goals, obviates the need to distinguish different modes of cultural identity formation in a way that is subversive not only of critical but also of any meaningful political judgment. It is some questions raised by these different modes of cultural identity formation that I address in this chapter.

To assert that cultural identity is ambiguous and the historical materials out of which it is constructed are invented is in some ways to state the obvious. The question is, what do different modes of identity construction imply intellectually and politically, and how do we construe the relationships they presuppose between the present and the past? The discussion is organized around three questions that I take to be critical to distinguishing among these identity formations: (a) What is their relationship to power? (b) Are the pasts out of which they are formed reified pasts or pasts recognized in their historicity? and (c) What relationship do they establish between the past as legacy and the past as project? My critique of the discourses on these questions, both in legitimations of power and in postmodern/postcolonial responses to it, is informed strongly by a perspective afforded by indigenism, the ideological articulation of the aspirations to liberation of those native peoples—designated the Fourth World in recent years—that I take to be the terminally marginalized of all the oppressed and marginalized peoples around the world. The discussion draws most directly on articulations of indigenism in North America and, to a lesser extent, among the peoples of the Pacific.

CULTURAL IDENTITY AND POWER

Leslie Marmon Silko prefaces her novel, *Ceremony*, with a song-poem (also entitled "ceremony") that tells the reader that the story she is to tell is more than just a story:

> I will tell you something about stories,
> [he said]
> They aren't just entertainment,
> Don't be fooled.
> They are all we have, you see,
> all we have to fight off
> illness and death.

> You don't have anything
> if you don't have the stories.
>
> Their evil is mighty
> but it can't stand up to our stories.
> So they try to destroy the stories
> let the stories be confused or forgotten,
> They would like that
> They would be happy
> Because we would be defenseless then.[2]

There may be a postmodern ring to the idea that stories create reality, a notion that drives Silko's narrative, but the intention is anything but postmodern. *Ceremony* is about the recovery of identity destroyed by war and cultural incoherence through a reliving of ancient stories, and as a story itself, it seeks to create a reality for native peoples different from the one that is in the process of destroying them. The theme of restoring an indigenous identity by salvaging the native past from its distortions in Euro-American historiography is a common one among indigenous peoples from Native Americans to the Australian aborigines, from Hawai'ians to the Indians of Chiapas. As the Hawai'ian sovereignty movement leader Haunani-Kay Trask puts it:

> Burdened by a linear, progressive conception of history and by an assumption that Euro-American culture flourishes at the upper end of that progression, Westerners have told the history of Hawai'i as an inevitable if occasionally bitter-sweet triumph of Western ways over "primitive" Hawai'ian ways. . . . To know my history, I had to put away my books and return to the land. I had to plant taro in the earth before I could understand the inseparable bond between people and *'aina* [land]. I had to feel again the spirits of nature and take gifts of plants and fish to the ancient altars. I had to begin to speak my language with our elders and leave long silences for wisdom to grow. But before anything else, I needed to learn the language like a lover so that I could rock with her and lie at night in her dreaming arms.[3]

"Indigenous peoples," according to the Cree author George Manuel, who is also the founding president of the World Council of Indigenous Peoples, are peoples "descended from a country's aboriginal population and who today are completely or partly deprived of their own territory and its riches."[4] They have been described also as "the fourth world: the world on the margin, on the periphery."[5] Annette Jaimes describes the various aspects of indigenism as follows:

> In terms of economics, the Native peoples tend to have communal property, subsistence production, barter systems, low impact technologies and collective production.

... In terms of political relations, Native people have consensual processes, direct "participatory" democracy, and laws embedded in oral traditions. ... In respect to their social relations, they differ [from modern society], generally, in terms of matrilineality versus patriarchy, extended versus nuclear families, and low versus high population density. ... Finally, regarding differences in world view, the Native peoples are polytheistic, derive an understanding of the world from the natural order's rhythms and cycles of life, and include animals and plants as well as other natural features in their conceptions of spirituality.[6]

The goal of indigenism, then, is to restore these features of native life that have been associated in Euro-American historiography with "primitivism." Fundamental to indigenism is the recovery of land and, with it, the special relationship to nature that is the hallmark of indigenous identity.

"Indigenous ideology," as its proponents present it, defies all the protocols associated with postmodern/postcolonial criticism—to the point where it could be said fairly that it replicates the colonizers' views of indigenous peoples. Not only does it affirm the possibility of "real" native identity, but it also asserts as the basis for such identity a native subjectivity that has survived, depending on location, as many as five centuries of colonialism and cultural disorientation. Not only does it believe in the possibility of recapturing the essence of precolonial indigenous culture, but it also bases this belief on a spirituality that exists outside of historical time. The very notions of Indian or Hawai'ian that are used to describe collective identities take for granted categories invented by colonizers, and imposed upon the colonized, in remapping and redefining diverse peoples in a Euro-American reconstruction of space in the process of colonization. An articulate spokesman for indigenous ideology such as Ward Churchill not only utilizes this terminology but also insists that the collectivities thus depicted are "referents" (to recall Bhabha's term in the quotation above) for Indian nationhood, or peoplehood.[7] In all these different ways, indigenous ideology would seem to provide a textbook case of "self-Orientalization" that replays the features ascribed to the Others of Eurocentric modernizationism that have been analyzed by Fabian in his *Time and the Other*.[8] What Nicholas Thomas says of "New Age primitivism" in Australia could describe equally well the self-essentialization that is a feature of indigenous ideology in general: "Constructing them as culturally stable since the beginning of humanity does imply an ahistorical existence, an inability to change and an incapacity to survive modernity; this essentialism also entails stipulations about what is and what is not appropriately and truly Aboriginal, which marginalizes not only urban Aboriginal cultures, but any forms not closely associated with traditional bush gathering."[9]

Not surprisingly, indigenous ideology has come under criticism from postcolonial positions, or positions that share certain basic premises with postmodern/postcolonial criticism. A prominent Australian proponent of postcolonial criticism, Gareth Griffiths, wonders of the protests against oppression of "subaltern people" that, "even when the subaltern appears to 'speak' there is a real concern as to whether what we are listening to is really a subaltern voice, or whether the subaltern is being spoken by the subject position they occupy within the larger discursive economy." Griffiths goes on to state that his goal is not to question

> whether the claim of Aboriginal peoples in Australia and elsewhere to restitution of their traditional lands and sacred places, or to the voices and practices of their traditional cultures, is legitimate. Nor do I question the importance of locality and specificity in resisting the generalizing tendencies and incorporative strategies of white society. . . . [I]t is not my business to comment on this. What I am concerned with is the impact of the representation of that claim when it is mediated through a discourse of the authentic adopted and promulgated by the dominant discourse which 'speaks' the indigene within a construction whose legitimacy is grounded not in their practice but in our desire.[10]

Similarly, but obviously with fewer qualms about offending indigenous sensibilities, a Canadian postcolonial critic writes:

> While post-colonial theorists embrace hybridity and heterogeneity as the characteristic post-colonial mode, some native writers in Canada resist what they see as a violating appropriation to insist on their ownership of their stories and their exclusive claim to an authenticity that should not be ventriloquized or parodied. When directed against the Western canon, post-modernist techniques of intertextuality, parody, and literary borrowing may appear radical and even potentially revolutionary. When directed against native myths and stories, these same techniques would seem to repeat the imperialist history of plunder and theft. . . . Although I can sympathize with such arguments as tactical strategies in insisting on self-definition and resisting appropriation, even tactically they prove self-defeating because they depend on a view of cultural authenticity that condemns them to a continued marginality and an eventual death. . . . Ironically, such tactics encourage native peoples to isolate themselves from contemporary life and full citizenhood.[11]

Nicholas Thomas has observed that cultural studies in the United States have been largely silent on the question of native Americans: "In U.S. journals that address race, more reference is made to racism and colonial conflicts elsewhere—in South Africa or Britain—than to Native American struggles."[12] One noteworthy exception that is pertinent to the discussion here may be the questions raised by the anthropologist Jocelyn S. Linnekin on the claims to cultural authenticity of the Hawai'ian independence movement. In an article published in 1983, "Defining Tradition: Variations on the Hawaiian Identity," Linnekin argued not only that Hawai'ian society was internally differentiated (and hence not to be homogenized) but also that the "traditions" that served as symbols of Hawai'ian nationalism—such as Hawai'ian seafaring capabilities or the "love of the land"—were invented traditions. Especially damaging were the questions she raised about the traditional sanctity of the island of Kahoolawe, used by the U.S. Navy for bombing practices, and the use of the practices by the navy as legal evidence to justify continued bombing.[13]

Whether these critiques are based on sufficient readings of indigenous ideology is a question I will take up below. It is necessary here to examine more closely the relationship of indigenous self-assertion to its context in a colonial structure of power. Griffiths's concern that the dominant discourse "speaks" the indigene raises the important question that the reification of indigenous identity not only replicates the assumptions of the dominant discourse but also opens the way to the "consumption" of indigenism by the dominant society; after all, people who are outside history are more easily placed in museums and theme parks than those who are part of a living present, and exoticized cultures provide a ready-made fund for the production of cultural commodities.[14] What he overlooks, however, is that it is the power context rather than the reification that may be the more important problem. As the case of Linnekin shows, the denial of reified pasts is equally open to exploitation by power. Disney these days justifies its constructions of the past or of the Other on the grounds that since all pasts are invented or constructed, their constructions are as valid as anyone else's. It is arguable that postmodern/postcolonial denials of historical or cultural truths render the past or other cultures more readily available for commodification and exploitation by abolishing the possibility of distinguishing one invention from another. The premise that all truths are "contingent" truths, without reference to the structures of power that inform them, opens the way to silencing the subalterns who cannot even claim authentic custody of their own identities against their "construction" by academic, commercial, or political institutions of power.

The importance of accounting for power relations in judgments on identity formation may be illustrated further by placing indigenous ideology within the context of the current proliferation of cultural nationalisms, with which it shares much in terms of intellectual procedures. There has been a resurgence in recent years of fundamentalistic nationalisms or culturalisms against Euro-American ideological domination of the world that range from Islamic fundamentalism to Pan-Asianism, from assertions in Japan of an ideology of "Japaneseness" to the Confucian revival in Chinese societies. These revivals, while antihegemonic in some respects, are also fueled by newfound power in formerly Third World societies that have achieved success in capitalist development and all of a sudden find themselves in a position to challenge Euro-American models of development. They are also motivated, however, by efforts to contain the disintegrative consequences of such development. The assertion of homogenized cultural identities, on the one hand, celebrates success in the world economy but also, on the other hand, seeks to contain the disintegrative threat of "Western" commodity culture, the social incoherence brought about by capitalist development, and the cultural confusion brought about by diasporic populations that have called into question the identification of national culture with the space of the nation-state. Thus the Confucian revival among Chinese populations points to Chinese success in capitalist development to argue that the Confucian ethic is equal, if not superior, to the "Protestant ethic" that Max Weber had credited with causative power in the emergence of capitalism in Europe; a "Weberized" Confucianism in turn appears as a marker of Chineseness regardless of time or place. In the idea of a "cultural China" that has been promoted by proponents of a Confucian revival, cultural essence replaces political identity in the definition of Chineseness. At the same time, the idea is one that Chinese states, capital, and academic intellectuals (mostly in First World institutions) have played a crucial part in promoting. No less important is the fact that non-Chinese academics in the United States closely connected with academic and commercial institutions of power have participated in this revival and have even played an important part in legitimizing it. Confucianism, reduced to a few ethical principles conducive to social and economic order, has been rendered in the process into an ideology of capitalist development, superior to the individualistic ideology of Euro-American capitalism in its emphasis on harmony and social cohesiveness. The latter aspect prompted the government of the People's Republic of China in 1994 to declare a "Confucian renaissance" on the grounds that with socialism having lost its ethical power to counter undesirable social tendencies, Confucianism might serve as a suitable native substitute.[15] Naturalized as a marker of Chineseness, Confucianism also serves to erase memories of a revolutionary past.

The tendencies toward the proliferation of fundamentalisms and culturalist nationalisms were no doubt on the mind of Samuel Huntington when he wrote in his celebrated 1993 essay that

World politics is entering a new phase. . . . [T]he fundamental source of conflict in this new world will not be primarily ideological or primarily economic. The great divisions among humankind and the dominating source of conflict will be cultural. Nation states will remain the most powerful actors in world affairs, but the principal conflicts of global politics will occur between nations and groups of different civilizations. The clash of civilizations will dominate world politics. . . . With the end of the Cold War, international politics moves out of its Western phase, and its centerpiece becomes the interaction between the West and non-Western civilizations and among non-Western civilizations. . . . Civilization identity will be increasingly important in the future, and the world will be shaped in large measure by the inter-actions among seven or eight major civilizations. These include Western, Confucian, Japanese, Islamic, Hindu, Slavic-Orthodox, Latin American and possibly African civ-ilization.[16]

A critique of cultural essentialism that offers no articulated means to distin-guish between the essentialism of indigenous ideology and the essentialism of a Confucian revival or Huntington's vision of war among civilizations may be methodologically justifiable; but it is, to say the least, morally irresponsible and politically obscene. Indigenous claims to identity are very much tied in with a desperate concern for survival, not in a "metaphorical," but in a very material sense. Indian lands in the United States, or what is left of them, are not just reminders of a bygone colonial past; they are still the objects of state and cor-porate destruction in what Churchill describes as "radioactive colonization."[17] In accordance with racist policies established since the nineteenth century, according to Annette Jaimes, Indian identity in the United States is determined either by the recognition of tribal governments or by what has been described as "the blood quantum," the degree of "Indian blood" in any one individual as certified by the Bureau of Indian Affairs (the minimum for qualification set at "quarter blood").[18] Churchill, who describes the implications of the "blood quantum" as "arithmetical genocide," writes:

> The thinking is simple. As the historian Patricia Nelson Limerick frames it: "Set the blood quantum at one-quarter, hold to it as a rigid definition of Indians, let inter-marriage proceed as it has for centuries, and eventually Indians will be defined out of existence." Bearing out the validity of Jaimes' and Limerick's observations is the fact that, in 1900, about half of all Indians in this country were "full-bloods." By 1990, the population had shrunk to about twenty percent. . . . A third of all Indians are at the quarter-blood cut-off point. Cherokee demographer Russell Thornton estimates that, given continued imposition of purely racial definitions, Native America as a whole will have disappeared by the year 2080.[19]

Cultural identity, under such circumstances, is not a matter of "identity pol-itics" but a condition of survival, and its implications may be grasped only by reference to structures of power. There is a world of difference between a "Con-fucian identity," promoted by states and capital and intended to carve out a place in a global structure of political and economic power, and an indigenous identity that may be essential to survival as a social and cultural identity against the depredations of power. Postmodern/postcolonial criticism, especially in the United States, has not only been insensitive to such differences in its unquali-fied affirmation of "hybridity and heterogeneity" but also, as the quotation from Brydon above suggests, quite intolerant of any efforts to "construct" the past differently than is allowable to "postcolonial critics"; in fact, it is difficult to see how Brydon's "join up or shut up attitude" differs in any significant sense from that of colonialist attitudes toward indigenous peoples.[20]

What renders indigenous ideology significant, however, is not what it has to reveal about postmodern/postcolonial criticism. Its intellectual and political significance rests elsewhere: in its claims to a different historicity that challenges not just postcolonial denials of collective identity but also the structure of power that contains it. To criticize indigenous ideology for its reification of culture is to give it at best an incomplete reading. It also disguises the complexity of what indigenous authors have to say about the relationship between culture and history, which is considerably more radical ideologically than is suggested by its apparent culturalism.

CULTURAL IDENTITY/HISTORICAL TRAJECTORY

One of the celebrated conflicts in U.S. letters in recent years is that between the Chinese American writers Frank Chin and Maxine Hong Kingston. Following the publication of Kingston's *Woman Warrior* in 1976, Chin launched an attack on the book for its misrepresentation of Chineseness. The attacks continue to this day but have been broadened now to include other prominent Chinese American writers such as Amy Tan and David Hwang. Chin has accused all of these authors of stereotyping Chinese culture and distorting its realities by adopting what he takes to be a "missionary" view of Chinese society.[21]

Chin's attacks on these authors have been ascribed to his misogynistic attitudes and his envy of these writers' success. Whether or not there is any merit to such charges, his own refusal to bring any kind of subtlety to his criticisms has not helped his cause. His insistence that his is the only viable and authentically "Chinese" position has further isolated him and, unfortunately, obviated the need for elaborating on a critique that, I feel, has much to say about the problem of history in a minority group's construction of its ethnicity.[22]

At the heart of this particular controversy is Kingston's (mis)use of Chinese legends and the liberties she took with the interpretation of Chinese characters (namely, the association of the character for woman with the character for slave) in *Woman Warrior*. Kingston has conceded the liberties she took but has explained them in terms of literary license. Chin has refused to accept this excuse. Legends, to him, represent cultural truths that are not to be tampered with. Kingston's distortions of Chinese legends were all the more serious because, at the insistence of the publisher, she consented to having *Woman Warrior* classified as autobiography rather than fiction, as originally intended, further endowing her distortions with the status of truth. She thus played into the hands of the dominant society's stereotypes of Chineseness.

Kingston herself has expressed regrets that *Woman Warrior* was indeed received as a description of Chinese society, contributing to the image of an exotic China. This may have something to tell us about the plight of minority literature, but it will not do to ascribe it just to the parochialism of the dominant society, as Frederick Buell has suggested recently.[23] The problem with Kingston's representation of Chineseness may lie, not in the distortions of Chinese legends or characters (although these are certainly problems), but in the manner in which the relationship to the past is represented in *Woman Warrior*. A comparison with Chin's representation of this relationship may lend us a clue. Chin's own work engages in a stereotyping of Chineseness by associating it with certain primordial characteristics; indeed, it is arguable that Chin's notion of the cultural endowment of Chinese in his formal statements is one-dimensional in contrast to that of Kingston, who perceives in Chinese culture the location both for oppression and for the struggle against it, as personified in the woman warrior.[24] Nevertheless, in his fiction, Chin presents a relationship to the past that resists appropriation into the image of an exotic China. Why one representation should lend itself to appropriation while the other should resist it is an important question that has been sidestepped in the whole controversy.

The part history plays in mediating the Chinese American relationship to the Chinese past is crucial, I think, to understanding the difference. While complex, Kingston's representation of the past relegates it to a Chinese space, which then haunts the Chinese American as burden or promise, but in either case as a legacy from a different time and place ("haunts" in an almost literal sense, as she uses the metaphor of ghosts to depict the presence of the past in the present). Chin in his fiction is relatively unconcerned with Chinese culture—except in relationship to the Chinese American; it may be suggested even that he substitutes the culture of the Chinese American as he understands it for Chinese culture. The relationship of Chinese American to Chinese culture in his representation is a relationship both of sameness and difference, mediated by a history that is grounded in a U.S., not a Chinese, temporality. The difference between the two representations is the difference between Chinese culture as a past legacy that continues to haunt the American Chinese and Chinese culture as a source of struggle to define a Chinese American identity that defies "death by assimilation" while reaffirming its irreducible Americanness. In this latter case, the past serves not merely as legacy to be left behind as the ghosts of China themselves eventually recede to invisibility. Rather, it is a fundamental moment in the creation of a Chinese American history even as that history is distanced from its sources in China. What makes Chin's version resistant to exoticism, as well as to assimilation, I think, is its claim to a Chinese American historicity that derives its trajectory from the reworking of past legacy within an American topography. This makes it as American as any other history but at the same time proclaims a historicity that is different from, and challenges, American history as represented in dominant historiography—one that has written the Chinese American out of history and has denied the Americanness of the Chinese American in doing so. Also, in this representation, we might note, there is a shift of emphasis (in spite of Chin's own longings) from cultural legacy that resists history to a historical legacy that rephrases the question of cultural identity in terms of its historicity.[25]

Despite his insistence on his being the only "real" Chinese around, it is arguable, therefore, that Chin is the most "American" of all the Chinese American writers, and it is his alternative vision of being American, rather than his insistence on his Chineseness, that endows his work with a radicalism that resists appropriation. The complexity of Chin's notion of Chineseness may be gleaned from the following passage from his novel *Donald Duk:*

> A hundred years ago, all the Chinatowns in America were Cantonese. They spoke Cantonese. The only Chinese Donald has any ears for is Cantonese. Donald does not like the history teacher, Mr. Meanwright. Mr. Meanwright likes to prove he knows more about Chinese than Donald Duk. Donald doesn't care. He knows nothing about China. He does not speak Mandarin. He does not care a lot about Chinatown either, but when Mr. Meanwright talks about Chinatown, Donald Duk's muscles all tighten up, and he wants Mr. Meanwright to shut up.[26]

It is Chinatown culture that is Chinese American culture, and while Chin has taken liberties by representing this culture as a metonym for Chinese culture as a whole, it is Chinese American culture that has been his major preoccupation. Early on in his career, he not only acknowledged that Chinese Americans were not recognized as "real" Chinese by those from China, but he also complained about the confusion of Chinese American with Chinese culture.[27] Interestingly from our present vantage point, the happy in-betweenland of postcolonialism appeared at the time as no-man's land. He and Jeffrey Chan wrote of the concept of "dual personality" (the unblendable "blending of east and west") that pervaded studies of Chinese Americans at the time:

> The concept of the dual personality successfully deprives the Chinese-American of all authority over language and thus a means of codifying, communicating, and legitimizing his experience. Because he is a foreigner, English is not his native tongue. Because he was born in the U.S., Chinese is not his native tongue. Chinese from China, "real Chinese," make the Chinese-American aware of his lack of authority over Chinese, and the white American doesn't recognize the Chinese-American's brand of English as a language, even a minority language, but as faulty English, an "accent." The notion of an organic, whole identity, a personality not explicable in either the

terms of China or white America . . . has been precluded by the concept of the dual personality. . . . [T]he denial of language is the denial of culture.[28]

The realization of just such a personality, one that is not a hybrid of two cultures but a product of historical experience, emerges then as the goal (this may be the reason that Chin consistently uses the derogatory term "Chinaman" to describe his characters, turning the tables on racist usage). The grounds of the experience are very much American, but to resist assimilation the experience must draw upon the Chinese past, the authenticity of which then becomes crucial to the plausibility of a Chinese American identity. An underlying theme of a novel such as *Donald Duk* (as well as Chin's other writings) is the erasure of Chinese from American history (literally absent from the photograph at Promontory Summit, Utah, where the Union Pacific met the Central Pacific, after Chinese workers had done so much to build the railroad from Sacramento). The goal is to restore that history, but as Chinese, not as shadows of white society:

> "I think Donald Duk may be the very last American-born Chinese- American boy to believe you have to give up being Chinese to be an American," Dad says. "These new immigrants prove that.They were originally Cantonese, and did not want to be Chinese. When China conquered the south, these people went further south, into Vietnam, Laos, Cambodia, Thailand. They learned French. Now they're learning English. They still speak their Cantonese, their Chinese, their Viet or Lao or Cambodian, and French. Instead of given anything up, they add on. They're including America in everything else they know. And that makes them stronger than any of the American-born, like me, who had folks who worked hard to know absolutely nothing about China, who believed that if all they knew was 100 percent American-made in the USA Yankee know howdy doodle dandy, people would not mistake them for Chinese."[29]

In *Donald Duk*, legendary Chinese heroes appear as railroad foremen, and the 108 outlaws of the Chinese novel *Water Margin* offer their aid in the semblance of "the ghost riders in the sky."

The historicity of identity does not make it any the less whole, nor does the constructedness of the past make it any the less significant in shaping history. Each generation may rewrite history, but it does so under conditions where it receives as its historical endowment previous generations' constructions of the past. For the marginalized and oppressed in particular, whose histories have been erased by power, it becomes all the more important to recapture or remake the past in their efforts to render themselves visible historically, as the very struggle to become visible presupposes a historical identity. In the face of a "historiographic colonialism" that denies them their historicity, capturing the truth of history, of oppression and the resistance to it, is a fundamental task that for its accomplishment requires constant reference to the precolonial past.[30] But it is also the case that those who are engaged in a struggle for identity can least afford to dehistoricize or reify the past, for the struggle is always the struggle for the present and must address not just the legacy of the past but also problems of the present. Cultural identity itself, then, is a terrain of the very struggles that it inspires. Whether it is reified, hybridized, or historicized, the meaning to be attached to alternative constructions of cultural identity is inseparable from the totality of the struggle that provides its context. The Confucian revival, Kingston's feminist construction of China, and Chin's use of popular religious and literary traditions all construct Chineseness differently but also with different implications for the relationship between culture and history. They also imply different relationships to social and political power.

Chin's use of the past provides a cogent illustration that cultural construction is not a "zero-sum" process (either Chinese or American) or a matter of hybridity or in-betweenness (neither Chinese nor American) but a historical process of production in which the dialectical interaction between past legacy and present circumstances produces cultural identities that are no less integrated for being historical, that derive their trajectories of change from the accretion of experiences that may be shaped by the legacies of the past but also transform the meaning of the latter, and in which local experience interacts with structural context to produce at once forces of difference and unity. Cultural essentialism does not consist merely of defining cultural essences; it requires the isolation of culture from history, so that those essences come to serve as abstract markers that have little to do with the realities of cultural identity. Notions of cultural purity and hybridity alike, ironically, presuppose a cultural essentialism; from a perspective that recognizes the historicity of culture, the question of essentialism becomes quite irrelevant. In this sense, assertions of hybridity or in-betweenness as well as claims to cultural purity are equally culturalist, the one because it rejects the spatiality and temporality of culture, the other because it renders into spatial differences what are but the temporal complexities of the relationship between the past and the present. The historicization of culture against such culturalism is also quite radical in its consequences, in that it opens the way to an insistence on different histories that, unlike the insistence on different cultural spaces or spaces in-between, are not to be contained within a cultural pluralism, let alone assumptions of cultural unity; hence the resistance of a historicized insistence on culture to appropriation.

Historicizing Chinese culture, Chin's account seeks also to indigenize it in the topography of a new location for history, where it challenges the claims of the dominant culture. But its own claims are those of one group of settlers against other settlers, an assertion that the one group of settlers has the same claims on history as another. What, if any, alternative vision of the future is embedded in this alternative history remains unclear.

This is where the radicalism of indigenous ideology comes in. If Chin indigenizes Chineseness in a new historical location, indigenous ideology historicizes indigenism in the face of a new historical situation, but without conceding its topographical claims, and an alternative way of life embedded in that topography. Not only does it insist on a different history, in other words, but also as it refuses to distinguish temporality from spatiality, it does so through a repudiation of the very idea of history promoted by the settlers. I suggested above that readings of indigenous ideology that ascribe to it a simple cultural essentialism may not be sufficient. Contrary to critics wedded to ideas of "heterogeneity and hybridity," who see in every affirmation of cultural identity an ahistorical cultural essentialism, indigenous voices are quite open to change; what they insist on is not cultural purity or persistence but the preservation of a particular historical trajectory of their own. In this case, however, the trajectory is one that is grounded in the topography much more intimately. And it is one that is at odds with the notions of temporality that guide the histories of the settlers.[31]

Silko might be echoing Chin when she writes:

> The people nowadays have an idea about the ceremonies. They think the ceremonies must be performed exactly as they have always been done. . . . But long ago when the people were given these ceremonies, the changing began . . . if only in the different voices from generation to generation, singing the chants. You see, in many ways, the ceremonies have always been changing. . . . At one time, the ceremonies as they had been performed were enough for the way the world was then. But after the white people came, elements in this world began to shift; and it became necessary to create new ceremonies. . . . [T]hings which don't shift and grow are dead things. They are things the witchery people want. That's what the witchery is counting on: that we will cling to the ceremonies the way they were, and then their power will triumph, and the people will be no more.[32]

Change is necessary, but it is to be contained within the history of the ceremonies. And, in this case, the ceremonies are inseparable from the land. Silko's narrative is a confirmation of the coexistence of the timeless and the temporal, a sensibility of timeless validity and the changes that are necessary to sustain that sensibility. The Indian is responsible for both. It was Indian witchcraft that "invented" the whites, who threaten the eternally valid. While the Indian invention of the whites points to the Indians' responsibility for their own fate (rather than blaming the whites for it), it also reverses the historiographical relationship by making whites into creatures of a quintessentially Indian history.[33] Only by overcoming witchcraft can the Indian once again restore the sensibility that is necessary to the sustenance of life.

Indigenism thus conceived is both a legacy and a project (as is ethnicity, when viewed in this perspective). Arguing against the "determinism" of culturalism, Jean-Paul Sartre wrote in his *Search for a Method*:

> The project, as the subjective surpassing of objectivity toward objectivity, and stretched between the objective conditions of the environment and the objective structures of the field of possibles, represents in itself the moving unity of subjectivity and objectivity, those cardinal determinants of activity. The subjective appears then as a necessary moment in the objective process. . . . Only the project, as a mediation between two moments of objectivity, can account for history; that is, for human *creativity*.[34]

The project, Sartre noted, contains a "double simultaneous relationship. In relation to the given, the *praxis* is negativity; but what is always involved is the negation of a negation. In relation to the object aimed at, *praxis* is positivity, but this positivity opens unto the 'non-existent,' to what *has not yet been*."[35]

To an indigenist such as Ward Churchill, indigenism is a "negation of the negation," which also affirms "that which is most alive and promising for the future of the Indian people."[36] By indigenism, Churchill writes,

> I mean that I am one who not only takes the rights of indigenous peoples as the highest priority of my political life, but who draws upon the traditions—the bodies of knowledge and corresponding codes of values—evolved over many thousands of years by native peoples the world over. This is the basis upon which I not only advance critiques of, but conceptualize alternatives to the present social, political, economic and philosophical status quo. In turn, this gives shape not only to the sorts of goals and objectives I pursue, but the kinds of strategy and tactics I advocate, the variety of struggles I tend to support, the nature of alliances I'm inclined to enter into, and so on.[37]

The point of departure for this indigenism is the present, and its goal is not to restore a bygone past but to draw upon the past to create a new future (which also explains why Churchill uses the term "Indian," fully aware of its colonial origins, as does Frank Chin with "Chinaman" and Trask with "Hawai'ian"). In working out the scope of indigenism, moreover, Churchill also strives to account for challenges that are very contemporary, such as problems of class, sexism, and homophobia.[38]

Likewise, Annette Jaimes describes indigenism as a "reworking of . . . concepts which are basic to an American Indian identity on the threshold of the

Twenty-first century," and Trask, like most indigenous writers, links the struggles for Hawai'ian independence to the struggles of oppressed people around the world.[39] The same is true of writers of the Pacific, such as Albert Wendt and Epeli Hau'ofa, who have affirmed that the effort to recapture a native identity and history may proceed only by struggles against colonialism that nevertheless recognize the historical transformations wrought by colonialism.[40] The effort to overcome Eurocentrism and colonialism does not require denial of an immediate past of which Euro-American colonialism was an integral part but presupposes an identity through a history of which Euro-American domination was very much a reality.[41]

What is of fundamental significance here (and distinguishes these arguments from postcolonialism), however, is a recognition that the common history that united the colonizer and the colonized was also a history of division. What the colonizer may have experienced as unification the colonized experienced as an oppressive denial of native identity. The insistence on a separate historicity is driven by this sense of division: to liberate native history from "historiographic colonialism," it is necessary not just to revive memories of a precolonial past but to write the ways in which the precolonial past was suppressed, as well as the ways in which it informed past struggles against colonialism. As the Australian aboriginal writer Mudrooroo Narogin puts it:

> It is no use declaring, as some Aborigines do declare, that the past is over and should be forgotten, when that past is only of two hundred years duration. It is far too early for the Aboriginal people to put aside that past and the effects of that past. Aboriginal people must come to realise that many of their problems are based on a past which still lives within them. If this is not acknowledged, then the self-destructive and community-destructive acts which continue to occur will be seen as only resulting from unemployment, bad housing, or ill-health, and once these are removed everything will be fine.[42]

Mudrooroo's comments show that the struggle over history is no longer just a struggle between colonizer and colonized but among the colonized themselves, between those who would forget the immediate past and those who insist on remembering.[43] Indigenism's insistence on remembering the immediate past distinguishes it from reifications of precolonial cultural markers and renders it fundamentally threatening to the status quo, even when that status quo is redefined in terms of cultural diversity and difference. As Gillian Cowlishaw writes, "Forty thousand years of history and spiritual links with the land gain a more sympathetic hearing than accusations of past injustices and displaying of old wounds received in the struggle for equality."[44] The reasons are not very complex: the reification of the precolonial past may be accommodated within a cultural pluralism much more easily than the insistence on the construction of alternative futures that draw not only on primordial traditions but also on the struggles of the immediate past. The difference is the difference between a multiculturalism that enables assimilation without challenge to the social, political, and economic status quo and a multihistoricalism that questions the totality of existing relations and the future of the history that legitimizes them.

The indigenous historical challenge, moreover, is not "metaphorical" but deeply material. The insistence on a special relationship to the land as the basis for indigenous identity is not merely spiritual, an affirmation of an ecological sensibility, but also calls for a transformation of the spatial arrangements of colonialism or postcolonialism. Indigenism, in other words, challenges not just relations between different ethnicities but also the system of economic relations that provides the ultimate context for social and political relationships: capitalist or state socialist. In this challenge also lie the possibilities for opening up indigenism to other radical advocacies of social change. Instead of a multiculturalism that presupposes coexistence of multiple ethnicities identified by ahistorical cultural markers, which elevates ethnicity to a determining principle of social life without saying much about the political and economic system as a whole, the historicity of the indigenous argument permits the design of open-ended projects that promise a return to a genuinely common history once the legacy of the colonial past has been erased—not just ideologically but materially as well.

CONCLUSION

In his critique of Jocelyn Linnekin's criticisms of the Hawai'ian independence movement, Jeffrey Tobin has called for greater attention to context in evaluating political movements and their constructions of native identity. "It is important," he writes, "to distinguish between discourses that naturalize oppression and discourses that naturalize resistance."[45] Similarly, responding to critiques of "essentialism" by James Clifford and Edward Said, Nicholas Thomas writes that

> what . . . these critiques pass over is the extent to which humanism and essentialism have different meanings and effects in different contexts. Clifford writes as though the problem were merely intellectual: difference and hybridity are more appropriate analytically to the contemporary scene of global cultural transposition than claims about human sameness or bounded types. I would agree, but this does not bear upon the uses that essentialist discourses may have for people whose projects involve mobilization rather than analysis. Said might be able to argue that nativism as a political programme or government ideology has been largely pernicious, but nativist con-

sciousness cannot be deemed undesirable merely because it is ahistorical and uncritically reproduces colonial stereotypes. The main problem is not that this imposes academic (and arguably ethnocentric) standards on non-academic and non-Western representations, but that it paradoxically essentializes nativism by taking its politics to be uniform.[46]

Thomas also recognizes that "nativist-primitivist idealizations can only be productive . . . if they are complemented by here-and-now concerns, and articulated with histories that do not merely recapitulate the 'imperialist nostalgia' of the fatal-impact narrative."[47]

The insistence of the postcolonial argument on history, ironically, conceals a deeply ahistorical reluctance to distinguish anything but the local, imbedded in an ideology of "heterogeneity and hybridity." It is also an argument that undercuts the ability to resist oppression except on the level of "identity politics." It is ironic that the insistence on the inventedness and the constructedness of the past should not be accompanied by a more acute self-awareness of the inventions of postcolonialism itself, but instead should be disguised, as in the case of Linnekin, by claims to a disinterested search for truth. Viewed from these perspectives, postcolonialism itself appears as a project among competing projects that reifies into the eternal condition of humanity the endowments of a limited group.[48] In this case, however, the project is one without a future, one that condemns everyone without distinction to existence in ethnic margins—including those in the margins whose efforts to overcome their marginality are subject to immediate condemnation.

The call for greater attention to political context in evaluations of identity construction is commonsensical to the point of being trivial. Common sense, unfortunately, is never transparent but is loaded with ideological assumptions. The postmodern/postcolonial questioning of identity is itself quite commonsensical; it is when it is generalized and universalized to the point where it will brook no deviation from its own assumptions that it becomes intellectually counterproductive and is driven into a political dead-end that extinguishes the possibility of political alternatives. Sharpened awareness of the constructedness of identity or of history may have rendered political and moral choice more complex and difficult; it has not eliminated the necessity of choice. Postmodernism may be an ideology of defeat, as Terry Eagleton suggests, or a "matter of class," as Aijaz Ahmad puts it; in either case, it reifies into a general analytical or political principle what may be but a condition of our times.[49]

In a recent essay, I suggested that indigenism may be of paradigmatic significance in contemporary politics globally.[50] This is not to suggest that indigenism provides a ready-made utopia, as in New Age constructions of indigenism. Indigenous proponents of indigenism are quite aware of the problems of native societies: that they have been disorganized by centuries of colonialism and reorganized in accordance with the political and cultural prerogatives of colonialism, which has led to a social and political disintegration, as well as a nearly total incoherence of native identity that will take enormous effort to overcome; that their cultures continue to be cannibalized by tourist industries and New Age cultural consumerism, often with the complicity of the native peoples themselves; and that the dream of recovering the land, crucial to both material and spiritual existence, may be just that, a dream.[51] It may be out of this deep sense of the historical destruction of their societies that indigenous writers insist on recovering the process of history "as it really was"—for them. As indigenous people were written out of history for being "unhistorical," it becomes all the more necessary to document meticulously the process whereby they were erased from history in order to recover historicity.[52]

The insistence on a separate history is itself not without problems, especially these days, when tendencies to the ethnicization or even the biologization of knowledge threaten not only a common understanding of the world but also the possibility of common political projects. While the cannibalization of indigenous cultures (by tourist or anthropologist) is very real, the fact remains that its very reality divides indigenous from nonindigenous projects, especially when issues of identity are framed around spiritualities that are accessible only to those on the inside.

Nevertheless, it is arguable that indigenism is as much a utopian aspiration that seeks to contain and overcome these problems as it is an expression of native sensibilities. The same utopianism—history as project—also offers possibilities of common struggles and aspirations. Indigenous ideology, while insistent on a separate history, also finds common ground with other histories in the problems it addresses. What makes it particularly pertinent in our day are the questions it raises about the whole project of development, capitalist or socialist; while some indigenous writers have pointed to common features between socialism and indigenism, this is a socialism that is far removed from the state socialisms as we have known them, grounded in the reassertion of community.[53] The indigenous reaffirmation of a special relationship to the land as the basis of a new ecological sensibility obviously resonates with growing ecological consciousness worldwide. The indigenous reassertion of ties to authentic pasts is not as divisive as it may seem but may contain a lesson that is broadly relevant. If the past is constructed, it is constructed at all times, and ties to the past require an ongoing dialogue between present and past constructions—except in linear conceptions of history where the past, once past, is irrelevant except as abstract moral or political lesson. The repudiation of linear temporality in indigenous ideology suggests that the past is never really past but offers "stories" that may be required to resolve problems of the present, even as they are changed to answer present needs.[54] The notion of dialogue between past and present also suggests the possibility of dialogue across present-day spaces, among indigenous peoples and with the nonindigenous as well, in which lies the possibility of common understanding as well as common historical projects.

If indigenous ideology claims as its basis an indigenous sensibility, it also opens up to others through problems that cut across any ethnically defined identity, those of class and gender oppression in particular. Just as local political movements in our day have had to reconsider such problems as class, gender, and ethnicity in light of ecological and community needs, indigenous ideology has had to reconsider the meaning of indigenism in light of those problems. Surely such movements may learn from, and cross-fertilize, one another while respecting their different identities. If indigenism does have paradigmatic significance, it is because it shares with other political movements in our day both common problems and the necessity of common action to resolve those problems.

I cannot think of a better way of concluding this discussion, and illustrating what I have just said, than to quote the eloquent words of a leader of a contemporary movement for indigenous self-assertion that has caught the attention of many in these bleak political times:

> Not everyone listens to the voices of hopelessness and resignation. Not everyone has jumped onto the bandwagon of despair. Most people continue on; they cannot hear the voice of the powerful and the fainthearted as they are deafened by the cry and the blood that death and misery shout in their ears. But in moments of rest, they hear another voice, not the one that comes from above, but rather the one that comes with the wind from below, and is born in the heart of the indigenous people of the mountains, a voice that speaks of justice and liberty, a voice that speaks of socialism, a voice that speaks of hope . . . the only hope in this earthly world. And the very oldest among the people in the villages tell of a man named Zapata who rose up for his own people and in a voice more like a song than a shout, said, "Land and Liberty!" And these old folks say that Zapata is not dead, that he is going to return. And the oldest of the old also say that the wind and the rain and the sun tell the campesinos when they should prepare the soil, when they should plant, and when they should harvest. They say that hope also must be planted and harvested. And the old people say that now the wind, the rain, and the sun are talking to the earth in a new way, and that the poor should not continue to harvest death, now it is time to harvest rebellion. So say the old people. The powerful don't listen, the words don't reach them, as they are made deaf by the witchery that the imperialists shout in their ears. "Zapata," repeat the youth of the poor, "Zapata" insists the wind, the wind from below, our wind.[55]

The choices may be complex, but they are ours to make.

NOTES

1. Homi Bhabha, "The Postcolonial and the Postmodern: The Question of Agency," in *The Location of Culture* (London: Routledge, 1994), 171–97, 172.

2. Leslie Marmon Silko, *Ceremony* (New York: Penguin Books, 1977), 2.

3. Haunani-Kay Trask, "From a Native Daughter," in *From a Native Daughter: Colonialism and Sovereignty in Hawai'i* (Monroe, Maine: Common Courage Press, 1993), 147–59, 149–54. Roger Moody, ed., *The Indigenous Voice: Visions and Realities* (Utrecht: International Books, 1993), offers the most comprehensive selection I am aware of of indigenous problems and perspectives. See also Ward Churchill, "A Little Matter of Genocide: Sam Gill's *Mother Earth*, Colonialism, and the Expropriation of Indigenous Spiritual Tradition in Academia," in *Fantasies of the Master Race: Literature, Cinema, and the Colonization of American Indians*, ed. M. Annette Jaimes (Monroe, Maine: Common Courage Press, 1992), 187–213; Albert Wendt, "Novelists, Historians, and the Art of Remembering," in *Class and Culture in the South Pacific*, ed. Antony Hooper et al. (Auckland: Centre for Pacific Studies of the University of Auckland, in collaboration with the Institute of Pacific Studies, University of the South Pacific, 1987), 78–91; Epeli Hau'ofa, "Our Sea of Islands," in *A New Oceania: Rediscovering Our Sea of Islands* (Suva, Fiji: School of Social and Economic Development, University of the South Pacific, 1993), 2–16; and Alan Duff, *Once Were Warriors* (Honolulu: University of Hawaii Press, 1990).

4. Quoted in Ward Churchill, "I Am Indigenist: Notes on the Ideology of the Fourth World," in *Struggle for the Land: Indigenous Resistance to Genocide, Ecocide, and Expropriation in Contemporary North America* (Monroe, Maine: Common Courage Press, 1993), 403–51, 410.

5. Quoted in Churchill, "I Am Indigenist," 411.

6. M. Annette Jaimes, "Native American Identity and Survival: Indigenism and Environmental Ethics," in *Issues in Native American Cultural Identity*, ed. Michael K. Green and Roberta Kevelson (New York: Lang, 1994).

7. Ward Churchill, "Naming Our Destiny," in *Indians Are Us? Culture and Genocide in Native North America* (Monroe, Maine: Common Courage Press, 1994), 291–357, 300.

8. Johannes Fabian, *Time and the Other: How Anthropology Makes Its Object* (New York: Columbia University Press, 1983).

9. Nicholas Thomas, *Colonialism's Culture: Anthropology, Travel, and Government* (Princeton, N.J.: Princeton University Press, 1994), 176.

10. Gareth Griffiths, "The Myth of Authenticity," in *De-Scribing Empire: Post-Colonialism and Textuality*, ed. Chris Tiffin and Alan Lawson (London: Routledge, 1994), 70–85, 75, 83. The title suggests, in spite of Griffiths's disclaimer, that what he says in this passage would apply to aboriginal claims as well, and not just to the dominant discourse. An earlier work leaves no doubt that, under postcolonial conditions, "the demand for a new or wholly recovered pre-colonial reality," while "perfectly comprehensible . . . cannot be achieved," because "post-colonial culture is inevitably a hybridized phenomenon involving a dialectical relationship between the 'grafted' European cultural systems and an indigenous ontology, with its impulse to create or recreate an independent local identity." Bill Ashcroft, Gareth Griffiths, and Helen Tiffin, eds., *The Empire Writes Back: Theory and Practice in Post-Colonial Literatures* (London: Routledge, 1989), 195.

11. Diana Brydon, "The White Inuit Speaks: Contamination as Literary Strategy," in

The Post-Colonial Studies Reader, ed. Bill Ashcroft, Gareth Griffiths, and Helen Tiffin (London: Routledge, 1995), 136–42, 140–41, originally published in *Past the Last Post: Theorizing Post-Colonialism and Post-Modernism,* ed. Ian Adam and Helen Tiffin (New York: Harvester Wheatsheaf, 1991). Brydon's arguments are largely directed at Linda Hutcheon, who is much more sympathetic toward indigenous claims against the "settlers." See Diana Brydon, "Circling the Downspout of Empire," in *Post-Colonial Studies Reader,* Ashcrofts, Griffiths, and Tiffin, 130–35. Brydon reveals more cogently than Griffiths that what postcolonial critics have to say on the subject of indigenism could be said easily without the aid of a "postcolonial consciousness." Thus, a former Smithsonian historian writes: "Those who decry the intrusion of the white presence in Indian history are often simply unwilling to recognize that Indian history is, for good or ill, shaped by the white presence, whether physically, in terms of European immigrants, or intellectually, in terms of Western historical or anthropological theories." Wilcomb E. Washburn, "Distinguishing History from Moral Philosophy and Public Advocacy," in *The American Indian and the Problem of History,* ed. Calvin Martin (New York: Oxford University Press, 1987), 91–97, 92.

12. Thomas, *Colonialism's Culture,* 172. This is not to say that such discussions do not exist. Thomas has in mind progressive cultural critics. As noted in note 11 above, there is no shortage of criticism of indigenous ideology, albeit without the marker of "postcoloniality." For a more sympathetic criticism that points out the origin in Euro-American power and the Euro-American mapping of the world of the concept of "Indianness" itself, see Robert F. Berkhofer, "Cultural Pluralism versus Ethnocentrism in the New Indian History," in *The American Indian and the Problem of History,* Martin, 35–45.

13. Linnekin, "Defining Tradition: Variations on the Hawaiian Identity," *American Ethnologist* 10 (1983): 241–52. For a discussion of the case and the controversy it provoked between Linnekin and Haunani-Kay Trask, see Jeffrey Tobin, "Cultural Construction and Native Nationalism: Report from the Hawaiian Front," in *Asia/Pacific as Space of Cultural Construction,* ed. Ron Wilson and Arif Dirlik, special issue of *Boundary 2* 21, no. 1 (Spring 1994): 111–33.

14. See also Thomas, *Colonialism's Culture,* chap. 1, for a discussion of this problem. In the United States, the New Age craze drew extensively on "tribal cultures" for its lore.

15. For further discussion, see Arif Dirlik, "Confucius in the Borderlands: Global Capitalism and the Reinvention of Confucianism," *Boundary 2* 22, no. 3 (November 1995): 229–73. For the role of the state in this revival, see Allen Chun, "An Oriental Orientalism: The Paradox of Tradition and Modernity in Nationalist Taiwan," *History and Anthropology* 9, no. 1 (1994): 1–29.

16. Samuel P. Huntington, "The Clash of Civilizations?" *Foreign Affairs* 72, no. 3 (1993): 22–49.

17. Ward Churchill, "Radioactive Colonization: Hidden Holocaust in Native North America," in *Struggle for the Land,* 261–328. Where Indians refuse the use of reservations as dumping grounds, the state uses its power to "disestablish" the reservations, as is the case most recently with the Yankton Reservation in South Dakota. See *Indian Country Today,* 3 August 1995. "Radioactive colonization" is also an ongoing threat in the South Pacific.

18. M. Annette Jaimes, "Some Kind of Indian: On Race, Eugenics, and Mixed Bloods," in *American Mixed Race: The Culture of Microdiversity,* ed. Naomi Zack (Boston: Rowman & Littlefield, 1993), 133–53, 137.

19. Churchill, "Nobody's Pet Poodle," in *Indians Are Us?* 89–113. See 92–93 for the quotation.

20. In case this seems like an exceptional case, we may take note here of the special issue of *Public Culture* (6, no. 1 [1993]) devoted to the critique of Aijaz Ahmad's *In Theory*, which also came under severe attack for its "transgressions" against postmodern/postcolonial criticism. Rather than address the issues raised by *In Theory*, most contributors to that special issue engaged in ad hominem attacks on Ahmad. Especially noteworthy are the red-baiting comments by Peter van der Veer and the religious bigotry displayed by Marjorie Levinson.

21. Frank Chin, "Come All Ye Asian American Writers of the Real and the Fake," introduction to *The Big AIIIEEEEE! An Anthology of Chinese American and Japanese American Literature*, ed. Jeffrey Paul Chan, Frank Chin, Lawson Fusao Inada, and Shawn Wong (New York: Meridian, 1991), 1–92. All the above-named authors were excluded from this collection.

22. For a discussion of these issues, see Edward Iwata, "Word Warriors," *Los Angeles Times*, 24 June 1990, sec. E, pp. 1, 9.

23. Frederick Buell, *National Culture and the New Global System* (Baltimore: Johns Hopkins University Press, 1994), 180–81.

24. Chin, "Come All Ye Asian American Writers," passim.

25. I do not wish to overlook here the different experiences of oppression that inform the works of the two authors. Chin is concerned almost exclusively with the oppression of Chinese in general and the "feminization" in the process of Chinese men in particular. Kingston is concerned with the "double" oppression of Chinese women, as Chinese and women, the latter including oppression sanctified by Chinese cultural tradition. While Chin is right to point out that Kingston's portrayal of Chinese tradition as relentlessly oppressive of women plays into the hands of Euro-American stereotypes of China, he nevertheless goes overboard in presenting a portrayal himself of idyllic gender relations in Chinese history. All I would like to say on this issue here is that gender relations, too, must be rescued from cultural stereotyping and placed within historical context, as has been argued by writers on Third World gender relations since the publication of *Woman Warrior*.

26. Frank Chin, *Donald Duk* (Minneapolis: Coffee House Press, 1991), 34.

27. See the interview in Victor G. Nee and Brett deBary Nee, *Longtime Californ': A Documentary Study of an American Chinatown* (New York: Pantheon, 1973), 359, for the interview. For the confusion of Chinese Americans with Chinese, which ignores "the obvious cultural differences," see Frank Chin and Jeffery Paul Chan, "Racist Love," in *Seeing Through Shuck*, ed. Richard Kostelanetz (New York: Ballantine Books, 1972), 65–79, 77. This article, incidentally, should put to rest the notion that Chin's recent criticisms of Chinese American writers are motivated by envy, because he and Chan raise here all the questions that have been brought up again in recent years. At the time, Chin was the only well-known Chinese American writer.

28. Chin and Chan, "Racist Love," 76.

29. Chin, *Donald Duk*, 41.

30. Calvin Martin, "The Metaphysics of Writing Indian-White History," in *American Indian*, 27–34, 33.

31. The very notion of "first nations," which is especially common in Canada and Australia, in this sense represents a compromise, since it makes it possible to speak of a second, third, etc., disguising within an ordinal succession of arrivals of fundamentally irreconcilable

ways of life and a history of colonization and repression. Against this compromise, however, we might note a historicization, as in the case of Annette Jaimes, who proclaims that Indian tribes have been open all along to outsiders, as shown in marriage practices, etc., which skirts around the issue of "openness" while making the quite valid point that racial differences were not the most important criteria of difference.

32. Silko, *Ceremony*, 126.

33. Silko, *Ceremony*, 135. This appropriation of whites for Indian history seems to have an interesting parallel among Australian aborigines, who have appropriated white social scientists for their own "traditions." Says one, "I am thrilled at the knowledge that has come through archeologists and scientists about the Aborigines. To me, it is as though the ancients are trying to relay a message not only to the Aboriginal race, but to the human race." Quoted in Robert Ariss, "Writing Black: The Construction of an Aboriginal Discourse," in *Past and Present: The Construction of Aboriginality*, ed. Jeremy R. Beckett (Canberra: Aboriginal Studies Press, 1994), 131–46, 136.

34. Jean-Paul Sartre, *Search for a Method*, trans. Hazel E. Barnes (New York: Vintage, 1968), 99, 101.

35. Sartre, *Search for a Method*, 92.

36. Churchill, "Nobody's Pet Poodle," 107.

37. Churchill, "I Am Indigenist," 403.

38. Churchill, "I Am Indigenist," 418–20.

39. M. Annette Jaimes, "Native American Identity and Survival," in *Class and Culture*, Hooper et al., 276; and Haunani-Kay Trask, "Hawai'i: Colonization and Decolonization," in *Class and Culture*, Hooper et al., 154–74, 169–70.

40. Epeli Hau'ofa, "The Future of Our Past," in *The Pacific Islands in the Year 2000*, ed. Robert C. Kiste and Richard A. Herr (Honolulu: Pacific Islands Studies Program Working Paper Series, 1974), 151–70; and Albert Wendt, "Towards a New Oceania," in *Writers in the East-West Encounter: New Cultural Beginnings*, ed. Guy Amirthanayagam (London: Macmillan, 1982), 202–15.

41. I am paraphrasing here Geoffrey M. White, *Identity through History: Living Stories in a Solomon Islands Society* (Cambridge: Cambridge University Press, 1991).

42. Mudrooroo Narogin (Colin Johnson), *Writing from the Fringe: A Study of Modern Aboriginal Writing* (Melbourne: Hyland House, 1990), 25.

43. Klaus Neumann writes, "These days, Papua New Guineans . . . do not appear overtly interested in being told about the horrors of colonialism, as such accounts potentially belittle today's descendants of yesterday's victims." "'In Order to Win Their Friendship': Renegotiating First Contact," *Contemporary Pacific* 6, no. 1 (1994): 11–145, 122. Likewise, Deirdre Jordan notes the complaints of adult Aboriginal students in Australia about emphasis on white oppression, "which seems designed to call forth in them responses of hostility and racism and which they believe causes a crisis of identity." "Aboriginal Identity: Uses of the Past, Problems for the Future?" in *Past and Present*, Beckett, 109–30, 119. There are others, needless to say, who would suppress the past for reasons of self-interest.

44. Gillian Cowlishaw, "The Materials for Identity Construction," in *Past and Present*, Beckett, 87–107, 87–88.

45. Tobin, "Cultural Construction and Native Nationalism," 131.

46. Thomas, *Colonialism's Culture*, 187–88.

47. Thomas, *Colonialism's Culture*, 189.

48. Buell, *National Culture and the Global System*, provides an example of the fetishism of hybridity. Buell is intolerant of any argument that suggests the possibility of integrated identity, and the main targets of his argument are those who would foreground divisions between oppressor and oppressed.

49. Terry Eagleton, "Where Do Postmodernists Come From?" *Monthly Review* 47, no. 3 (1995): 59–70, 66; and Aijaz Ahmad, "The Politics of Literary Postcoloniality," *Race and Class* 36, no. 3 (1995): 1–20, 16.

50. Arif Dirlik, "Three Worlds or One, or Many? The Reconfiguration of Global Relations under Contemporary Capitalism," *Nature, Society, and Thought* 7, no. 1 (1995): 19–42.

51. Churchill writes of the "go it alone" approach that he advocates: "I must admit that part of my own insistence upon it often has more to do with forcing concession of the right from those who seek to deny it than it does with putting it into practice." "I Am Indigenist," 432.

52. See, e.g., Ward Churchill, "Bringing the Law Back Home: Application of the Genocide Convention in the United States," in *Indians Are Us?* 11–63. The necessity of documentation is closely related to legal efforts to recover or protect treaty rights. It is also interesting that in a volume such as *The American Indian and the Problem of History*, while most of the nonindigenous contributors speak of different temporalities and conceptions of history, the distinguished indigenous scholar Vine Deloria Jr. stands out for his advocacy of old-fashioned historical documentation.

53. Churchill, "I Am Indigenist," 409.

54. The rewriting of history implied here is not merely a matter of writing indigenous sensibilities into existing history but of rewriting history in accordance with indigenous sensibility. Lenore Coltheart offers a challenging discussion of the distinction between "history about Aborigines" and "Aboriginal history," in "The Moment of Aboriginal History," in *Past and Present*, Beckett, 179–89.

55. Subcomandante Marcos, quoted in Alexander Cockburn, "Jerry Garcia and El Sup," *Nation*, 28 August–4 September 1995, 192.

9

PLACES AND TRANSCOMMUNALITY:

A COMMENT ON JOHN BROWN CHILDS'S

IDEA OF THE TRANSCOMMUNAL

John Brown Childs's case for transcommunality is most significant for its courage to hope. Hope in a better future does not come easily these days, when what remains of an earlier left despairs of the relevance to a changed world of the solutions it once espoused, and its putatively radical successors wallow variously in self-inflicted, if not self-serving, agonies of identity or in the euphoria of corporate-sponsored sensory overload ("tittytainment," in the words of that coiner of puerile slogans, Zbigniew Brzezinski), neither of which allows for anything beyond an eternal, and eternally fractious, present. Idealism and utopianism are the undesirables of the age, viewed with cynical disdain by sophisticated cultural theorists when they are not actually blamed for the ills of past efforts to change the world, as is the case, most notably, with subjects of former communist regimes. It seems especially risky under the circumstances to espouse a vision that claims the legacy of left radicalism, for there is no apparent end to the revival, under the guise of cultural diversity, of the most reactionary practices masquerading as expressions of alternative cultural visions.

Transcommunality appears in Childs's presentation as such a vision, one that seeks to redirect radical left practice in response to present challenges but also calls as a precondition for a reevaluation of long-standing leftist assumptions with the help of inspiration drawn from indigenous pasts conventionally ignored, or even disdained, by leftists. What Childs has to offer is not a a blueprint for the future drawn from the past, as in traditionalist and right-wing revivalisms that refuse to recognize their own historicity and reject in the name of cultural autonomy the aspirations born of the experience and promise of modernity. On the other hand, his insistence on the inescapable historicity of social practices and the indispensable transformative vision that must inform all radical practice distinguishes what he has to say from liberal or New Age appropriations of indigenism. For Childs, if I read him correctly, indigenous practices of transcommunality serve most importantly as an inspiration for going about radical practice differently than in the past: not repudiating fundamental questions of material circumstances and needs, but redirecting attention away from a persistent economism to the conjuncture between the material, the social, and the cultural to rethink political practice. What he has to offer is not a solution but a new beginning to solutions yet to be imagined and a few considerations that may help us along the way. This is what a transformative, nondogmatic radicalism is all about.

The source of the inspiration is interesting and also has much to tell us about our times. If the fall of socialist regimes, the revelations of their misdeeds, and the social and political transformations that have accompanied the global victory of capital have discredited, rendered irrelevant, or called into question earlier left solutions, they have also made it possible to ask hard questions about a socialist legacy that was in many ways informed by the same assumptions about the world as the capitalism that it challenged. The "politics of conversion" in the subtitle of Childs's essay refers to a socialism that proposed identical paths for all into the future, and presupposed homogenized constituencies, mostly around the paradigm of the laborer under capitalism (the proletariat), in order to realize such a future. It also shared in the developmentalist assumptions—an unquestioning faith in the necessity of a technologically advanced economy for human salvation—of a capitalism of which it was the progeny. To be sure, leftists of all stripes, from Marxists to anarchists, have been driven by an urge to place real, living people at the center of questions pertaining to the economy and society, but it is hardly deniable that socialisms in practice aspired to development with even greater faith than under capitalism, and engaged through the image of the proletariat in even more egregious abstractions of living people than the capitalism they opposed. It is fashionable these days to repudiate socialist histories as deviations of one kind or another, which serves to justify the invasion of the globe by the forces of capital. Such repudiations, most notably by postsocialist regimes, ignore not only that there were good historical reasons for socialist revolutions but also, more important, that it might have been impossible to gauge the effects of socialism without first going through it. Most important, they ignore the extent to which the ills of socialism may have been the products of those economistic assumptions that socialism shared with capitalism, which a bureaucratized path to development rendered into an instrument of social homogenization and repression, in the process obstructing the very development to which it aspired. As remaining socialist states such as China seek to remake themselves by abandoning the revolutionary vision that brought them to power, all that remains of socialism is state-led national development. The ills that were particular products of socialist regimes may be a thing of the past, but the ills that they sought to overcome are still with us. The fall of socialisms as we have known them makes it possible to ask once again if the best way to overcome the ills of capitalism is by replicating its assumptions about human salvation.

The latest phase in the globalization of capital, ironically, has served not to unify humanity in a march toward an identical, or even a common, future, but on the contrary has resulted in the further fracturing of societies worldwide along lines of religion, nation, and ethnicity. This very fracturing allows for challenges to conceptualizations of the future in terms of models derived from the advanced capitalist societies of Europe, North America, and Eastern Asia (divisions among which are also expressive of such fracturing). The challenge to Eurocentrism must be welcomed, but with an appreciation of its contradictory consequences. The cultural reassertion of social practices around the world, once thought to be remnants of the past, is not an unmixed blessing. In many cases, it issues in the revival of retrograde and repressive social practices in the name of cultural diversity. But it may also serve as an inspiration for reconsidering the whole project of modernity and the oppositional practices informed, not by the negativities of contemporary intellectual life, but by the search for practices that may help recapture the vision of human liberation that is also a fundamental aspect of modernity.

Indigenous practices are especially important to this end.[1] To be sure, indigenous claims to identity may be as open to reification and abuse as any other. On the other hand, conceived historically with due recognition of the need to respond to changing social circumstances and the new social challenges they bring, indigenism may have a fundamental contribution to make to a contemporary radical discourse on economic and political transformation. We may recall here that within a U.S. context, some of the earliest challenges to the developmentalism built into socialism came from radical Amerindian scholars who were products themselves of the radical ferment of the 1960s and were sympathetic to its social goals.[2] Indigenous insistence on the fundamentalness of the relationship of humans to nature to any consideration of social change has acquired wide currency in radical thinking since then as ecological concerns have become central to radical consciousness. This is also a predicament, however, as the absorption of indigenous ideas into a diffuse radicalism may also take the critical edge off a critique that is driven not merely by a vague concern for nature but also by a conviction that a harmonious relationship with the environment is possible only with social arrangements that give priority to everyday human needs and welfare. The indigenous critique of developmentalism is not just another reminder to include ecological concerns in the radical agenda; it is radically social in its implications and forces a reconsideration of the dimensions and modes of radical practice.

No less important is the indigenous challenge to ideas of political sovereignty based on the nation-form. Arguments for national sovereignty ignore that the nation-state itself is a product of colonialism both in its replacement of more localized sovereignties by the sovereignty of the nation and in its homogenizing cultural policies that erase local diversities. In no case is the colonial nature of the nation-state more evident than with indigenous peoples whose ways of life have been totally marginalized, if not actually eradicated, by nationalist political and cultural homogenization. The restoration of indigenous sovereignty, as indigenous scholars argue, is a precondition for any meaningful end to colonialism. On the other hand, if indigenous forms of organization in the past inspired political forms such as federalism in the United States, those forms may be more relevant than ever at a time when the nation-form is under attack from the inside and the outside and its future status less certain than ever.[3]

Indigenism, Childs reminds us, represents more than just another expression of identity politics that calls into question cultural and political boundaries. And it is not to be contained within a liberal multiculturalism that sees one form of resistance as much the same as another in a quest for a new politics of which diversity is the goal—and the ultimate political horizon. Indigenous practices and the very meaning of indigenism are subject to the ideological pressures of the age and are by no means immune to the threat of fragmentation internally, making it necessary to distinguish a radical transformative indigenism from its accommodationist forms. The possibility of indigenous self-expression at present may owe much to globalist ideologies that call into question earlier ideas of sovereignty, but indigenism in its very insistence on the groundedness of everyday life ultimately presents a radical challenge to a developmentalism that nourishes off-ground cultural and institutional arrangements. And if we may no longer recapture an innocently holistic way of conceiving life in which the economic, the social, the cultural, and the political are indistinguishably blended together, we may at the very least insist on conjoining the various spheres of life in arrangements that take different forms in accordance with the diverse needs of different places. What indigenism is about, ultimately, is a radical reconceptualization of cultural and political space from the bottom up.

Although one would scarcely guess it from the record of socialist regimes in power, the creation of democratic spaces from below has been a crucial component of most radical projects associated with socialism, including Marxism. While dismissed as utopian (or, alternatively, backward) in the tradition of so-called scientific socialism, insistence on the importance of local control over local economic and political resources has refused to disappear. Socialist states such as China, products of guerrilla revolution, did indeed struggle with the problem, but to no avail in a hostile environment that inevitably reinforced considerations of national power in socialisms that were already marked by an urge to national liberation from colonial or imperial oppression and exploitation. It is important to revive this alternative tradition once again. State socialism may have had a progressive part to play within the historical circumstances that gave rise to it, but at this particular historical juncture there are at least three important reasons that a radical agenda should turn to local control over local economic and political resources in order to achieve more egalitarian and democratic ways of living, mindful of the ecological conditions of human existence.

First is the necessity of abandoning the illusion that these progressive goals can be achieved through the agency of the state. It is not that state action is irrelevant, but rather that the role the state has to play needs to be considered historically: state-centered policies that are progressive at one historical juncture may inhibit further progress at another. Where the socialist experience is concerned, it seems apparent that while socialist states did achieve certain ends for their constituencies, the achievements came at the very cost of the professed ideals of equality and democracy. Even in less bureaucratized states, progressive measures may prove in the end to be meaningless unless they allow for local diversity and are internalized locally.

A second illusion that needs to be abandoned is that somehow an abstraction that goes by the name of socialism may replace another abstraction that goes by the name of capitalism to remake society globally. As it becomes increasingly difficult to locate a center to capitalism, it becomes even more difficult to imagine that such a center may be captured in the name of socialism; this seems to hold as much for individual nation-states as it does for that totality called capital. It is not that totalities need not be accounted for; what needs to be recognized is that the totalities themselves are fractious and contradictory and do not allow for the identification of "centers" that may be captured for the revolution in the manner, say, that V. I. Lenin envisaged it. One of the most contradictory consequences of the contemporary globalization of capital is the simultaneous decentering of capital (to be distinguished from the continued centrality politically and militarily of certain states) and the production of new localisms. Any sense of totality needs to be accompanied by this sense of fracturing and the generation of new diversities. A radical agenda must in turn respond to such diversity and abandon developmental and social teleologies.[4] The recent preoccupation in radical circles with the global and the local indicates that this awareness is already quite prevalent, although it seems in general to lead to a sense of helplessness rather than to its articulation to the alternative socialist tradition discussed above.

Finally, to the extent that there is visible radical activity in our day, it takes the form of place- or community-based social movements, the so-called new social movements, that nourish off diverse radical traditions (including homespun traditions of protest against injustice) but share common goals of survival and control over everyday life. From the United States to Latin America, Europe, Africa, and Asia, there has been a proliferation of localized movements against global capital, against the alliance between states and capital, and against the policies of supranational institutions such as the World Bank and the International Monetary Fund that make no allowance for local needs and circumstances. Rather than dismiss these movements as expressions of backwardness or mourn their proliferation as signs of the breakdown of socialism, radicals need to rethink inherited ideas of socialism to account for these new movements from the bottom up. To be sure, not all such movements are necessarily progressive or benign. Community itself appears more often than not as a location for inequalities and oppressions inherited from the past, which need to be overcome in the process of the struggle for life against the ravages of states and capital. It is for this reason that I myself prefer "place-based" over "community" in describing this mode of politics: place-based in the sense of grounded but with open boundaries both within (among the constituencies of the place) and in the relationship to the outside.[5] Places, if they are to serve as the locations for progressive rather than regressive politics, need to allow for negotiations of such inherited inequalities and oppressions (whether of class, gender, race, ethnicity, religion), as well as ally with other places that share their goals. Simply to be against capital and the state is not sufficient; it is also necessary in the process to generate new, more democratic and egalitarian ways of living. It is equally necessary to recognize that the very diversity of places calls for diverse resolutions of these problems in different places. The abandonment of the illusions of past socialisms only reveals the complexity and difficulties of social change to progressive ends.

Perhaps the most intractable difficulty, often pointed out by left theorists who prefer more conventional left politics, is the helplessness of places against the control of spaces by capital, states, and even diasporic ethnicities. In other words, if places are to be able to fulfill any progressive role, they need to be able to project themselves into the spaces of power without losing their own grounded diversities. This may be the most important challenge to radical politics in our day. Supraplace organizations (from labor to gender to radical associations all the way to the more progressive and less government-controlled nongovernmental organizations) may be essential to connecting places in alliances that may counteract the power of globalizing forces that erase places or manipulate them against one another. In order to achieve this end, however, such supraplace organizations need to be able to reorient themselves from the centers of power to the needs of the powerless and be more mindful of place-based needs against corporate identities of one kind or another. We need to remember, as numbers of writers have pointed out, that even capital and states need places for their operations, and their personnel, too, live in places.

On the other hand, what today passes for radicalism itself has become an obstacle to the radical reconceptualization of politics that a place-based imagination requires. I am referring here to the preoccupation with identity politics that has been a prominent feature of "radical" intellectual life in the United States over the past decade. While the question of cultural identity is by no means a trivial one, *where* identities confront one another and seek the resolution of difference is equally important. In its attachment to globalist ideologies, as is the case with many contemporary discussions of identity, identity politics is biased toward the reification of off-ground "diasporic" identities that contribute further to divisions between the constituencies of places that otherwise have to live and deal with one another. The diasporization of identity not only is divisive at the level of the local but also conceals unequal relations of power among the constituents of diasporas and is open to all manner of self-serving manipulation. The grounding of identities at the level of everyday life may be a precondition to resolving the many conflicts over identity, especially ethnic and racial identity; otherwise they may contribute to perpetuating the very divisions and oppressions that they seek to overcome. Whether self-assumed or imposed from the outside, moreover, a sense of cultural, class, or gender identity may be a necessary condition of countering the oppressive practices that are the legacies of the past. The problem with cultural politics at present is not its insistence on the need to account for the recognition of diverse identities but its rendering of diversity into an end in itself, which also makes possible its appropriation for liberal, and even managerial, ends that leave intact existing arrangements of power.[6] From a radical perspective, however, the ultimate goal of identity politics is not to establish boundaries to identity, which only further contributes to setting people against one another on the basis of some identity or other, but to enable them to live together with all their differences—which presupposes some sense of the historicity of identity. If identities are products of histories, they are also subject to change with changing historical circumstances. It may be important, therefore, to speak less of identities, as if they were carved in stone, and speak more of identifications, with some sense of human agency in self-definition and the definition of relations to others. This, too, may well be achieved best at the level of concrete everyday social relationships.

The idea of transcommunality may be pertinent to resolving questions raised by relationships within as well as between places. The way I read it, "transcommunal" carries a deconstructive sense similar to what Edward Said calls "contrapuntal": a decoding of a text, a culture, or whatever with the aid of its acknowledged or suppressed Other, while recognizing the integrity (and even the boundaries) of both.[7] Childs's goal, however, is also fundamentally reconstructive and goes beyond the reading of texts or cultures to find grounds for common action to resolve concrete problems of everyday life. While he stresses the ethical bases of transcommunality, we may note that transcommunality is also quite relevant as a principle of flexible associations that allows for diversity even as it promotes alliances for the common good. I do not mean to imply in suggesting this that the epistemological or the ethical dimension is subsidiary. If transcommunality as an organizational principle is to be viable, it will take a fundamental reorientation of our thinking on what are progressive ends and what may be the best means to achieve them. It calls for educational work at the most fundamental level, but educational work that addresses questions of basic human needs and not corporate needs or the needs of corporate identities. Such educational work, if it is to be effective, cannot be satisfied with abstract formulations but, as Childs points out, must be informed by the concrete practices in the context of which people may learn to live with one another in different ways.

NOTES

1. It is not my intention, in discussing indigenism as a radical option here, to assimilate indigenism to general problems of radicalism as one more radical paradigm, erasing in the process the specific meaning it has for indigenous peoples themselves. Nevertheless, I feel it is important that indigenous peoples, and indigenous paradigms, be brought into the dialogue on social change not as "resources" but as subjects of their own fates.

2. Ward Churchill, ed., *Marxism and Native Americans* (Boston: South End Press, 1982).

3. Franke Wilmer, *The Indigenous Voice in World Politics* (Newbury Park, Calif.: Sage Publications, 1993).

4. For further discussion of this problem, see Arif Dirlik, *After the Revolution: Waking to Global Capitalism* (Hanover, N.H.: University Press of New England for Wesleyan University Press, 1994).

5. For further discussion, see Arif Dirlik, "Place-Based Imagination: Globalism and the Politics of Place," *Review* 23, no. 2 (Spring 1999): 151–87.

6. For a discussion of this problem, see Henry A. Giroux, "Rethinking Cultural Politics: Challenging Political Dogmatism from Right to Left." I am grateful to Henry Giroux for sharing this (as yet) unpublished paper with me.

7. Said has discussed "contrapuntal" in a number of places. For one discussion, see the preface to Edward Said, *Culture and Imperialism* (New York: Alfred A. Knopf, 1994).

APPENDIX: JOHN BROWN CHILDS

ON TRANSCOMMUNALITY

Transcommunal cooperation emphasizes coordinated heterogeneity across "identity lines" not only of those such as "ethnicity," "race," "class," and "gender," but also of organizationally, philosophically, and cosmologically diverse settings. Transcommunality entails a changed way of thinking, a paradigm shift, or to use the Andean indigenous terminology of *pachukutiq,* "a change of direction," that moves beyond the classic Eurocentric progressive emphasis on homogenizing "unity" based on the leadership of a "vanguard party," while also escaping from the aimless ever-splintering relativism of post-modern perceptions of "diversity" and multiculturalism.

Transcommunality emphasizes a general ethics of respect in which mutual recognition and acceptance of diverse even divergent perspectives occurs among partners. Transcommunality sees distinct group locations with their often clear-cut boundaries and well-developed internal senses of communal integrity as essential. It is precisely from these clearly defined rooted locations that diverse communities can reach out to one another, so creating constellations of cooperation that reinforce rather than undermining a positively interactive heterogeneity.

These ethics of respect can lead to some transformation of interacting participants as they learn more about one another. However, this transformation is not a one-sided conversion to a single perspective, but rather involves an opening up to shared understandings. My development of the concept of Transcommunality, drawing in large part from Indigenous models of alliances in the Americas, offers a flexible approach in which the autonomy of of cooperating participants rather than uniformity is key. . . .

Transcommunality does not negate the communities and perspectives from which interacting participants emerge. Rather, it involves a form of responsiveness in which the participants' mutual awareness of each other is enhanced and modified. . . . Transcommunality entails a process of self-transformation among its participants as they interact and communicate with one another. . . . The glue holding these Transcommunal ties together is that of face-to-face interpersonal relationships of mutual trust, built up through "Shared Practical

Action," in which people from what I call different "Emplacements of Affilia-tion" can work together around shared tasks and objectives. . . . There is . . . [a] significant area of concern for those seeking to act Transcommunally. This involves what I call fundamentally distinct *Emplacements of Affiliation.* An Emplacement is a site of collective life shared by a group of people, which pro-vides them with a rooted and demarcated sense of shared perspective and affil-iation. An emplacement may be geographically located (or from the point of view of some communities, spiritually located in a particular geographical set-ting). Or, an Emplacement may involve dispersed members who nonetheless feel solid commonality based on "sites" defined in terms of religious, ideologi-cal, philosophical sets of shared beliefs, values, and objectives. . . . Such Emplacements are significant in part because each has its own distinct "rules of the game" in which goals, methods, and outlooks are uniquely theirs.

(From John Brown Childs, *Transcommunality: From the Politics of Conver-sion to the Ethics of Respect* [Philadelphia: Temple University Press, forthcom-ing], 31–39.)

INDEX

ABOUT THE AUTHOR

Arif Dirlik is professor of history and cultural anthropology at Duke University and Distinguished Adjunct Professor of the Centers for Contemporary Literature and European Studies at the Beijing Language and Culture University. His area of specialization is modern China, but he has ventured in recent years into Pacific and Asian American Studies, as well as studies of globalization, postcolonial criticism, and what may vaguely be described as cultural studies. His works have been translated in Chinese, French, German, Japanese, Korean, Portuguese, and Turkish. His most recent book-length works include *Quanqiu ziben shidaide houzhimin piping* (Postcolonial criticism in the age of global capitalism) (2000); *Chonchikuchok chabonchuuie Nundduki* (Waking to global capitalism) (2000), a Korean translation of *After the Revolution: Waking to Global Capitalism* (1994); *Hougeming fenwei* (The postrevolutionary aura) (1999); and *The Postcolonial Aura: Third World Criticism in the Age of Global Capitalism* (1997). Recently edited volumes include *Places and Politics in the Age of Global Capital*, with Roxann Praxniak (2000); *History after the Three Worlds*, with Vinay Bahl and Peter Gran (2000); *Chinese on the American Frontier: A Reader* (2000); *Postmodernism and China*, with Zhang Xudong (2000); *What Is in a Rim? Critical Perspectives on the Pacific Region Idea* (1998); and *Critical Perspectives on Mao Zedong's Thought*, with Paul Healy and Nick Knight (1997).